Social Justice and the Power of Compassion

Social Justice and the Power of Compassion

Meaningful Involvement of Organizations Improving the Environment and Community

MARGUERITE GUZMAN BOUVARD

ROWMAN & LITTLEFIELD
Lanham • Boulder • New York • London

Published by Rowman & Littlefield
A wholly owned subsidiary of The Rowman & Littlefield Publishing Group, Inc.
4501 Forbes Boulevard, Suite 200, Lanham, Maryland, 20706
www.rowman.com

Unit A, Whitacre Mews, 24-36 Stannary Street, London, SE11 4AB

British Library Cataloguing in Publication Data Available

Names: Bouvard, Marguerite Guzman, 1937-author.
Title: Social justice and the power of compassion : meaningful involvement
   of organizations improving the environment and community / Marguerite
   Guzman Bouvard.
Description: Lanham : Rowman & Littlefield, 2016. | Includes
   bibliographical references and index.
Identifiers: LCCN 2016005005 (print) | LCCN 2016012508
   (ebook) | ISBN 9781442266803 (cloth : alk. paper) |
   ISBN 9781442266810 (Electronic)
Subjects: LCSH: Social justice—United States. | Social action—
   United States. | Social service—United States. | Community
   development—United States. | Nonprofit organizations—United States.
Classification: LCC HN59.2.B696 2016 (print) | LCC HN59.2 (ebook) |
   DDC 303.30973—dc23
LC record available at http://lccn.loc.gov/2016005005

♾™ The paper used in this publication meets the minimum requirements
of American National Standard for Information Sciences—Permanence
of Paper for Printed Library Materials, ANSI/NISO Z39.48-1992.
Manufactured in the United States of America.

Contents

CONTENTS

Acknowledgments

Many thanks to Professor Michèle Cloonan, Renée LaCasse, Rajashree Ghosh, Mei Mei Ellerman, Professor Ethel Morgan Smith, Rachel Salmond, and Linda Bond.

Introduction

Service to others is the payment you make for your
space here on earth.
                                    —Mohammed Ali

This book is about social justice. It celebrates what Vaclav Havel
has called "The Power of the Powerless"—how a single person
or an organization founded by one or two people can make great
strides in helping the marginalized and bringing them back into
the community. It is not only about what one person or a small
organization can accomplish, but also how people who have
been helped to feel valued and part of society go on to play similar roles. Among the marginalized are the homeless, people who
live in poverty, the victims of trafficking, and those who suffer
from experiences of racism and oppression. The book also tells
of the achievements of those who seek to halt the plunder of our
very earth, the destruction of its biodiversity and the threatened
loss of countless species by extracting resources, or by eliminating the forests. Tropical forests play a central role in stabilizing
the climate by recycling more carbon dioxide into oxygen than

forests in the temperate regions. In addition, a warming Arctic Ocean has caused dramatic changes in the upper atmosphere. The polar jet stream, an upper atmospheric river of air that normally hugs the North Pole, has been affected by the warming of the Arctic Ocean heat, causing it to migrate and creating unpredictable weather of epic proportions, including unusually heavy snowfalls, massive flooding, and high winds. Drought is a big issue. But trees retain water in their bark and the soil, and that is why reforestation is an important path to save our earth.

The achievements of these wonderful people prove that we are not powerless—although the political and social systems that try to define us make too many of us believe in the contrary. Jonathan Moore has written that in this country we prefer to settle our differences in narrow negative terms that divide, divert, and obstruct us from common purpose. He also has written that we lack a national ethos about our common effort, and our commitment to public good.[1] In fact, in this country the working poor and the lower-middle class are struggling to keep afloat, and the gap between the very rich and the poor has widened considerably in recent years. Yet a shift from self-preoccupation to caring for others is a form of growth and understanding. Racial profiling in criminal justice, the pervasive use of guns causes both physical and emotional suffering, and together with the issues of immigration, are complex problems facing our society. Yet a single individual can make a difference in helping the invisible regain their space in our collective consciousness.

Several people in this book have either witnessed suffering firsthand or experienced it themselves, and that has transformed their perspective, and helped them understand that we are deeply connected to people in difficult circumstances. Their accounts remind us of the importance of moving beyond our personal lives, and are about respect and inclusion, teaching us that we can grow in new ways by reaching out to those individuals society deliberately ignores.

Václav Havel, who created and led the Velvet Revolution that brought down the communist regime in Czechoslovakia peacefully, has written in his wonderful book, *Living in Truth*, how it is possible to take space that will improve the way we live in society, "if an organization is to serve people, people will have to be liberated and space created so that they may organize themselves in meaningful ways."[2] He has also written "Historical experiences teaches us that any genuinely meaningful point of departure in an individual's life usually has an element of universality about it."[3] The organizations in this book both large and small have taken space in our society in many ways that transform and improve it, despite the ethos of the political culture. Compassionate action is a way of helping the many groups that we turn away from to gain the confidence they need to use their talents, and become part of the community. We live in a society where "personal success" is of paramount importance, ignoring the sense of accomplishment that arises from compassion. In her description of Emmaus, a shelter for the homeless that she founded, Sister Lucille MacDonald lists the reasons for homelessness, and added, "It could be you or me." What each of these chapters reveals is that working on behalf of people who desperately need help is a source of change in the world that occurs despite political disagreements.

The founders of these efforts have not only improved the lives of those they serve, but have made connections with important organizations that have supported their work in many different ways. For example, Wendy Young's organization, KIND (Kids in Need of Defense), has received much needed financing from corporations. Sam Polk who works with people who live in dangerous neighborhoods and need help to acquire healthy foods and build their self-esteem, received funding from his former boss in an important Wall Street firm as well as support from Gregory Boyle who established Homeboy Industries for young people who live in dangerous neighborhoods.

This book addresses the main issues that are affecting our country—many of which are the subject of political contentions: climate change; homelessness which is rising at an unusual rate in most cities; health care for the homeless; young people suffering from gunshot wounds; a surge of immigration; and sexual trafficking which has been discussed in the government. It also covers racism and criminal justice that has raised national concern through the use of mobile phone videos of police brutality that have gone viral. The Cedar Foundation addresses the discord among religions that occurs throughout the world and in the United States in its efforts to create peace and understanding among them. The fact that a fourteen-year-old boy, Ahmed, brought a clock he designed to his school in Dallas and was arrested because his teacher thought it was a bomb, would not have resulted in national attention and outrage if our negative perception of Muslims had not become an important issue. Some Republican candidates for president have posted anti-Islamic tweets.

The book has a section of chapters about the survival of our earth, and of peace and mutual respect; a number of chapters are about working for people who suffer from climate change, such as MADRE, which partners with sister organizations in the developing world. Women around the world who are caught up in warfare and oppression are in touch with MADRE, which was established to give them health care, political space, and aid in dealing with environmental change, in addition to ensuring their safety. This book reveals that while women are on the front line for being abused, they are also making the world a better place. Women and girls who have been sexually trafficked and were helped by the Polaris Project moved on to create their own organizations. Women living in forced marriages can turn to an organization that provides services for them, and women who live in male-dominated societies have become successful university students who not only find good employment but also work for the needy in their country.

David Milarch and the Archangel Ancient Tree Archive he cofounded have accomplished the unimaginable. Twenty-five years before the emergence of studies in science, and nature publications, and the rise of groups like Union of Concerned Scientists, and the Pentagon's research on climate change, David Milarch, a nursery farmer, had a near death experience. He had a revelation that the earth's forests were disappearing and received a solution of how to protect them. The greatest of earth's surviving ancient trees, such as redwoods, could be cloned. Their DNA could be preserved for future generations and their clones could be planted around the world. When his sons became adults, they joined him in climbing trees to capture a small living graft of a tree that was shipped, cooled, and then placed in a container with hormones in their nursery until it grew roots. When the roots sprout, they are potted until they become saplings ready to plant. First David created the Champion Tree Project in 2001, and then the Archangel Ancient Tree Archive in 2008, working to save our planet from environmental destruction. David and his sons sent many thousands of saplings of different trees throughout the United States and in places where they would prosper given the geographical changes in climate. Each tree, depending upon its size, recycles 200 pounds of carbon annually, and filters air and water pollutants as well as toxic wastes in the soil. That a farmer and his two sons, working in a tree nursery, can achieve global reach and clone and plant ancient trees around the world is proof that we can contribute a great deal to the problem of climate change. David Milarch's work achieved recognition in newspapers, television programs, and social media around the world, and continues to grow. He is a rare person who has devoted his life to future generations, and to the health of our planet.

Adam Seligman used to be a professor of sociology, but turned to theology to create peace and understanding among different religions around the world at a time of warfare based on religious differences. He created CEDAR (Communities Engaging with Differences and Religion), which brings together members of different religions and creates mutual respect among them. What motivated him to start this organization was how affected he was by the wars in 1992 and 1995 in Bosnia-Herzegovina and Croatia. Professor Seligman was so preoccupied with this terrible period that he wrote a book, *The Problem of Trust*. A sociologist who was living in Bosnia gave the book to Rusimir Mahmutčehafić who had served as the Deputy Prime Minister and Minister of Munitions during the war. He was so moved by the book that he invited Adam to Sarajevo where he, an observant Muslim, and Adam, a practicing Jew, became fast friends. As a result of the time he spent there, Adam founded the International School on Religion and Public Life in Sarajevo in 2002 that gave rise to CEDAR. It organizes conferences that foster discussions on how one can be tolerant while believing deeply in one's religion. He organized a number of conferences throughout Europe and eventually in Africa. The CEDAR program started with a small staff of four; a person from Israel; a Muslim from Bosnia; a Catholic from Croatia; and a former graduate study student who worked with Adam, and is an active member of the Presbyterian Church. The program combines lectures with site visits to different churches, mosques, and synagogues followed by intense discussions in small groups. The CEDAR schools have taken place in many countries where religion and ethnicity are important issues. Religion, politics, and economics are closely intertwined around the world. Climate change has also become part of the tension between ethnic and religious groups as they come to blows over land, water, food, and worldviews. CEDAR has become a pioneering global network in which, in every country and program it organized, its fellows who remain behind often create their own programs as a result of changing their perspectives. This amazing organization has created peace, respect for diversity, and mutual understanding in some of the most turbulent places around the world.

Dr. James O'Connell has spent his whole working life providing medical care for the homeless. It is a complex task that required him to learn about a number of different illnesses that date back to World War II, and even centuries earlier. He is truly multidisciplinary in his work, and in his thought. He studied philosophy and theology in graduate school when he was young, also working as a bartender that put him in touch with many different kinds of people. His work with the homeless began when he was about to leave Boston for New York to study oncology on a fellowship he was granted but was called into his chief of medicine's office. Boston had been awarded a grant to care for homeless people and to integrate their healthcare into the mainstream of medical care. The coalition that worked with the mayor to create this program wanted a full-time doctor. This position turned out to be yet another education and a long career where Dr. Connell became a true visionary. He began to work in a clinic at a homeless shelter, The Pine Street Inn, run by Barbara McInnis who was the head nurse. There he learned how to work with mentally ill people, and deal with trench foot, for example, a condition that affected soldiers from the two World Wars. Soon the team Dr. O'Connell worked with realized that they needed to treat the homeless throughout the city, rather than just give care in the shelters. They also found that they needed to be connected with the hospital because so many homeless people were seriously ill. During his first years, he worked from a van that would run every night from 10:00 p.m. to 5:00 a.m. Dr. O'Connell and his team have been doing this for twenty-seven years. His clinical practice is part of a team that takes care of street people who won't come to the clinic. An important breakthrough came in 2005 when Dr. O'Connell and the medical staff secured an empty building that is right across from the Boston Medical Center. It became a hospital with 104 beds for people who are on chemotherapy or suffer from serious illness and are unable to return to sleeping under a bridge. Dr. O'Connell loves his work because he feels that he is doing something that people really appreciate as well as pointing out the increasing number of vulnerable street people.

Sister Lucille MacDonald is a founder and director of the Emmaus Homeless Shelter in Ellsworth, Maine. It is truly a home, unlike homeless shelters that require their residents to leave at seven o'clock in the morning and return in late afternoon. It has rooms for families, a living room, a kitchen were guests prepare their meals, as well as a play area for children. There are twelve people on the staff at Emmaus. During the day there are four and the rest work at night. Sister Lucille operates the shelter like a CEO, using technological tools to further her cause, and expertly funding the shelter by holding annual events such as the Spring Fest, which combines a lunch with an auction, and music from local musicians who donate their time. She is in close touch with a number of organizations, as well as with local people, and protestant churches where she is highly regarded. Given the number of people who live in poverty in Ellsworth, the shelter's second mission is to serve them food on a regular schedule. Twice a week people come into the shelter to pick up boxes of fruit, vegetables, and desserts. The Shaw's supermarket donates a great deal of food that is transported by the National Association of Letter Carriers. She also provides backpacks for school-children, crayons, pencils for the younger ones, and calculators for high-school students. Sister Lucille's greatest contribution is the unconditional love she gives to people at the shelter based on the acceptance of everyone, regardless of their problems and situations. She has also brought together the whole community that takes great joy in helping her mission.

Sam Polk spent eight years working on Wall Street as a senior trader for one of the largest hedge funds in the world. Yet he became unsure of his life and was wracked with conflict and distress, as over time he changed his perspective and no longer felt comfortable with his lifestyle or employment. He began to see a counselor twice a week, and these sessions helped him to reflect on his life and get in touch with his deepest feelings. He began meditating, writing in a journal, and reading spiritual books. His counselor told him that he had lost touch with his inherent value, and that his need to become successful was a way to prove to himself and to the world that he mattered. He was very close to his twin brother who recommended a book to him *Tattoos on the Heart*, by Father Gregory Boyle, a priest who started Homeboy Industries to create jobs for young people who led deprived lives in a poor and violent neighborhood. As a result, Sam quit his job and moved to Los Angeles with his wife, Kristen, who is a physician. They watched a documentary on hunger, which revealed how, in the richest country in the world, millions of people didn't know where they would be able to have their next meal. That's what inspired Sam to start an organization to help struggling families. He not only wanted to help poor families buy healthy groceries, but also to educate people about nutrition. He educated himself on healthy eating and contacted Father Boyle who became a mentor to Sam. He created an organization, a logo, website, and found a lawyer—his twin brother, who decided not to become a corporate lawyer but to work for good causes. Sam also read about the connection between the rampant obesity in the United States and race, ethnicity, and poverty. He raised money to start the program Groceryships, which didn't prove difficult for a former Wall Street employee. For six months, participating families receive money to buy fruits, vegetable, grains, seeds, and have access to a program of education and support to empower them to increase their health. The families' progress is monitored by clinic partners who follow changes in the participants' weight, cholesterol, and glucose levels. The program's participants sit in a circle with Sam and share their stories about the difficulties in their life. They not only have become close friends, but after their feted graduation, members started their own groups for healthy eating. The space where participants meet is not about service provider and service recipient, but about everybody coming together. To understand how deeply we are connected despite the differences that appear on the surface is a way of honoring our universal humanity

Wendy Young, a lawyer, founded KIND (Kids in Need of Defense), in 2008, along with Angelina Jolie, and Brad Smith, Executive Vice President and General Council of Microsoft. KIND is an organization of pro bono lawyers who take on the complex and politically sensitive cases of child migrants who are brought to court without a lawyer to defend them. Not many people realize that children as young as seven flee countries in Central America because they are afraid of being killed and have had their parents and siblings murdered by gangs and drug traffickers. They wind up being held in juvenile jails and often deported without consideration of their immigration cases. It was an issue Wendy started working on in 1989, when it was receiving little attention, because the number of children arriving alone was not very high. Previously, she had spent most of her career working on advocating on civil rights advocacy and immigration. She also worked at the United Nations High Commission for Refugees, as a representative in Washington, D.C. As president of KIND, she is concerned about the abuse by border agents of children crossing the border. Between 2013 and 2014, there has been widespread reporting of the cruel treatment in many newspapers such as *Huffington Post*, *Tucson Sentinel*, and *New York Times* and airing on National Public Radio. The major issue is not just the treatment of these unaccompanied children, but also preventing their deportation to dangerous situations where they might be murdered. KIND has accomplished a great deal despite the problems it faces. It has helped more than 7,500 unaccompanied minors referred to them. And it has partnered with more than 250 law firms, corporations, and law schools that represent unaccompanied children in their immigration proceedings. As well as helping them in their court proceedings, the attorneys give them the compassion and care that many of them have never experienced in their lives. KIND has represented children who have fled to the United States from sixty-six countries, trained more than 9,500 lawyers, and has received more than $50 million in pro bono assistance. Wendy has also shown this country the value of children in distress and that when they are well treated they become important members of our society.

Our soldiers returning from wars in Iraq and Afghanistan are suffering from posttraumatic stress disorder (PTSD), a condition we have become familiar with through social media. Yet, not many people are aware of the youngsters who survive gunshot wounds in dangerous neighborhoods also suffer from PTSD.

David Crump is a Violence Recovery Specialist in the trauma and surgery unit at the Brigham and Women's Hospital in Boston. While we focus on the Newtown slaughter in a Connecticut elementary school, and too many mass shootings, what happens in Dorchester and Roslindale, Boston doesn't affect our views. Yet, in a typical five-month period, approximately fifty people are maimed and killed by gunfire. At the hospital and in their homes, David has helped more than one hundred victims of street violence. Only a very few of them have returned to the hospital with violence related injuries, and this represents great progress. Besides being present to help the wounded, David has also taught the medical staff about the street violence that affects patients, and how to help them in ways that go beyond medical care. Since staff members spend only the time it takes to stitch up a wound or the few days a youngster is in the hospital, David is an important part of their lives. He not only works at the hospital with the injured and their families, but also visits them in their homes, and keeps up the close relationships he forged until he feels that they have the help they need from other sources or have made progress. What he has accomplished is to help these young people feel safe and cared for, that they are valuable members of society.

Jodi Rosenbaum worked in child welfare and juvenile justice and was a teacher in the nonprofit Teach for America that recruits people to serve in schools with few resources. Her background in working with at risk and deprived young people prepared her to start a bookstore that would employ them, and give them the skills they needed to thrive, finish school, and find employment. She began this project by renting a 150-foot square office in Waltham, Massachusetts, with a few teenagers who were living in a group home with the foster care system. In 2004 she began selling books on the Internet with youngsters that never liked or worked with books or had any experience with technology. Nor did they like to be held accountable for showing up on time and acting professionally. But when the books began to sell, they became intrigued and felt empowered, because they were responsible for shipping the books and the money that was coming in. That is how her social enterprise, More Than Words (MTW), started. In just a few months, MTW moved to a larger office. The young people painted the walls, put up the shelves, and helped create some of the organization's policies. It was a challenging experience for Jodi and her colleagues, who were learning how to run the business on the one hand, and on the other helping with the significant issues young people faced, such as their need for housing, acquiring a GED, dealing with health problems, and substance abuse. As the years passed, MTW put out a monthly digital newsletter listing the major accomplishments of its young people, and the recognition it achieved such as a visit of a Congresswoman. Jodi sees this wonderful program where young people stay from six to twelve months, as a transition for youth development. It involves several stages of working with young people, until they can acquire the skills of showing up on time and keeping a bank account, and have gained self-confidence and feel empowered. The staff helps them map out a plan to get back in school, or stay in school, and to set specific goals for their future education, work, and life. Having role models at MTW, who have come from similar backgrounds yet achieved so much is a way of helping these young people believe in themselves. MTW helps them after they graduate and is committed to supporting them for at least two years in the graduate program. MTW has become a nationwide model for helping at-risk youth and there are now thirteen chapters in eleven states that provide local networking and collaboration opportunities and also influence social policy.

The Polaris Project is widely known both nationally and internationally for helping young women and girls escape the pimps who have sexually trafficked and abused them. It is one of the top charities that changed the world in 2014, and received an award for its work in International Peace and Security. It was founded in 2002 by two students at Brown University, Derek Ellerman and his friend Katherine Chon. What caught Derek's attention was reading an article in the *Providence Journal* about five Korean women who had been trafficked into a massage parlor that was only ten minutes away from where he and Katherine were living. They had cigarette burns on their arms and slept on concrete floors without bedding. Derek wrote up a business plan for Polaris (North Star) a nonprofit and moved to Washington, D.C., to set up their organization in a small apartment. Derek acquired an insight into the different ethnicities and how sexual trafficking was run. By talking with women and working on their cases, Polaris developed a sophisticated understanding of how these girls are recruited, how they are controlled, and how the money moves. Soon Derek and Katherine were training the police, who called them in the middle of the night so that Polaris could make sure that potential traffic victims were not sent to jail as prostitutes. Polaris acquired Congressional support in its early years. Over time that support has grown and the organization now partners with the Department of Health and Human Services, the Department of Justice, and the State Department. Polaris started with victim outreach and also developed a client service program in Washington, D.C., and New Jersey in 2005. Anyone who comes out of being trafficked has a great need for emergency services. Polaris has a twenty-four/seven hotline for victims that it publicizes, and has also created a number of signs that show how traffickers have victimized a person. Texting is a good way to contact Polaris because women, children, and trafficked laborers can delete the text afterward. Also Polaris has partnered with similar groups around the world. Not many people realize how widespread sex trafficking is and that it happens in affluent communities. While the statistics may seem overwhelming, Polaris and its partner organizations have changed the fate of the victims and responded to their needs, helping them heal and reenter society.

MADRE (mother) is an international organization based in New York City. It is headed by Yifat Susskind and has a multilingual staff of eleven women. MADRE is committed to human rights around the world and has partnered with local women's groups because it sees woman as the backbone of their communities and that positive change depends upon them. Its programs reflect the needs of the grassroots populations in twenty-seven countries, within which it works with numerous community groups to achieve their goals. Through this important work, the organization is making the politically invisible visible, and empowering women in the world, who are viewed as socially, politically, and economically powerless. MADRE works with sister organizations whose work support survivors of war, the politically repressed, the economically and sexually exploited, and victims of national disasters. These organizations have worked with MADRE to build health clinics, nutrition programs, create shelters for women subjected to domestic violence, literacy campaigns, and programs to improve women's political participation. Rather than accepting the dichotomy between victims and advocates, MADRE has found that survivors of abuse are often the most powerful advocates for change. In addition, given that climate change impacts the most vulnerable communities, MADRE has become involved in environmental programs because some of the biggest threats these women are facing are coming from environmental degradation. It is concerned that the international community has overlooked the connection between gender and climate change. Women provide subsistence for their families and are dependent on free clean water, on growing medicinal plants, and on a predictable climate for their farming. Rural women's work increases dramatically as they are forced to trek longer distances to collect food, water, and firewood. The range of MADRE's services are wide and innovative. For example, the organization brought Bosnian women they had worked with to share their experience with Syrian women's groups so that they could exchange strategies and tactics. Such exchanges are emotional because during a civil war people feel that they have been forgotten and that nobody understands what they have endured. The accomplishments of MADRE's eleven staff members are remarkable and bring hope to troubled parts of the world.

Dr. Alan Lightman, a professor at the Massachusetts Institute of Technology, accompanied his friend, a Unitarian minister, to Cambodia in 2003. That trip changed his life dramatically. His friend, Frederick Lipp, had founded a nonprofit organization in Cambodia to help twelve- and thirteen-year-old girls, who have been taken out of school to work in rice fields, resume their educations. When Alan Lightman saw what the minister's organization was accomplishing, he decided that he too would create a humanitarian project in Cambodia. After that trip he spent a great deal of his time fundraising and built a school in a small village. Because this project was so successful, he created the Harpswell Foundation dedicated to helping women achieve a university education. Alan Lightman felt that educating women was the best way to rebuild a country mired in poverty and led by an authoritarian government. Historically and culturally, women are supposed to be deferential to men in Cambodia, so there is a great need to empower women. World Bank studies have revealed that educating and empowering women is the most effective way to help developing countries. Alan Lightman built the first dormitory for women in 2006 and a second in 2009. He also created an in-house academic program for the students to attend during the evenings and weekends when they are not at their universities, which includes English classes, leadership, and history seminars, classes on debating, analytical writing, South East Asian geography, and genocide studies in which the genocide committed by the Khmer Rouge is put into international context with other genocides. National and international news is also discussed to sharpen their critical thinking skills. The eighty-four women in the two dormitories come from poor families in villages without electricity or running water. For the past five years, the foundation had brought four graduates to the United States for a one-year certificate program, in which students can take any course they want at an American university. Alan Lightman is pleased that his graduates have become project managers at nonprofit governmental organizations, journalists in some of the major newspapers in Cambodia, employees in law firms and in the government's Ministry of Women's Affairs, and teachers in both high schools and universities. The students not only find important work, but also share their experiences in rural communities that reduce the isolation of villages. In addition, the Harpswell Foundation has formed partnerships with other organizations around the world that are devoted to the empowerment of women.

We live in a multicultural society, yet many of us believe that arranged marriages only happen abroad; few of us have ever heard of forced marriages. Marriages that are forced are an invisible form of gender violence and a matter of human rights and social justice. Its victims hide in the shadows, so their plight has been socially invisible. Vidya Sri was brought up in New York City and was enjoying her life when her parents sent her back to

India to a forced marriage. After she finished college there, her father told her that, unless she married the man he chose, she could not return to the United States. The pain of forced marriage was evident in Vidya Sri's married life and in the years preceding it. In fact, she lived a double life. She found a job to pay for her master's in business administration, and then worked at a bank where she became a regional manager of sixteen branches with over a billion dollars in assets. At the end of each day, she would come home to a new identity where she didn't matter and felt invisible. Then she read about forced marriage and that opened a door for her. Before that she didn't have the words for what she experienced, believing that she had failed her family. She divorced her husband, and endured hostility from her family, but she founded Gangashakti (Ganga for the Ganges River, which signifies the life-empowering planetary energy of Mother Earth, and Shakti, meaning the power within). Forced marriage takes place in communities across the United States, crossing religious, cultural, and socioeconomic lines. Gangashakti partners with many different groups that help women and performs a number of important supportive actions, such as managing individual cases and assisting survivors by transporting them across state lines, helping them acquire new identities, and changing their social security numbers. Vidya not only supports women in forced marriages, but is also raising awareness about that practice around the country, and the world, since she travels widely. Like Yifat Suskind of MADRE, Vidya has found that her experience has taught her that without grassroots efforts, international law is not effective in countries where there are many different ethnic groups and practices.

Eric Adams experienced horrific racial discrimination when he was only fifteen years old and was arrested on a criminal trespass charge for unlawfully entering and remaining in the home of an acquaintance. He was taken to a police precinct where he was assaulted and kicked repeatedly in his groin. A week after he was released, there was blood in his urine. This experience led him into a career where he has worked from the "inside" to reform policing and the criminal justice system. Fifty years after Martin Luther King, Eric Adams has become an important part of our contemporary conversation on racism, which should have taken place decades ago, and is conveyed in videos, newspapers, and online messages from organizations such as Color of Change and Black Lives Matter. Today, even though we have the first black president and the second black attorney general to head the department of justice, we still live in a nation that is divided by institutionalized racism that affects voting rights, jobs, poverty rates, racial profiling, incarceration, and education. Eric Adams has worked to bridge that gap in his consecutive careers.

Eric Adams spent twenty-two years in the New York Police Department (NYPD), where he became a captain and cofounded 100 Blacks in Law Enforcement Who Care. The organization has grown and understands that social problems are at the core of too many criminal actions and unfair responses. Eric Adams and 100 Blacks in Law Enforcement Who Care, work for policies to address racial disparities such as poverty, poor housing, struggling schools and poor access to jobs. Then Eric Adams became a state senator in the New York Senate where he proposed a number of laws, such as one to place cameras on police guns, and spoke about the need for transparency in policing. He became the first black American to become the president of the Brooklyn borough, speaking out on the many problems of racial profiling and especially about police stops when racial minorities are questioned, handcuffed, and searched at dramatically higher rates than whites. While one person cannot change a racially divided country, his voice has become a very important one, not only in speaking out for justice, but in educating white people about the oppression they impose.

What this book reveals is that while wealth, social standing, and political clout are a source of power, caring for people in need can create substantial changes. They include changing social and political perspectives about the marginalized and the oppressed, and helping them reenter society. In addition, networking with a diversity of groups and individuals helps people who have been excluded from our social consciousness acquire a strong presence in our country at all levels. Working at the grassroots in partnership with people who have survived difficult times is also the road to great accomplishments, one that may be propelled by anger at injustice, but is open to everyone who wants to make this world a better place. Many of these groups have created countrywide changes, and are also working on the international level such as Polaris, CEDAR, KIND, and MADRE. Some of them serve as models such as More Than Words, The Archangel Ancient Tree Archive, and 100 Blacks in Law Enforcement Who Care, serve as models for further initiatives.

Beyond the political discord that has been exacerbated in the past few years, and a government that is also blocked in so many important areas are these organizations that accomplish significant social progress and provide much needed hope.

ONE

David Milarch and the Archangel Ancient Tree Archive

Trees

In the days of old, when the Creation was young,
The Earth was filled with giant trees,
Whose branches soared above the clouds,
And in them dwelled our Ancient Fathers,
They who walked with the Angels,
And who lived by the Holy Law.
In the shadow of their branches all men lived in peace,
And wisdom and knowledge was theirs,
And the revelation of the Endless Light.
We shall guard and love one another.[1]

David Milarch cofounded the Champion Tree Project with his son Jared, and then the Archangel Ancient Tree Archive. He had a near-death experience and believed that he was sent back to this earth to save the forests that are essential to this planet's survival. He had a long experience with trees because he grew up as the son and grandson of nurserymen, working on his father's shade tree farm where ash, maple, oak, birch, and locust trees were cultivated. In fact, his father put him to work when he was only seven years old, weeding, hoeing, digging, pruning, and planting trees every day after school and weekends. David describes these years as a stern, brutal, and harsh upbringing. His father believed that hard work was the center of life. David and his brothers experienced unusual childhoods for the time, but not for past centuries when children were treated as indentured servants. David saw it as a lifestyle that either makes or breaks a person. "It was like being Nelson Mandela and a prisoner of war at the same time."[2]

But David also felt a deep rebellion and anger at the life he was living and took it out in street fighting and arm wrestling, drinking and joining a street gang. At fifteen he started fighting and at seventeen he joined a motorcycle club. What he didn't realize at the time was that his childhood labors were a training period for the task he would undertake later in life to save our dying forests by cloning trees. When he became an adult, he realized that his father taught him a great deal to make him a strong person who could deal with adversity. "My father forced me out into nature and kept me out there. I communed with the beauty and the laws of nature. I got a deep understanding of how things worked."[3] His father told David, "When you absolutely have to get something done, it's do or die." And he added, "When you find yourself in a situation where you have to do something with only half enough money and half enough time, you should ask an American farmer to do it." Those were the guides for David's own career.

When he was eighteen years old David crossed the country from his home in Michigan to the redwood forests of California. He and his friend parked at the Muir Woods National

Monument and walked into the old-growth forest of coast redwoods (sequoia). These were the tallest trees on earth, over 300 feet tall and among the oldest—some two thousand years old. The coast redwood is one of three living descendents of a 240-million-old tree family from the Triassic era, when Earth's continents were part of a single landmass. The Giant Sequoia of the Sierra Nevada Mountains and the Dawn Redwood family also descend from this primordial tree family.[4] David was deeply moved by the soaring, misty woodland and its haunting majesty. He felt that he was on holy ground. But his teenage amazement was shattered because beyond Muir Woods' protected acres stretched a wasteland of hundreds of miles of stumps. He felt physically ill as he and his friend drove through it.

Before the mid-nineteenth century, the coast redwoods grew on more than two million acres of the United States' Pacific coastline. It was a natural carbon sink, absorbing carbon dioxide and exhaling oxygen. The redwoods and other forests circling the globe were what kept the earth in balance.[5] According to the botanist Diana Beresford-Kroeger "A functioning forest is a complex form of life. It is interconnected by its own flora and driven by the mammals, the amphibians and insects in it. . . . The primogenitors of the forests are trees. They communicate by carbon-coded calls and mass-market themselves by infra-sound. The atmosphere links the forests into the heavens and the great oceans. The human family is both caught and held in that web of life."[6] In other words, trees are the lungs of the planet. Diana Beresford-Kroeger, a medical and agricultural researcher, lecturer, and scientist in the fields of medical biochemistry, organic chemistry and nuclear chemistry, studies trees from a multidisciplinary perspective. She became one of the science advisors of the Archangel Ancient Tree Archive that David would create with his sons in 2008.

David was devastated when he left this scene and returned to his father's shade-tree farm, a job that no longer appealed to him because of what he experienced at Muir Woods. He was thinking that people were destroying the entire ecosystem, cutting down all the trees and bulldozing the topsoil to clear the way for cities, suburbs, factories, and agribusiness. He and his father worked with non-native species, cloning them, and selling the clones. The trees were not selected for their size, or indispensability to life, but for their attractive leaves and flowers.[7]

When he grew up, David married Kerry, a schoolteacher, and had two sons, Jared and Jake who were precious to him. They moved to the Milarch family farmhouse in Copemish, Michigan, a town of two hundred where they still live. As he took over the family business, David was drinking heavily. One day when he was forty-two, he tripped and fell down drunk at his youngest son's ball game. Looking up, he realized that he had become an embarrassment and an alcoholic. After that incident, he told his boys that he would never drink again and locked himself up in the bedroom that night, telling his wife that he wouldn't come out until he was sober. He stayed in the room for three days with no food or alcohol, only water. He then became very weak and ill.

A friend came by to see him and knew that something was very wrong. David had trouble breathing and was in great pain, so his friend carried David to his car and drove him to an emergency room. The physician found that the fluid his kidneys could no longer process was filling the lower thoracic cavity and pressing against his lungs and heart. The physician told him that he had to give him a blood transfusion because his blood wasn't coagulating. A syringe, eight inches long and around an inch in diameter, was put in his chest, an inch from his heart. The physician did that several times and withdrew the fluid from his chest.

When David began to recover, he told his physician that he wanted to go home. The physician was very angry and told him that they would be lucky to keep him on dialysis for twenty-four hours, or he would die. David refused because he could breathe again. His friend literally lifted him over his shoulder, carried him out to the car and drove him back home, about forty minutes away, where his family took care of him.

Sitting by his bed, his family thought that he had died because he seemed to be in a coma. What David remembers is that he was lifted out of his body and aware that he was dying. He was filled with sorrow at the thought of missing his boys whom he loved so much. Then an angel appeared before him and told him that he was not alone, and not to be afraid. Angels accompanied him as he went through a tunnel of light and arrived in the most beautiful place he had ever seen. He saw light beings and he felt surrounded by unconditional love. He didn't really want to stay because his sons were in the fifth and sixth grade, and he asked them if he could go back to see them graduate from high school. Then an archangel approached him and told him that he needed to return to his body because he had important work to do. After plummeting back into his body he sat up, shocking his wife and everyone who was in the room.

It was six weeks before he could get out of bed and walk again because his feet had turned black and the nerves on the bottom on his feet created great pain. Gradually he became stronger and could walk a few steps. When he visited his physician again, the doctor told him that his feet would need to be amputated. David refused, saying, "I've grown attached to them. They'll be fine." He kept them in an ice water bucket for a few hours at a time to kill the pain.

That was more than twenty years ago. His project came to him as a revelation from his near-death experience that the earth's forests were disappearing and he was given a solution. The greatest of earth's surviving ancient trees, "champion trees" could be cloned. Their DNA could be preserved for future generations and their clones could be planted around the world. Without realizing it, David was born with the knowledge of a scientist and a light-filled soul.

After that, David returned through what he called the "tunnel" every night between 2 a.m. and 3 a.m. A white light would wake him up and he would go into the living room for two hours of training with the light beings. He heard a voice telling him to "get a pad and a pen and write this down." Once when he went to wake up his sons for school, he saw ten pages of an outline. When he showed what he had written to his wife, she was amazed and told him, "You couldn't have written this, there aren't any spelling mistakes and you can't spell."[8]

David learned about genetics and cloning from his meetings with what he refers to as "the light beings." In fact, he describes himself as having one foot in this world and one foot and two arms in the next. He continues to go into another room at night. He says his family knows how he has changed, and that his work is also in the next world, bringing what he learns back into this dimension. He has told people, "You are not just your body, and your emotions, but a powerful spiritual being incarnated in that body. You are here for lessons and a mission. I am a global voice for the trees and the earth because the trees and the earth speak and need an interpreter. Time is an illusion and it is also in the third dimension. All our past lives and future lives are like parallel lives on a sheet of music and all affect each other. There isn't any beginning, middle or end. It's infinite. As we live this third dimensional life, it reflects our past and future life."[9]

Another man, who battled climate change, had an experience similar to David Milarch's. In 1991, the same year as David

Milarch first had his vision, Lonnie G. Thompson saw that the world's largest tropical ice cap was starting to melt. He became one of the first scientists to witness and record a global melting of land ice. His long cylinders of ice proved that this sudden coordinated melting had no parallel in the past several thousand years. But in the autumn of 2011, he became so ill he could barely walk. He wound up in the hospital, drifting in and out of consciousness. More than once his wife and daughter were told that he might not survive the night. During one of those comatose periods, he jumped through space, landing in a beautiful vista filled with flowers and streams. There, a figure in white spoke to him, "It's not your time. You have another purpose." He then received a heart transplant that allowed him to recover ice cores in Antarctica and to develop a detailed reconstruction of the planet for the past eight hundred thousand years.[10]

Raymond A. Moody Jr., MD, wrote a book about the thousands of people he interviewed who returned back to life after what he refers to as a near-death experience. He discovered that many of them returned with a newfound respect for nature and a sense of connection with all things.[11] He also found that many people expressed a sense of urgency in a world where vast destructive powers are in the hands of people.[12] David Milarch and Lonnie Thompson were working for the safety of our planet when few people were thinking about our forests or our warming earth.

One exception was NASA scientist James Hansen who first warned Congress about global warming in 1988. Over time he became more outspoken and active. Yet he was forbidden to talk about climate change in public, revealing the attitude of the government toward that life-threatening problem. He was arrested at a White House protest against the XL Pipeline on February 20, 2013.[13] He worked for forty-seven years in the government, many of which were devoted to the scientific study of climate change, and was the forerunner of the work of climate scientists, many of them hemmed in by lobbyists and politicians. For example, the glaciologist Jason Box spent many years studying the Arctic at the Byrd Polar and climate research center at Ohio State University. He discovered that the warming ocean creates methane. Defying the stereotype of scientists as unemotional, he tweeted his discovery in a very direct and emotional way. The media criticized him to such an extent that he moved to Denmark with his family where he continues his research.[14] A number of other climate scientists have come under fire from the media, but they just shrugged their shoulders and continued their important work.

But at the time of David's experience with light beings, not many people were worried about the disappearance of the world's virgin forests that were being harvested around the world and few people realized that many animal species were being extinguished in those forests. Tree roots that are near streams cleanse toxins, which among other things, give forests a vital role in our planet. He saw that the ancient trees held a unique wisdom and were the crown of the creation.

David Milarch was ahead of his time in his concern about the loss of many forests. It was only years later that deforestation was formally studied. In 2014, the Center for Global Development found three causes of deforestation: population growth, proximity to cities, and proximity to roads.[15] In 2015 Oxford University researchers came out with a working paper entitled, *Stranded Carbon Assets and Negative Emissions Technologies*, which found, among other conclusions that planting new forests, and soil carbon improvement would help mitigate climate change.[16] Neither of these two studies mentioned forests as a source of profit. A biologist, Rodolfo Dirzo, who works in the

Amazon and writes about biodiversity, insects, plants, birds, and mammals and species of trees, has studied how deforestation that is resulting from resource extraction is destroying the biodiversity of the Amazon and threatening to wipe out countless species. Roads enable access to untouched areas, bringing massive deforestation and threats to Amazonian cultures. In fact, 95 percent of deforestation in the Amazon takes place on land less than five kilometers from a road.

Of course angels don't provide funding or help create large, well-funded organizations to study important issues. But David Milarch had his two sons who began working closely with him and continue to do so. Today they both have jobs but also work tirelessly on cloning the biggest and oldest trees. David describes his older son Jared as wise, steady, and deep. Even at an early age he knew about his father's mission, and what lay ahead for him. His younger brother has the same personality as his father, and is determined and hardworking. David recalls that, without Jake, no redwoods or sequoias would have been cloned because he was the one who found them and cloned them. David searched for ten years, but the trees that he found were on federal or state lands where he was denied access. While people who were in forestry were telling David that cloning would not work, Jake replied, "We'll make it work." His sons worked continuously on their own terms, scouring the Internet, experimenting and making important breakthroughs so the world would have the ability to rebuild a redwood. For them, it wasn't a job, but a lifestyle they believed in throughout the years. They experienced a lot of negative comments. "You can't do this. It won't work. You are from a small village in North Michigan, just dumb farmers."[17] Because of their exposure to such negativity, David saw them develop stamina, and rebellious attitudes. He sees them as having had a lifetime of training in persistence. When he was twelve years old, Jared found a tee shirt with a pelican standing with a frog in its beak, but the much smaller frog had a chokehold on the pelican's neck. Below were the words, "never give up." In 1997 Jared and David founded the nonprofit Champion Tree Project International with the mission of preserving, propagating, and planting old growth forest genetics. Following college, Jared helped collect, propagate, and plant champion trees around the country and in 2004, decided to continue his family's growing tradition into another generation. He purchased the family farm and established Milarch Brothers Nursery and Landscaping. Since 2008 Jared has been executive director and chairman of the board of the Archangel Ancient Tree Archive, taking no pay while holding a full-time job. Jake has worked half time for the archive on half pay as a Propagation Specialist and Climber. Thomas Brodhagen is a part-time paid consultant and Propagation Specialist, and Jen Milarch is a part-time paid consultant and bookkeeper. Lack of money doesn't stop this family. David Milarch's wife, Kerry, has been the rock of the project, the steady hand in lean times.

David and his sons began their work in Michigan. With permission from private landowners they cloned the national champions—ash, elm, and maple. Jake and Tom Brodhagen worked in the greenhouse to push the frontiers of tree-cloning science. As clones sprouted and took root, saplings were shared in Michigan. Propagation is a method of producing genetically identical plants from a single parent plant. The resulting plant is a clone, meaning that 100 percent of its DNA matches the DNA of the plant from which it was propagated and that it yields the exact genetic traits of the parent tree. Propagation by seed collection, in comparison may yield only 50 percent of the genes of the seed-producing tree since the seeds may have been pollinated from another tree.

David and his sons then ventured into other states to continue their work. In Mount Vernon, the Milarchs were given access to trees planted by George Washington. The ash, hemlock, tulip poplar, cedar, and eight other species were cloned. Champion Trees donated twenty-five saplings of each of the species to Mount Vernon, and planted one of them ceremonially on the grounds of the U.S. Congress.[18] David has planted them ceremonially at a firemen's memorial in New York City, at the Pentagon a year after 9/11, at the Ford Motor Company, as well as in botanical gardens and college campuses.

David remembers that ten years ago when he was first speaking to the major media outlets around the world, the presidents in office at the time did everything in their power to deny climate change. Nevertheless, he and his sons were interviewed by the *Washington Post, London Times*, and *New York Times*, carrying his message of our need to reforest our planet to prevent destroying it. They also talked to timber companies, paper companies, and government agencies, telling them that 98 percent of old growth forests are gone and 96 percent of redwood forests have been cut down.

Yet in 2001 the Champion Tree Project that preceded the Archangel Ancient Tree Archive was lauded on the cover of *American Nurseryman Magazine, Washington Post, Chicago Tribune, Forbes, National Geographic, Smithsonian Magazine, London Times, Der Speigel*, and *The Guardian*. David appeared on television and radio shows such as *The Today Show, Good Morning America, All Things Considered*, and numerous other media outlets that brought him to public attention and elicited support from around the country.

David continues to work toward revitalizing stressed urban and watershed forests with selected robust strains of trees. He has propagated more than 130 species of trees including the tallest redwoods, and the oldest bristle cone pines, white oaks, and silver buttonwoods. He first worked with coast redwoods in 2008, collecting material from the stumps of trees felled in the late nineteenth and early twentieth century. His team collected and successfully propagated material from more than fifty old-growth trees.

In 2009 the Milarchs began their giant sequoia project. David and Jake made frequent trips to California in search of coast redwoods and giant sequoias. The trees he found in 2010 were on public lands that state and federal authorities blocked access for cloning. Jake is the person who climbs trees to gather cuttings of new sprouts for the greenhouse, and he traveled to the Sierra Nevada Mountains hunting for giant sequoias. By stopping in small towns and asking people where the biggest trees were located, he and his friend found an intact giant sequoia forest of 800 acres. Jake called his father who immediately flew out to meet him. The land was owned by a former logger who refused to let anyone near his trees but was open to David and Jake because of their project. One of the largest trees was the Stagg Tree, the fifth largest tree in the world; another was the Waterfall Tree which has the largest circumference of any giant sequoia at its base (155 feet) of any giant sequoia in the world and is the fourth largest tree on earth. The oldest giant sequoia ever cloned was eighty years old,[19] but the archive wanted to clone trees that were two to three thousand years old and they did.

It took many months for Jake and Tom to clone the magnificent tree, but Jake was successful and presented it to his father with great pride. The harvested material is cool-shipped overnight to Archangel's propagation facility where it is processed into small jars filled with a concentrated solution. In their greenhouse the cuttings are placed in tubes filled with hormones, fertilizer, and nutrients. Trays of tubes sit on heat mats until roots sprout. The process is the vegetative propagation of cuttings of new growth from the tops of mother trees. It takes about eight to ten days for them to grow. There are a series of rooms in the Milarch greenhouse, one is for the cuttings that are placed in tubes that take about two months, and sometimes as long as two years, to root. Fostering their growth means controlling the environment. After they are rooted they are brought to another room where the potted cuttings receive eighteen hours of light, humidity, and are kept at a temperature of seventy-five degrees. When they have grown they are transferred to a cooler room with twelve hours of light. The greenhouse is frequently open to young people from one in the afternoon to five o'clock so that a new generation can learn how to create new forests.

David and his sons also cloned thirty thousand black willows that clean the water better than any other trees. Obtaining genetic information isn't always easy. The best material for propagating and cloning is often at the top of the tree, and since some of these trees grow over four stories high, it can be dangerous work. Planting these potentially genetically superior clones in the wild allows the champion trees to cross-pollinate with other trees and produce sturdy offspring. These events could not have occurred without David Milarch's mystical powers he acquired after his visit with light beings. He discovered "on the other side" that science and the divine are connected.[20]

In 2012, a film crew from Brazilian TV network, Globo, traveled to northern California and northern Oregon to film a movie about the world's biggest trees and the role that Archangel Ancient Tree Archive is playing in restoring giant trees. David Milarch recalls that, when they were filming at the propagation facility, the crew kept saying that they loved to feel the energy in that building. The producer told Milarch that if the crew could capture that energy they seek around the big trees in the forest or the magic they feel around the propagation facility they could make a superior film and even win an award. They asked David "Can you show us how to pick up the energy we're feeling and the magic and why we feel better when we are near the trees?"[21] He replied, "You have to understand that they are living beings like human beings and animals, living, breathing, feeling, and communicating." He also told this to the person who inter-viewed him for a television program.

One morning David told the TV Globo crew that it was the magic moment. The six film people accompanied David to a lo-cal park where there were some massive redwoods near a river. David had learned years ago that a person is able communicate more effectively if he or she backs into the trees. He told a climber that she should turn around and put her heels in the ground, then lean against the tree, put her tailbone into the trunk, and the back of her head against the tree. Then she should put her hands on the tree, palms down, and breathe deeply in through her nose and out through her mouth three times, ask the tree to take any negative energy out of her aura or her body in order to communicate with the tree. After about five minutes while the crew was filming, she was breathing faster and deeper and there was a big smile on her face. David told her that when she was finished with the tree, she should thank it. She opened her eyes and started to stand up, groggy, but she had a big smile on her face and was wide-eyed.[22] She felt that she had really connected with the tree. The rest of the others and a couple of bystanders were both shocked and moved. Another one tried it, and then another member of the crew and had the same response. They believe that it was one of the most powerful footages they were able to film.

Globo's documentary, *Planeta Extremo-Sequoias Gigantas*, appeared on March 10, 2015, and was distributed to 130 countries reaching one hundred million viewers daily.[23] It gives a very good view of the propagation and cloning process as well as of the climbers who reach the top of the tall trees.

The TV crew members were exhilarated and almost frightened because, later that day, they saw a rainbow above one of the giant sequoias they were filming, although it was a very clear day. That same morning, the secretary of Archangel Ancient Tree Archive saw a rainbow and took a photo of it above their propagation facilities. David said that in the middle of winter, these rainbows were affirmations. David has found that there is scientific documentation of the way trees communicate what they are feeling. He claims that for thousands of years, the trees have been collecting stellar energy from many of the galaxies and believes that they are solar collectors photosynthesizing from the stars as well as the sun. Energies inside the earth are transmuted and transmitted into the cosmos by the trees, so the trees are like antennas, senders and receivers of earth energies and stellar energy. Many recent scientists and scholars are coming to the same conclusions on the galactic influence of trees and the reverse. University of Edinburgh researchers found that galactic cosmic rays were the biggest predictor of ring growth, rather than precipitation or temperature.[24] David told the TV crew that what that did was to put their bodies, their cellular structure and organs in a circuit that vibrates a lot higher than humans and is more intelligent. He added that they light up our DNA and memories will start to come forward, rendering a person more multidimensional.[25]

When the crew returned to Brazil, they emailed David to tell him that they had changed, that they felt that they had acquired more knowledge and a deeper consciousness. David realized that we don't think of ancient trees as conduits and teachers of an expanded consciousness, and he sadly remarked that we had cut almost all of them down. Yet he planted trees in England, Wales, and New Zealand, as well as throughout the United States. Many times people have told him that what David and his sons have accomplished is like Noah's Ark. He told everyone concerned that they are building that ark for the genetics of the great trees to rebuild the forest.

David has found that redwoods are drought-resistant, fire-proof, disease-proof, and have withstood many droughts over the thousands of years of their lives. They have a genetic memory of how to survive thousands of droughts. Trees are very powerful and much needed in this time of climate change. Also, on average, depending on their size, each tree stores two hundred pounds of carbon annually, filters air and water pollutants and toxic wastes in the soil. The flooding we have experienced throughout the world is exacerbated by deforestation and building on marshes. He found that we have cut what he refers to as mother trees that produce seeds to keep the forests alive. In addition, there are many beneficial aerosols that emerge from the leaves, and from the roots into the soil and the water that are natural disinfectants. The Archangel Ancient Tree Archive warehouse hosts thousands of cuttings, tissue samples, and cloned saplings of sequoias and redwoods, the world's largest carbon and water sequesters. In early 2015 they sent one thousand young trees to Oregon to start new forests. They chose to plant the trees north of the current range of coast redwoods as an assisted migration effort because they are unlikely to be able to survive in their current location as the climate continues to change.

Then there is phytoremediation, the use of green plants and trees to remove pollutants from the environment or render them harmless. The roots of certain plants such as Alpine pennycress and corn for example remedy heavy metals, dioxins, lead, toxins in our water, and soil.[26] Trees also absorb harmful metals and toxic wastes and are powerful water filters through a dense community of microbes around their roots. David Milarch's goal is to restore the ecosystems of our planet. He discovered that not only have we destroyed most of our forests around the world, but that we have also urbanized our planet by rivers, lakes, streams, and the oceans, where watersheds are the most predominant. He told a studio audience during one of his television interviews that one tree over fifty years gives services that are worth $162,000 and suggested that we plant trees in our own yards.

Through his connection with light beings, David Milarch has learned that the timeline of human habitation on this planet is a lot longer than what scientists understand. There have been three or four times during our lives on this planet when cultures and most of humanity were reduced to just a small number. And he believes that a few will be left behind and that we will start again. He has remarked that "this is the fourth time and, that we are heading to the same precipice for similar reasons—greed, arrogance, and lack of love—but that our energy and consciousness are opening simultaneously, and that the darkness will be replaced by the light."[27]

By 2013, David Milarch's work had become widely known. He and his team have been contacted with inquiries from 150 countries in the past three years. Keith Park, the leading expert of the redwood variety that was planted by John Muir in the 1880s, the John Muir Giant Sequoia, asked him to clone a John Muir Giant Sequoia. Although the tree looked healthy to the untrained eye, internal fungi that can't be eradicated infested it. Park was concerned that if the tree died, the world would lose a living link to a notable man, so he tried, unsuccessfully, to clone the redwood. Then in early 2013, he read a newspaper article about David Milarch and his plan to launch a worldwide movement with people planting millions of cloned trees, mitigating the effects of pollution and climate change, thus saving the plant.[28] He contacted David Milarch and asked him to clone the tree. David and his sons spent six months caring for the cuttings until the cuttings sprouted roots.

Although initially, many scientists and tree experts said that reforestation couldn't be accomplished by cloning, David's team has successfully cloned some of the world's oldest trees. Among the dozens of unique individual trees to be planted in a forest will be a duplicate of the Fieldbrook Redwood, a giant tree cut down in 1890, that measured 32.5 feet in trunk diameter and would have surpassed the General Sherman Sequoia as the largest tree on earth.

David's team's accomplishments include archiving the Brian Boru Oak, a legendary thousand-year-old common oak in Raheen Woods, County Clare, Ireland. At Ted Cook's house where the remote wilds of West Cork meet the slopes of Lee Valley were oaks that contain the precise DNA of the last remaining native and common oaks around Ireland. The Archangel Project sent people to clone trees to the tops of about 130 of all the oldest trees in Ireland. They successfully cloned the ancient oak, hazel, holly, and yew. As the oaks are the direct descendents of the ancient Irish forests that flourished after the Ice Age, they contain the genetic material best equipped to thrive. "We want to help Ireland reforest itself," said David Milarch. "It's imperative to reforest the planet and it makes sense to use the oldest, most iconic trees that ever lived."[29]

Another amazing feat is the Hippocrates Sycamore from Greece. When our country's original clone tree was dying, David's team took still living cuttings from the trunk and made genetic duplicates. There are now fifty Hippocrates Sycamores clones growing in their greenhouse. On Earth Day 2014, there was a ceremony in front of the National Institutes of Health in Bethesda, Maryland, and one was planted.[30]

The Milarch's old growth forest restoration is an integral part of an approved forest conservation plan that provides a focal point for ongoing sustainability initiatives within the local community stewardship area and surrounding Curry County, Oregon. It is a rare place on earth where scenic rivers rush through steep canyons on their way to the Pacific Ocean, and where the tallest and largest carbon-sequestering forest in the world still exists.

Rama Nemani, an earth scientist wrote, "It's amazing for one layman to come up with the idea of saving champion trees as a meaningful way to address the issues of biodiversity and climate change. This could be a grass roots solution to a global problem. A few million people planting and selecting the right trees for the right places could really make a difference."[31]

The major successes of the Archangel Ancient Tree Archive in 2013 included cloning ancient champion coast redwoods and planting them in seven different countries around the world Australia, New Zealand, Great Britain, Ireland, Canada, Germany, and the United States.[32] The following year, Archangel sent one hundred coast redwoods to the Eden Project in England and ten clones of ten different ancient coast redwoods to create Europe's first old growth redwood forest. It had also established the world's first cloned champion redwood and sequoia grove in Oregon to assist migration during climate change. Traditionally, conservation biologists have sought to protect endangered plants and animals where they live, creating refuges where species can be protected from threats.[33] Now David is accomplishing assisted migration because of dramatic climate changes, and restoration might be in an area far from the tree's actual origin. For example, the proliferation of mountain pine beetles in the American West and in Canada has occurred because of the disappearance of bitterly cold winter nights that killed off the beetles. Instead, warming has allowed them to ravage tens of millions of acres, from forests. The pine beetles burrow beneath the bark and lay their eggs, from which larvae hatch and eat the moist membrane under the bark, the tree's life support. The damage is so severe that it can be seen from space.[34] The same destruction has occurred in New Jersey. Also because of specific pests, David Milarch has told supporters that a forest should include no more than 10 percent of any species, no more than 20 percent of any genus, and no more than 30 percent of any family. He has also emphasized an appropriate mix of native species and site-specifics, noninvasive exotics, and a mix of young and mature trees.

The archive's global media messaging has reached over two hundred million people in over 150 countries. It has created an international organization by establishing a registered charity in Europe. David Milarch offered to clone some of Britain's most important trees, oaks, yews, and firs. He planned to reproduce all of the United Kingdom's super-trees and to offer tens of thousand of their genetically identical offspring free to schools, cities, and landowners. David Milarch was in the United Kingdom for talks with specialists on ancient trees, and Prince Charles. He drew up a list of super-trees to start cloning in the summer of 2013. He planned to establish a complete archive of all of Britain's most important trees, which would be publicly available.[35] He also worked in New Zealand to reestablish giant Kauri trees and was commissioned to recreate a forest of all the greatest trees in Africa.

In 2015, David Milarch partnered with Sir Tim Smit, Executive Vice Chairman of the Eden Project, to plant one hundred redwood saplings as the foundation of Europe's first old-growth redwood forest in the United Kingdom. Inspired by the success of David's work, the Eden Project began to plan a United Kingdom–wide ancient tree cloning project. The United Kingdom has more ancient trees than the rest of northern Europe, with 130,000 already mapped. Any tree over four hundred years old is likely to be in the wild, and thus more diverse than modern forestry selections.

Because David Milarch and his sons are working for the future in a country that seems to live in the present, Archangel Ancient Tree Archive started to write a K–12 educational curriculum inspired by the book, *The Man Who Planted Trees: Lost Groves, Champion Trees and an Urgent Plan to Save the Planet.* In 2013, the University of Michigan Permaculture Design Team received a four-thousand-year-old sequoia tree clone from David and his sons' organization. In January 2014 University of Michigan students partnered with Chiwara Permaculture Research and Education, an Ann Arbor–based firm that investigates permaculture solutions in food, energy, water, building, transportation, and waste to conduct research into the number of champion sequoia trees required to offset the University of Michigan's carbon footprint.[36]

Archangel Ancient Tree Archive is now partnering with Michigan schools and universities to offer hands-on, learning programs in nature awareness, agro-forestry, and Permaculture design from the Archangel research and education facility in Copemish. Both programs, We Are the Forest, and Tree School, engage students in problem solving through community reforestation projects. We Are the Forest teaches technology, engineering, arts, and mathematics through civic-service learning and includes nature awareness permaculture design, biomimicry and agro-forestry solutions, forestry arts, music and movement, tree propagation, and reforestation, tree planting at either school site or Archangel facility.

The Tree School is for grades nine through twelve, as well as for university and adult education. It also includes four parts that are conducted at the Archangel facility or a school greenhouse. Activities include tree identification and native tree libraries, polycultures, tree climbing equipment and fieldwork, tree propagation techniques, permaculture design, and agro-forestry installation and planting trees.

The programs are offered throughout the state and establish a partnership with leading schools, while performing ecological reforestation, education and economic development projects. They now work at the grassroots level from which like a ripple on a lake, their message can spread for many miles and begin to change people's consciousness about what is taking place in our world and how to make a difference. Among the partners of the educational programs are fourteen universities and schools, including the Interlochen Arts Academy. A teacher at Interlochen, Mary Ellen Newport, wrote a thank-you note to David Milarch, in which she passed on her students' reaction to his talk about climate change. She found that it was very important to have the students introduce themselves to him, as it helped them to talk to each other about climate change rather than being "talked at by adults." After his talk she found them somber, reflective, and able to discuss their knowledge with their peers. Mary Ellen Newport and Marvine Stamatakis are developing an online course for students around the world to help them learn about climate change, ongoing scientific research on climate change, and understand the role of afforestation and reforestation in ameliorating atmospheric carbon, and the role of Archangel Ancient Tree Archive that makes it possible for children to plant trees wherever they live. This is a quiet and peaceful revolution to save our planet.

The Ford Foundation, which is helping to finance the project for education, sponsored Grand Valley University students to make a video of David for Ford's Go Further Campaign. His talk is an inspiration that shows how one person can make a difference in this world if he or she is passionate about their goals. The video had 1,500 viewers in just a few days. He and his sons have not only cloned 130 species of trees and had them planted around the world, but through their education programs have reached out to the younger generation to teach them about the lives of trees and how they can sustain and save our warming planet. In giving important lesson to young people around the world on how to plant trees and care for them, David Milarch uses his skills as an excellent communicator.

A 2014 report by an interdisciplinary team of professors from the University of California Los Angeles and five other universities came up with a number of approaches to dissipating greenhouse gases and reducing global warming. The study ranks a wide range of approaches to minimizing climate change in terms of cost effectiveness, risk, public acceptance, management, and ethics. Of the five options evaluated, sequestering carbon through biological means holds the most promise. The group calculated that curbing the destruction of forests and promoting the growth of new forests, could absorb as much as 1.3 gigatons of carbon annually.[37] This study confirms the work conducted by the Archangel Ancient Tree Archive more than twenty years later.

Finally, parts of our government are researching climate change. In 2007, the Pentagon's Military Advisory board prepared the first major study to make a connection between climate change and national security. It updated this study in 2014, linking the accelerating rate of climate change to the risk for global conflict. It found that climate change in the Middle East and Africa created conflicts over food and water and escalated regional and ethnic tensions into violent clashes. The CIA also established a center to collect information about climate change in 2013. CIA officials emailed environmental experts in Washington to seek their views on climate change impact around the world, and how the agency could stay abreast of what actions countries were taking to reduce greenhouse emission. It is interesting to compare what David Milarch and his sons have accomplished with the foreknowledge and expertise with the recent studies by those in power of the role of trees in stabilizing the climate, and of the connection between trees and stellar energy. The comparison makes all the more remarkable their extraordinary ability to clone thousands of trees from old, resilient trees such as redwoods.

Since early 2014, the Milarchs have partnered with PEM, Planetary Emissions Management Inc. CEO Bruno D. V. Marino's plan addresses the fact that "Climate change impacts on communities present a compelling case for afforestation with selecting tree species including Champion trees. We have to think outside of the box to get ahead of extreme events such as Hurricane Sandy."[38] PEM is testing a patented field instrument, the first of its kind to measure the three species of carbon dioxide in forest air. Its technology will provide a full accounting of the carbon sequestration dynamics of the new large-tree forest at Ocean Mountain Ranch in Oregon including its capacity to absorb carbon dioxide from fossil fuel combustions. It began a project to monitor, verify, and account for carbon in Maine's forests, which like every other forest, have changed substantially in the last two hundred years, resulting in widespread deforestation and growth related to agriculture, lumber production, the paper industry, and urban expansion. Original old growth forest represents a very small percentage of forest cover. PEM's goal is to leave a legacy of opportunity and sustainable benefits to landowners, which includes a new source of revenue to support land management while preserving and restoring biodiversity as well as providing the community and public with a working knowledge of forests.

Like Milarch's Archangel project, PEM was created out of a concern about the two perils of climate change and energy production that will shape the lives of future generations. What makes PEM's project so interesting is that it is a program for saving our planet that provides revenue so that people can earn their living by working on behalf of our earth. The first test of this technology combination will be at Ocean Mountain Ranch in Oregon where the world's first champion coast redwood and giant sequoia grove was successfully planted in 2012.

The Milarchs are also partnering with Ocean Mountain Ranch project manager Terry Mock, who acts as a part time sustainability consultant to the Archangel Ancient Tree Archive and served as executive director of the Archive's predecessor, Champion Tree Project International. He is overseeing the development of a sustainable carbon-negative project to demonstrate how landowners can be provided with incentives to regrow old growth forests. Ocean Mountain Ranch is a model mixed-use sustainable ecoforestry project overlooking the southern Oregon coast that is implementing a forest stewardship plan to meet the Port Orford Community stewardship area's environmental, social, and economic needs by using ecosystem-based best practice for natural resource management.

Archangel Tree Archive has supported several activities on Arbor Day, April 18, 2014. They included the planting of twenty-five cloned giant sequoias and one Hippocrates Sycamore by Interlochen Arts Academy students as part of a new earth science course, and a presentation by the University of Michigan students about their assessment of how many ancient trees it will need to offset the carbon footprint of the university. A Michigan food coop gave away 1,200 cloned willows and dogwoods as a gift to its local community while Northwest Michigan College gave away 250 cloned champion willows and dogwoods. The list of cloned champion trees planted as gifts in Oregon, Bethesda, Maryland, the United Kingdom, and Canada, is a long one.

Eighteen years ago David was approached by a number of Native Americans who were medicine people. A small group of Chippewa came to the farm unannounced wanting to talk to him and his sons. They shared what their visions had been for centuries about the forest, the animals, and the earth and told David that he and his sons had a role to play in reversing the damage they had suffered. Subsequently the chief Medicine Man of the Seminoles in Florida came to visit the Milarchs after he had heard about their work to save the giant trees, and requested a private meeting with David. He told David that in their legends and in their oral history, the Great White Bear of the North would come down and bring back the forest that we were destroying and that David was that very Great White Bear. Then the Sioux people came and then some of the tribes from the Pacific Northwest. David discovered that a lot of Native Americans, their shamans and leaders have known that a bear man would lead their project. Wherever the Milarchs have traveled, even when they are in Europe, indigenous people appear and tell them that they are so glad to see them because their oral history has foreseen him and his sons in these times and that our Creator would not allow the planet to be destroyed. What most of us are unaware of is that forests were not only a source of food for the First Peoples, but of medicine for every kind of ailment, including cancer. Because the water in the forests is contaminated, this natural medicine is no longer available.

Jonathan Lear has written about the cultural devastation of Native American nations and how they respond when their values, traditions, and ways of life are shattered. The Crow people once encouraged younger members of their nation to go off alone into nature and dream. The visions that resulted would give them an understanding beyond their daily lives and practice as well as giving them powerful insights into the future. Young Plenty Coups was called to go off and dream when he was nine years old. The young man reported, "I saw only a dark forest. A fierce storm was coming fast. The sky was black with streaks of mad color through it. I saw the Four Winds gathering to strike the forest and held my breath. Pity was hot in my heart for those beautiful trees. I felt pity for all things that lived in the forest, but was powerless to stand against the Four Winds that together were making war. I shielded my face with my arm when they charged. I heard the Thunders calling out in the storm, saw beautiful trees twist like blades of grass and fall in tangled piles where the forest had been."[39] The Crow people believed that because the Creator is good, his transcendence and good will occur.

The tree plays an important part in the spirituality of pre-Columbian Mesoamerican cultures. Several Amazonian peoples of eastern Peru believe that deities live in Ceiba trees throughout the jungle. The Maya civilization believed, Yaaxché, a concept of the central world tree is often depicted as a Ceiba trunk that connects the underworld, the terrestrial realm and the skies. Modern Mayans still often respectfully make sure that the tree remains when harvesting forest timber. The Ceiba tree is represented by a cross and serves as an important architectural motif in the Temple of the Cross Complex at Palenque. Ceiba Tree Park is located in San Antón, Ponce, and Puerto Rico. Its centerpiece is the historic Ceiba de Ponce, a five-hundred-year-old *Ceiba pentandra* tree associated with the founding of the city. It is also the national tree of Guatemala.[40]

Thomas Parkenham, aware that certain trees were disappearing too rapidly, traveled the world to photograph them. In New

Zealand he photographed two giant Kauris that were revered by the Maori as gods, Te Matua Ngahere (Father of the Forest) and Tane Mahuta (Lord of the Forest). Fewer than a dozen giant Kauari have survived two hundred years of logging.[41] He also traveled to Santa Maria del Tule near the Oaxacan city in the highlands of Southern Mexico to photograph El Arbol del Tule, one of the biggest girth tree recorded in the world. The Zapotec people gathered there, regarding it as a mother goddess whose many trunks spiraling from the base is an embrace. The Zapotec's story that the Pechocha, servant to Ehecatle, storm God of the Aztecs planted the tree 1,400 years ago, was confirmed by scientists.[42]

The first peoples of these lands cherished every plant, animal, the rivers, the ocean, and the trees, believing that human beings did not rule nature but were part of it and honored everything within it. When the Spaniards traveled to establish an empire in what is now known as Latin and Central America, they decimated many of the first peoples; Hernán Cortéz hung the Aztec emperor Cuauhtéemoc from the Ceiba tree. Centuries later, people around the world studied botany, and entomology and produced much that has been more than useful to our survival, but scientists and teachers did not perceive the connection between the divine and nature the way that David Milarch has.

In fact, Archangel Ancient Tree Archive's board includes experts from many disciplines to further their vision. Frank Ettawageshik believes that native people need to be rooted in their traditions in order to be prepared for the future. He served in a tribal-elected office for sixteen years. During his tenure as tribal chairman of the Little Traverse Bay Bands of Odawa Indians in Harbor Springs, he was instrumental in the adoption of the Tribal and First Great Nations Great Lakes Water Accord in 2004. Now serving as the Executive Director of the

United Tribes of Michigan, he is also the chairman of the United League of Indigenous Nations governing board. His forty years of public service in a number of fields have made him a valued member of Archangel Ancient Tree Archive Board. In fact, a Native American told David that Copemish is an Ojibwa word for big beech tree.

Another member of the board is Ian Ashken who is also a member of the boards of other businesses and charitable organizations. Dana King is an award-winning veteran journalist who has traveled extensively and reported on war, natural disasters, and inhumane conditions around the world. She is also an honorary board member of Sunnyhills Services; a nonprofit designed to meet the needs of emotionally and mentally disturbed, neglected youth. David's son Jared is executive director and chairman of the board.

As mentioned earlier, Diana Beresford-Kroeger speaks out for our planet in a way that is both scientific and mystical much as David Milarch views our forests.

> The bioplan is a blueprint for all connectivity of life in nature. It is the fragile web, which keeps each creature in balance with its neighbor. . . . It is the victor and victim in a vast cycle of elemental life, which is almost beyond our comprehension. It is the quantum mechanic of the green chloroplast without which we would all die. . . . It is the ultraviolet traffic light signaling system in flowers for the insect world. It is the terrene aerosol produced by plants in response to invasive damage. It is the toxin trick offered by plants for the protection of butterflies. It is the mantle of man, in his life and in his death, a divine contract to all who share this planet.[43]

Now newspapers like the *New York Times*, *Guardian*, *Huffington Post*, *Nature*, and other scholarly journals are filled with stories about climate change. In fact, at the end of 2014, the *New York Times* published a three-page article on how restored forests are making inroads on climate change. It included maps and color-coded marks that reveal the enormous losses of forests around the world and some of their restoration.[44] Many of the problems of deforestation that David and his team have been making public for so many years are now in the mainstream media.

Many groups have now organized for working against climate change including Physicians for Social Responsibility, the Union of Concerned Scientists (UCS), Earth Justice, Oceana, among many others. UCS has worked against the destruction of tropical forests for palm oil plantations because they play a crucial role in stabilizing the earth's climate, storing more carbon dioxide than forests in the world's temperate regions. Tropical forests also host two-thirds of the earth's biodiversity. The UCS has persuaded thirteen companies to use only deforestation-free palm oil in their products: Colgate-Palmolive; ConAgra foods; Danone; Dunkin' Brands; Procter & Gamble; General Mills; Hershey; Kao; Kellogg's; Krispy Krème; L'Oreal; McDonald's (which finally agreed in 2015); and PepsiCo. Taco Bell, however, still refuses to change its practice. UCS also helped spur a corporate exodus from the American Legislative Exchange Council (ALEC), which has attacked clean energy in more than a dozen states. Facebook is the newest addition to the list of more than eighty corporations, including technology corporations like Microsoft and Yahoo that have cut their support for ALEC. In June 2015 Pope Francis's encyclical "Praise Be to You," intones that everything is interconnected to God, to creation, and fellow humans. It repeatedly invokes "our Sister, Mother Earth," and "brother sun, sister moon," from the canticle of St. Francis of Assisi. Further, he comments that the proper relationship between humanity and the earth has been broken.[45] Pope Francis organized a two-day conference to combat global warming and help the poor deal with its effects, attended by about sixty mayors from around the world including two from the United States. His intent was to mobilize grassroots action and maintain pressure on world leaders for action ahead of a global summit meeting on climate change in Paris. Many people of different faiths have pointed out that the destruction of our planet is a moral issue. For example, the Reverend Sally Bingham started an organization the Regeneration Project and the Interfaith Power and Light Campaign. She has defined global warming as an ethical issue and has mobilized thousands of religious people to take action.

Despite the climate agreement signed in Paris on December 12, 2015, an agreement marking the international acceptance of the risks of climate change, the majority of members of the U.S. Congress and Senate still oppose working to save our planet, even though one-third of the Congress is Catholic, and most of our young people are concerned about climate change. This has made David Milarch and his sons' work all the more significant. It is remarkable to think that one man and his two amazing sons have been able to attract volunteers and businesses around the country and abroad, steadily and with spiritual rather than political goals. Their work preceded that of religious leaders and is about the power of hope, hard work, and raising people's awareness.

TWO

Adam Seligman and the Creation of the CEDAR Program

Communities Engaging with Difference and Religion (CEDAR) is an organization that seeks to bring together members of different religions and engender mutual respect and understanding. Everyone is aware of the conflict between adherents of different religions throughout the world that have caused war and horrific genocides. There have always been people who respected and took care of members of different religions who are suffering, such as the Catholic priest in Syria who created warm relations with the Muslims, sheltered them in his church, and was then killed by members of Islamic State of Iraq and the Levant (ISIL) in April 2014. When in July 2014, Christians fled Mosul, a city controlled by ISIL extremists, Muslims and Christians gathered under a church roof in Baghdad where both Muslims and Christians held signs "I'm Iraqi, I'm Christian."[1] And there have been heroines, like Vera Laska during World War II, who at the age of fifteen began accompanying Jewish people who were fleeing the Nazis and wound up in Auschwitz herself.[2] Adam Seligman and his organization are dedicated to creating widespread understanding to eliminate hatred, prejudice, and the terrible violence that ensues.

What motivated him to start this organization was the extent to which he was affected he was by the war in 1992 and 1995 in Bosnia-Herzegovina and Croatia. He claims that it made a huge impact on him, less than fifty years after the destruction of European Jews, thousands of people in the middle of Europe were still murdering people on the basis of their religion. According to Misha Glenny, there were three wars in Bosnia-Herzegovina; the first war involved Serbs and Croatians; the second war took place between Serbs and Muslims; and the third pitted Serb irregulars with a huge arsenal of heavy artillery against the urban dwellers of Sarajevo.[3] The Serbs left a horrific trail of blood and devastation in their wake. A book of writings about Bosnian women refugees, *Sjecam Se: I Remember*, edited by Radmilla Manojlovic Zarković,[4] is a collection of devastating stories of loss of husbands, home, rape, and also of the Women in Black Movement which objects to the war, militarism, nationalism, ethnic cleansing, and the rape of women during a war. Adam Seligman was so preoccupied with that terrible period that he wrote a book on trust.[5] He wrote the book to clarify the issue in his own mind and concluded "Trust is what you need when you cannot predict. We need trust when the other is free and has agency."[6] A sociologist living in Bosnia gave it to a man called Rusmir Mahmutćehafić who had been the Deputy Prime Minister and the Minister of Munitions during that war. He was so moved by the book that he invited him to Sarajevo where he, an observant Muslim, and Adam, a practicing Jew, got on famously.

As a result of the time he spent there, Adam Seligman founded the International Summer School on Religion and

Public Life in Sarajevo in 2002 that facilitated its growth into CEDAR. He and Rusmir Mahnutčehafič received funding for a project in Israel where Adam Seligman lived for many years, and in Bosnia to develop curricula in order to impart the values of democracy and pluralism for religious students in religious schools. It began with preparing elementary school teachers. He then organized two conferences, one in Berlin, Can One Have a Belief in Something Sacred and Still Be a Pluralist, which fostered discussions on how one can be tolerant while believing deeply in one's religion, and how one can be a devoted or ortho- dox member of his or her religion and yet be open to another religion without having to forgo one's interpretation of religion. Another conference on this topic took place in Vienna and gen- erated great interest. News of the conference was published in newspapers and journals printed in English, German, Bosnian, and Albanian. He then discovered that grants were being given to liberal religious initiatives, but didn't include grants to deal with religions that are recalcitrant and promote violence.

This experience led Adam Seligman to reexamine his per- spective on life. He was a professor of sociology for many years, before deciding to become a professor of religion. The concept of free will is very important to him and he believes that it can- not be reduced to psychology, or to a secular notion, but rather that it should be linked to transcendence, and a religious view of the world. He felt that there was a deep need to find a way out of pogroms, crusades, and inquisitions—all the hatred and strife that religion has brought. That is at the core of his establishment of CEDAR, of his work in that program, and in the books that he has written.

The CEDAR program started with a small staff of four: a person from Israel; a Muslim from Bosnia; a Catholic from Croatia; and a former graduate student of Adam Seligman,

David Montgomery, who is an active member of the Presbyterian Church. Their work focuses on the transmission of religious and cultural knowledge, expressions of everyday religious life, and social aspects of religious change in Central Asia and the Balkans. Today there are eight staff members, including Adam Seligman's wife, Rahel Wasserfall, who was born in France, but moved to Israel because she was deeply hurt by the anti-Semitism she experienced in France. Reflecting on her adolescent feelings, she said, "As a Jew I would never really belong to France. I loved France, but she did not love me back."[7] However, France is not as homogenous a country as many people believe; today there is amity among Christians and Jews, although it is indeed difficult for Muslims who are also immigrants. In Israel Rahel Wasserfall became a member of the Women in Black, which was organized to create peace between Israel and Palestine. She also supported the Peace Now movement at the beginning of the 1980s, an alternative voice that has grown to find a two-state solution.

Although she now lives in the United States, Wasserfall is especially concerned about politics in France, especially the success of Marine Le Pen's views, and she feels that today the Muslims who are not regarded as truly French citizens are experiencing what the French Jews experienced in the past. In fact, Marine Le Pen's right-wing National Front's party stunned France by winning its first mayoral elections on March 23, 2014. In the second round of municipal elections the party took control of eleven towns in France, giving Marine Le Pen's anti–European Union, anti-immigration, anti-Muslim, and pro-Russian party a strong showing.[8] Further, the National Front's strong showing in the elections for the European Parliament, with the Socialist Party and the scandal-plagued Union for a Popular Movement, has emboldened Ms. Le Pen to start working toward the presidency in 2017.

In fact, the right-wing parties all over Western and Eastern Europe are gaining votes. Adam B. Bartos, a thirty-four-year-old Czech journalist who is running for elections to the European Parliament, is campaigning with an anti-Semitic appeal and has called for the country to leave the European Union that he portrays as a "superstate" undermining Czech sovereignty. Parties outside the political mainstream are expected to win as many as a quarter of the 750 seats in the EU parliament. Leaders on the extreme right see the European Union as a gateway for illegal immigrants, and have been fueled by dissatisfaction with the economic situation in their countries.[9] In other words, the "other" has become a scapegoat for problems within these countries, which is another reason why CEDAR's work is so very important.

The program combines lectures with site visits to different churches, mosques, or synagogues, and there is intense discussion in small groups. The goal of these programs is to learn how to live with religious differences, to accept these differences and to build trust and solidarity among them. In 2003 Adam Seligman and his staff members traveled back to Sarajevo, where they saw huge crosses from the Christian part of the area trying to dominate the Muslim area. They even saw crosses in front of a mosque. That year the first CEDAR program was established in Bosnia to discuss issues of difference and tolerance. The theme of these events changed over the years and CEDAR staff working with locals dealt with other issues, such as gender and poverty, that came to the fore.

For each of its schools, CEDAR sends out a call for fellows on the Internet, usually receiving 150 applications for thirty places. These fellows are generally clergy, high school principals, high school teachers, teacher educators, nongovernmental leaders, politicians at the municipal level, and journalists. They come from all over the world. The criteria call for people of a general maturity who will carry on what they have learned in their own settings. CEDAR has had great success with high school teachers and principals. One fellow was the supervisor of citizenship education for Israel, who, in the following year, sent his deputy to Gaza. A program in Bulgaria included a high-school teacher from Rome, who discovered that the entire multicultural program in Rome's schools skirted the most important issues. As a result, she is working to redevelop it entirely.

Visiting sites is a very important part of the program. Adam remembers having a discussion about Palestinian refugees in Israel in 2005 that took place within a village abandoned in 1948. He remembers a Jewish member of the group telling him that he had been there thirty times, but had never been inside a Palestinian house. He believes that there is a special resonance in being in such places. In Bosnia, a Croatian woman, as she stood outside a former hospital that had been turned into a torture center and where Croatian fighters had tortured hundreds of men and boys, told Adam Seligman that standing in that place was the most difficult moment of her life.

CEDAR has brought these programs all over the world, each of them different, yet with the aim of mutual understanding and respect. For instance, it had a program in Birmingham, one of England's most diverse cities, with 47 percent of its population of Pakistani, Chinese, or Indian ethnic origin, which focused on how people from a mixture of ethnic and religious backgrounds live together. The staff and fellows worked with the Citizens of Birmingham that is an association of Muslims, Christians, and Sikhs. Fellows attended mosques, a gurdwara, and a metropolitan church with a gay and lesbian congregation. They saw a movie on being gay, Jewish, and Orthodox and followed it with a discussion. Many religions are not welcoming to homosexuals, but in some Muslim countries homosexuality is considered a crime, which makes it more than difficult for devout Muslims.

The fellows attend sessions from 7:30 a.m. to 10:30 p.m. sharing their meals and going to all events as a group. There are two principles and two rules. First, a fellow needs to attend every event. Everybody who participates comes with a lot of baggage, feeling that their ethnic, religious, tribal, racial, and gender group has some monopoly on suffering. Adam Seligman doesn't expect people to divest themselves of such feelings, but rather that, in their interaction with each other, they must not relate to another person as if they had a monopoly on suffering. Instead they should respect everyone. If they don't, he or she feels that "the other" is not present, but only a function of their needs. In other words, they must be able to temporarily step out of themselves and their personal experiences and be willing to challenge what they already know.

After the lectures, the fellows are divided into small groups for discussions; six groups of five people stay together throughout the two-week program. Every two days they are given a question that is connected to the themes that are discussed those days. The staff raises a question whose purpose is to allow the fellows to bring up their personal feelings. A typical question is "when did you ever feel uncomfortable with your own religious or ethnic group?" A member of the group then tells a story about how he or she was treated because of the beliefs he or she professed and practiced. The fellows sit in a circle to express themselves, and no one is allowed to interrupt another person because some people speak a lot and some don't speak at all. There is a protocol where people are allowed to speak for six minutes without being interrupted to guarantee that everyone speaks and everyone shares. These conversations are not shared outside the group. The members of a large group could be organizers, staff, or members of the group of fellows, but they are also members of the small facilitation group of five or six fellows so that they constantly have to negotiate those different identities. The idea behind this structure is to create the greatest possibility of diversity among them.

There are twelve days of lectures on a mix of academic and nonacademic topics. Afterward, the group of fellows will visit the community that is hosting the program. CEDAR had a program that encompassed the Roma community, whose abuse few people are aware of. The most notable example of their rejection in European society was President Hollande's ejection of the Roma community from France in 2013. The Roma are the European continent's largest minority of eleven million, who fight for survival on the fringes of society. Despite the lessons of Nazi history when the Roma (Gypsies) were rounded up for extermination, right-wing politicians continue to demonize Roma. For example, in Slovakia, four hundred mayors have created a movement using health and safety regulations to shut off or wall off Roma communities.[10] Like Hollande in France, the Hungarian government ejected the Roma from Hungary. The CEDAR program steps in where many people fear to go to address such terrible problems.

Rahel Wasserfall has wide-ranging experience in the evaluation of CEDAR's educational programs in complex multilingual and cross-cultural settings. She conducts the annual evaluation of programs and is part of the leadership team. She is also involved in training and leading new program developments and evaluations internationally. Her role as an internal evaluator of the group is to look at the impact of their action and how the fellows receive it. During each school she takes notes, interviews fellows, and gives them open questionnaires to see how they fared in their experience of the school. She then writes a report on what they learned and accomplished and what needs to be changed. Among CEDAR staff are a communications manager and a program advisor.

The fellows have to be able to speak English, as Adam Seligman feels that it would take too much time if interpreters were needed every moment of the two weeks and not having a common language would ruin the building of relationships among the fellows. In the small groups, some people do have difficulties with English and receive help from other members of the group, which is part of the group's bonding experience. Fellows are aged from their late twenties to late sixties. Seligman feels that anyone younger than his or her late 20s is not mature enough for CEDAR programs. Another important feature of these programs is that they bring together people from different troubled countries. For example, CEDAR brought people from Palestine and Israel to programs they held in the Balkans.

The first school provided fellows with a long reading list. Now CEDAR makes some basic information available online about the country they are going to visit, which is different every year. Lecturers are advised to send reading materials that are not more than twenty pages. One year, a staff member had a strong connection to poetry and taught in prisons in the United States. As a result, CEDAR started a program with him helping people to write poems at the beginning and the end of the program. Poetry is a wonderful way of expressing deep inner feelings that may be kept silent.

CEDAR is fortunate to have people who come to a program every year, give lectures and are sometimes able to show their commitment by paying for their transportation costs. One such person is Silvio Ferrari, a professor of Canon Law in Milan, who is an expert on church-state relations in Europe. Anver Emon gives annual lectures on Islamic Law. When CEDAR organized a program in Bulgaria, lecturers from Turkey came to discuss the school's theme, which was religious syncretism. The program asks such people to stay for three or four days so that they understand the nature of the group. Adam Seligman found that sometimes the hardest thing to do for academics is to talk like human beings and not in academic jargon. He understands that life experiences are a profound source of education.

CEDAR did have a program in Boston with the Boston Ten-Point Coalition, a coalition of African-American preachers and Boston police, groups that were natural enemies. The Ten-Point Coalition was started in 2001 by the Reverend Jeffrey Brown and calls upon church and faith-based agencies of Boston to work collaboratively to develop an action plan aimed at reducing violence and helping youth to develop more positive and productive life styles. Its program includes, among many other supports, commissioning youth workers to do street work with drug dealers and gang members. It is wide-ranging and deals with struggles of women and poverty, having established rape crises drop-in centers. Fellows from all over the world came to CEDAR's Boston program. One Saturday they went to an African-American Baptist church in Cambridge, and the following Monday they went to the police station in Roxbury and discussed issues from the perspective of the police. The next day the Reverend Brown and Chris Winship, a Harvard University professor who has written about the issues between these two groups, spoke at the event. The group heard many different perspectives, which is CEDAR's idea of developing knowledge.

An informative book by Alice Goffman, *On the Run*,[11] reveals how police and youth in impoverished neighborhoods are at odds. She spent six years living in a neighborhood where young African American men were in and out of prison and often on the run from police for major and minor infractions. She also experienced firsthand what it was like to be interrogated by the police and what happens when a SWAT team breaks down your door. Additionally, she experienced the death of a young man who was killed while leaving her car. Goffman observed how the intense police surveillance of the neighborhood often encouraged the criminal behavior it was designed to prevent, emphasizing a nationwide problem of relations between police and impoverished youth. While the book may be widely read, CEDAR is trying to fill a need that is not visible in the social media.

CEDAR schools have taken place in many countries where religion and ethnicity are important issues. For example, in 2007, they established their two-week school in Turkey, where they discussed the genocide of Armenians and the relations between Christians and Muslims. There was also a CEDAR program in Cyprus. As mentioned previously, CEDAR brings people from diverse places that have experienced a lot of conflict in their country, such as Pakistan, Bulgaria, and Poland.

Funding CEDAR is a very difficult aspect of its program. When it worked on a program for refugees, United Nations Relief and Rehabilitation Administration (UNRRA) sent two Palestinians to a program. CEDAR works very hard to come up with a few thousand dollars each year so it can bring its contacts in Jordan, Turkey, Bosnia, Palestine, Uganda, and Bulgaria to its programs. One university has funded people from its university, and United States Agency for International Development (USAID) who sent people over from Central Asia over the years. Paying for transportation and lodging is a burdensome task. The program is not aimed at the elite who can pay their own way. For instance, in Africa, those who pay their own way may be corrupt and have contact with political officials. If a priest needs to be brought from the Republic of the Congo to Tunisia, the program needs to pay for his bus fare and for his visa.

Adam Seligman's work is multitasked. In addition to designing the schools and working to fund them, he travels frequently, sending and receiving emails all day from 5 a.m. and using the telephone frequently. For instance, he will have a small meeting in Pittsburgh, Pennsylvania, with people from East Africa, Southern Africa, Bulgaria, and Canada. In other words, he is in constant contact with people he has worked with or will be involved with the CEDAR program.

CEDAR also has affiliate programs. Anver M. Emon, Director of the Connaught Summer Institute on Islamic Studies and author of books on Islamic law, heads one. He teaches tort law and offers specialized seminars on Islamic legal history, gender and Islamic law, law and religion. Dr. Schnitter is also a Director of the Balkan Summer School on Religion and Public Life. She is a native of Bulgaria, teaches throughout Europe, and is the Dean of the Faculty of Philosophy and History at the University of Plovdiv, Bulgaria. Her major publications are devoted to Orthodox ritual practices. Maximiano Ngabriano is the director of the Equator Peace Academy. He received his PhD in theology from the Catholic University of Leuven and is a senior lecturer at the Institute of Ethics and Development Studies at a university in Uganda. He is part of a team conducting research on diversity, marginalization, and pluralism. He and a nun, Sister Margaret, organized the Equator Peace Academy held in December 2014 to deal with the heart-aching issue of refugees in East Africa. An Anglican priest from Zimbabwe is organizing a school related to the CEDAR program, which is a further indication of its multicultural dynamic nature.

Thus, a wonderful result of the programs is that fellows use CEDAR's model and have created their own structure, and similar schools have now been established in Canada, Bulgaria, Zimbabwe, and Uganda which have their own staffs, directors, and websites. In the Balkans and in East and Southern Africa, local people have taken on the responsibility to create a program, raising funds, and vetting applicants. For the future, Adam Seligman wants as wide a network as possible of people running such schools and sharing the knowledge they acquired.

Adam Seligman's work enables people who are suffering to view similar experiences in different contexts, which is a very important approach for people to learn about themselves and the world. If a community has suffered and its members' only contacts are within that community, it is very difficult for that community to break away from a certain way of looking at the world. If, however, they are introduced to other people from another part of the world with a different skin color and a different religion that lived through similar experiences, community members can change their outlooks and see the world differently. This is a very creative way of learning that holds the world together. CEDAR's program has been running for twelve years and has taken place in twelve countries including Bulgaria, Croatia, Cyprus, Indonesia, Israel, Turkey, England, and the United States. The organization's remarkable achievements have been to change misunderstanding that often leads to hatred and violence, into trust and mutual respect. It is truly a global program that has inspired many people to live with those who are different from them in peace.

Religion, politics, and economics are closely intertwined all around the world, so addressing enmity and lack of understanding between religions is a very demanding task. Few people realize the extent to which issues in relation to oil, water, and land can exacerbate tensions between different religions and ethnicities, and few know that Christianity and Islam have a 1,500-year history in Africa and that in most of inland Africa, the majority Muslim, Arab-influenced North collides with the predominantly

Christian South, creating tensions that are exacerbated by difficult governments with well armed militias.[12] The divisions date back centuries and have been reinforced by colonial rule.

The power of religion is compounded by the fact that often the government of these nations, whose borders were drawn by colonial powers, means very little to its citizens, offering few services or political rights. Thus religion and ethnicity is an individual's safeguard in this world and in the hereafter. Growing populations intensify these competitions. There has been an explosive growth of Christianity over the past fifty years, so that 493 million Christians are living in Africa, who comprise nearly a quarter of the world's Christian population. Similarly, Africa's 367 million Muslims represent nearly a quarter of the world's Muslim people.[13] The Christians populations differ considerably and include evangelical Christians as well as Catholics and Protestants.

Climate change has also become a factor in the tension between ethnic and religious groups. Cycles of flooding and drought have become increasingly unpredictable, making it more than difficult for African nomads, who are Muslim, and farmers of all religions to rely upon centuries-old patterns of migration, planting, and harvesting. That means that they need to move into new territory to grow food and graze their livestock.[14] Two groups with different cultures and religions are facing off against each other over land, water, food, oil, and different world-views.

In a wonderful book by a Jesuit priest, *Say You're One of Them*, is a short story, "Luxurious Hearses," about a young Muslim boy fleeing conflict between religions after the death of his mother, and the stoning death of his brother, which opens with a beautiful saying from the Qu'ran.[15] Through the eyes of children the emotional toll of religious conflict is heartbreakingly clear. While fleeing from a terrible battle between Muslims and

Christians, that involved burning, killing, and hearing Christians yelling, "kill the infidels," the young Muslim boy shares his memories. Chased by people with guns and stones, he took refuge where Evangelicals were praying, and felt connected to his "newfound universe of diverse and unknown pilgrims, the faceless Christians. The complexity of their survival pierced his soul with a stunning insight: every life counted in Allah's plan."[16] The bus in which refugees are fleeing religious strife is like a stage where all the problems of African countries take place—police taking bribes, government officials supporting local chiefs, and military leaders. During the ride everyone argues over every issue intertwined with the grief of loss. As a Muslim child, he disguises himself as a Christian wearing a medal of Mary around his neck. Within that setting are ethnic as well as religious struggles, as well as the role of multinational oil companies. Due to decades of oil drilling, the soil is losing its fertility, the rivers no longer have fish, and oil fires have annihilated hundreds of people time and time again.

Sudan, for example, where there has been constantly war between the North and the South had another horrific massacre in South Sudan in April 2014. Before it split into two countries in July 2011, Sudan was Africa's biggest country, with a surface area of a million square miles. Successive governments in Khartoum decreed that Sudan must be an Arab and Muslim country, alienating millions of citizens. The failure to create a common identity was the chief cause of South Sudan breaking away.

Similar problems arose in the new country when rebel fighters from the Neur ethnic group took control of Bentiu, the capital of oil-producing Unity state. They slaughtered hundreds of non-Neur civilians in the town's mosque, hospital, and on the streets. Interethnic violence has been raging in South Sudan since 2013, when the president, Salva Kiir, an ethnic Dinka, fired the country's top military officer, isolating the Nuer group politically. A spokesman for the rebels claimed that the firing of the military officer and the director of military intelligence "mark the beginning of an imminent bloodbath, escalation and regionalization of the conflict."[17] About one million people fled their homes and thousands have been killed.

Enter a Catholic priest, from the Equator Peace Academy, Noel Nyombe Santo, of the Archdiocese of Juba who reflected on the situation and how he could handle it. He wrote that, once South Sudan gained its independence, the new leaders manipulated ethnic identities for their own interest. He saw this as the root causes of the ethnopolitical competition, discrimination, and violence. Father Santo believed that the government is incapable of managing the great ethnic diversity in the country by improving the ability of groups to live together peacefully despite their religious and sociocultural differences. He found it difficult for his countrymen to accept the "other" whom they viewed as being different, or to live in peace with him or her. He then wrote a paper for CEDAR outlining his growth and his change in perspectives:

> What occurred encouraged me to think about the other who is different from me—but is also a South Sudanese like me. Should I kill the other because he/she is different from me? Compete against the other because he/she is different from me? Is it possible for South Sudanese communities to recognize and accept their differences to build a peaceful civil society? . . . On January 15th, 2014, I was challenged to recognize and accept the other as different when my close friend and I were invited for a Thanksgiving prayer in the house of another friend of ours who was carjacked. . . . Luckily he got away with his life, sustaining only a small bullet wound in his ankle. To my surprise, some Muslims were called to lead

the prayers for Thanksgiving. At first I felt uneasy, but gradually accepted it. After the prayers, we had a shared meal . . . this situation challenged me because of the ethnic composition of the meal. Different ethnic groups were accepting each other and sharing the same dish. I came to understand that not accepting the other who is different from me is the result of seeing the negative in them. Instead of focusing on why someone is different from me, I should focus on how to live together in our diverse but one country, inhabited by people with very different religious, moral and political beliefs.[18]

The Equator Peace Academy is based in the Great Lakes region of Africa where horrific conflicts that took place in the past continue today. Two decades ago, Rwanda was the site of a genocide that few Western countries responded to and that France, a former colonial power, abetted by sending arms.[19] Ethnic violence occurred in Burundi, Uganda, and the Democratic Republic of Congo. Thousands of civilians were exiled or wound up in overcrowded Internally Displaced Person camps in Kenya.

In 2012, fellows of the Equator Peace Academy in Uganda traveled to the Northern and Central regions of the country. They witnessed the aftermath of two decades of war between the Lord's Resistance Army (LRA) and the Ugandan government. They connected with parents of abducted children of the Aboke Girls Secondary School, and met with survivors of the Barlonyo massacre in Lira district as well as former LRA commanders and Uganda People's Defense Force (UODF, the national army). Fellows also met with cultural, religious and civic leaders who work to provide leadership in addressing post-conflict issues in the aftermath of war.[20]

In Rwanda, fellows were learning about the aftermath of the 1994 Tutsi genocide and Hutu massacres. They traveled there two years before official mourning to commemorate the twentieth anniversary of the massacres. Paul Rusesabagina, the son of a Hutu farmer and married to a Tutsi, wrote about his experiences during the genocide in Rwanda. He describes how friends and neighbors turned against each other because radio programs promoted by the government, spread hatred. In his book he writes about racial hatred and its deadly consequences. Neighbors attacked each other, in some mixed-ethnicity marriages like his, husbands turned over wives to be killed. Even churches were not sanctuaries, as several Catholic Priests and nuns ordered killings. As a hotel manager, Paul Rusesabagina was able to hide 1,268 people in his establishment while their countrymen slaughtered eight hundred thousand people. He watched European colonists exploit the differences between these ethnic groups for a divide-and-rule strategy, and he lists all the failures in preventing this massive slaughter: the failure of Africa to get beyond its ethnic differences and form coalition governments; the failure of Western Democracies to step in and avert the catastrophe when evidence of it was clear what was going on; the failure of the United States for not calling what occurred a genocide; and the failure of the United Nations to live up to its commitments as a peace-keeping body.[21] His book became a renowned film, *Hotel Rwanda.*

It was important for the fellows to visit Rwanda not only because of what occurred there, but also because, although the country economy has rebounded, an international tribunal created to judge those who were involved in the genocide has delivered only forty-nine convictions out of ninety-five indictments since it began its work in 1995.[22] It is interesting that UN Secretary-General Ban Ki-Moon attended the memorial on the anniversary of the genocide to express the United Nation's remorse that its peacekeepers had failed to stop the genocide. Former President Bill Clinton apologized years later for America's lack of action. The U.S. delegation was headed by the UN ambassador Samantha Power, who won a Pulitzer Prize for her book on U.S. failures to respond to genocide. Yet the record of the reconciliation of Hutus and Tutsis is mixed. It is difficult for neighbors to even communicate, given their memories of family members killed in the genocide.

After the Equator Peace Academy fellows visited the National Genocide Memorial site, churches where the genocides took place and mass graves, they struggled with the consequence of those events in terms of memory, responsibility, and the construction of a postconflict community. Even though there have been some convictions of high-level figures who orchestrated the genocide, many Rwandans do not feel that justice has been done, which is why the fellows felt impelled to visit.

In Central Uganda, fellows met with the officials of the Kingdom of Buganda, which is central to the history of Uganda and from which the name, Uganda, is derived. As the British colonized Uganda, Buganda collaborated with the colonizers, an issue that every Ugandan government has had to deal with. The questions that fellows confronted in Buganda focused on the special status of the Kingdom of Buganda within the Ugandan state and its meaning for different notions of community and for historical identities in Buganda, Uganda, and the Great Lake region as a whole.

Fellows had an opportunity to compare and contrast the sites identified in the context of their Ugandan and Rwandan experiences, as well as with their experiences beyond the Great Lakes Region. Their hope is that CEDAR's unique mode of inquiry will open the way for communicating lasting solutions to policy makers in these two countries and influence the conversations dealing with the human condition.

CEDAR has worked in fifty different countries and changed the views of hundreds of people so that they repeatedly draw conclusions such as: "When we begin to appreciate each other's narratives, we can begin to live differently." "Our differences are our wealth. We have to cross over our boundaries sometimes but that doesn't mean that we are removing our boundaries." "People with significant differences can meet honestly but it takes more time and commitment than we usually give it."[23] CEDAR is a pioneering global network. Its growth is like ripples on the water. In every country in which it has organized programs it has left behind fellows who are transformed, whose perceptions of diversity are changed, and who often create their own programs in their own communities.

THREE

Dr. James O'Connell and Medical Care for the Homeless

Dr. James O'Connell has spent his whole working life providing medical care for the homeless. It is a complex task that required him to learn about a number of different illnesses that date back to World War I, and even centuries earlier. His work and thought are truly multidisciplinary. He studied philosophy and theology in graduate school when he was young, as well as working at a job that put him in touch with many different kinds of people.

It took Dr. O'Connell a long time to decide to become a physician. He attended graduate school, taught high school, and ran a restaurant in Rhode Island where he had worked since he was twelve years old. In his late twenties he decided he needed to select a career that would inspire him, although he had been thinking about medicine for some time. He attended Brown University for premed courses when he was twenty-eight. He then attended Harvard and started medical school at the age of thirty. He admits that the best training he had for medical school and for his career was "being behind the bar for many hours and nights, learning to listen to people and learning to be diplomatic as you listen. To hear what is going on is really a bartender's college."[1] It taught him how to reach out and help the homeless. He has done so by earning their trust, which requires patience, and by encouraging them to continue the medical care he has made available for them.

Dr. O'Connell's work with the homeless began with what he refers to as the "serendipity of life." When he was about to leave for New York to study oncology on a fellowship he had been granted, he was called into the office of his chief of medicine, who was with a physician who had mentored him. Boston had just been awarded a grant to care for homeless people and to integrate their health care into the mainstream of medical care. The community coalition that worked with Boston's Mayor to create this program wanted a full-time doctor, rather than just volunteers and were interested in establishing social justice, rather than charity. The two physicians told Dr. O'Connell that they would postpone his oncology fellowship if he would agree to participate in the program for the care of the homeless for a year. The Robert Wood Johnson Foundation, the organization that created the Boston Healthcare for the Homeless, provided the grant. The goal was to get physicians and nurse practitioners out of the hospitals and into the streets and shelters to take care of homeless people.

For Dr. O'Connell, this turned out to be the beginning of yet another education and a long career requiring new skills that he acquired as the program's founding physician with a small team. What he didn't realize then, and is now clear about his extraordinary career, is that this man who took so long to decide that medicine was his true calling became a true visionary as he struggled during his first years as a physician for the homeless.

The timing of his decision was also serendipitous because as a result of this country's deteriorating economic situation, the number of homeless people has risen dramatically. And while there are many good programs that have been serving them, cuts in financing enacted by Congress in 2011 and known as the Sequester have made states and cities as well as rural areas unable to care for all those who need shelter. Also, while the business news covers what in one *New York Times* article referred to as "the sinking middle class," the rising poverty in this country does not make the headlines nor does it enter into conversations about the issues facing people. Families who live in poverty and their advocates would like policy makers and the public to stop stigmatizing poverty and address the growing gap in opportunity affecting poor families and their need for decent jobs, housing, and higher minimum wages. Many residents of shelters around the country are working two jobs, but are still unable to afford to pay for permanent housing.

During President Ronald Reagan's administration, the expression "welfare queens," floated around. During the 2012 presidential campaign, a prominent candidate referred to people on welfare as "living in a hammock." One of the views frequently touted by politicians is that people should just pull themselves by their bootstraps and go to work, ignoring the fact that a large percentage of the people who live in shelters are disabled or mentally ill, or are already working very hard yet still can't afford to live without assistance.

According to the executive director of Care for the Homeless in New York, we ignore the need for a minimum wage that would make housing affordable for many people. The Department of Housing and Urban Development defines housing affordability as spending 30 percent of gross income for rent and utilities. Based on that definition, a New York City family would need to work 139 hours weekly, three-and-a-half full time jobs, to afford

a typical apartment including utilities.[2] The average poverty
threshold across the United States in 2011 was $23,280 for a
family of four. Equally shocking is the fact that the majority of impoverished families and individuals live below that poverty line.[3]

In Boston, a census that was conducted at the end of December
2012 found a total of 6,992 homeless men, women, and children,
a 5.2 percent increase over the previous year.[4] The number of
homeless families rose 7.8 percent from the previous year, partly
because of rising real estate prices that are out of reach for low-
wage earners. The greatest change occurred among runaway and
homeless young people; it grew from 27 to 36 percent.[5] In 2012,
Boston Mayor Walsh's predecessor, Mayor Menino's report on
homelessness revealed that, because of the high number of people
needing shelter, 20 percent of those who applied were turned
away for lack of space.[6] In 2012, the director of the Pine Street Inn,
a Boston shelter that draws people from cities and towns across
Eastern Massachusetts, which has 110 beds for women, noted that
in the previous year between ten and fifteen women had to sleep
on the floor every night; in 2012 that number rose to between
thirty and forty.[7] Given the lack of space and untenable sleeping
conditions available for the overflow, the city distributes vouchers for motel stays, but they too are short of space. According to
WBUR (Boston's NPR News Station), the number of families
seeking shelter in motels rose from 1,230 in April 2013 to 2,038
in October 2013.[8] In 2015, the year since the Long Island Shelter
closed in 2014, the homeless population grew by 5.6 percent and
family homelessness increased by a staggering 25 percent.[9]

There are short-term subsidies for families leaving shelters
as well as prevention programs, and Mayor Marty Walsh plans to
build permanent housing for these people, having set out a plan to
end homeless in Boston by 2018. The mayor's plan includes the
housing first model that gives the chronically homeless a home

as quickly as possible, and a centralized database that matches homeless individuals to appropriate housing and program vacancies.[10] However, the city is strained for resources and meanwhile people are finding themselves re-entering shelters multiple times.

The causes of homelessness in Boston are low wages and high housing costs, as revealed by the fact that 33 percent of the homeless are employed. Other causes include mental illness—which accounts for 36 percent—substance abuse, and domestic violence, which causes the need for shelter for another 15 percent. Twenty-five percent are physically disabled and 10 percent are veterans. Overcrowding and lack of affordable housing is a growing problem.

So many mentally ill people are homeless as a result of de-institutionalization of mental health care, which resulted in moving severely mentally ill people out of large state institutions and then closing part or all of these mental hospitals. That policy began in 1955 with the widespread introduction of the first effective anti-psychotic medications. Ten years later, it received further impetus with the implementation of Medicaid and Medicare programs. The policy was based on the principle that mental illness should be treated in the least restrictive setting possible, which is a laudable goal if those settings were available to all those released, including those without family or friends to support and care for them. By the mid-1990s about 92 percent of people who would have been previously committed to such institutions no longer existed. The result has been a catastrophe for too many people; those who were discharged or as time passed, could not enter an institution, as such institutions no longer existed, did not receive the medications and rehabilitation services necessary for them to live successfully in a community. Thus, many of the homeless suffer mental illness.[11]

Not included in the census are people who live in their cars or on the street, sleeping on park benches or under bridges.

I remember giving a talk at one of my colleague's classes when I was a college professor and finding out that a woman who was auditing the class was living in her car because of domestic violence. Afterward, she told me how her husband had thrown appliances, such as toasters, at her during his fits of temper. In that same period, one of the Catholic churches in my town allowed a homeless family to park their truck on church property, but that generous offer caused so much outrage in the community that the priest finally asked the family to leave.

Not only do we stigmatize poverty, but we also look down on the homeless. I used to see homeless people quietly sitting together on a heating vent for warmth in one of the side streets leading to Boston's Copley Square. The next time I walked by, I found that a cement wall had been erected around the vents to keep these people out. A friend living in Seattle told me that, in a part of the city, park benches where homeless people were sleeping had been removed to prevent them from doing so. Many cities use even more severe measures. It seems as if we want to keep the homeless out of sight and mind.

Then there is the issue of foreclosure. Boston's Mayor Menino created a program to prevent foreclosures through a number of ways, such as providing financial education to homeowners and buyers, foreclosures and helping reclaim foreclosed property. His program was successful, yet for all its accomplishments, the number of homeless keeps rising due to a variety of problems, especially because the economic recession has severely impacted very low-income households in Massachusetts. According to Dr. O'Connell homelessness is a symptom of failures in education, criminal justice, health care, the economy, and the housing market.[12]

Homeless people, especially those who are mentally ill, are desperately in need of medications and medical care. Those living on the streets or even in shelters are outdoors so much in all kinds of weather that they become ill with many different diseases. Homeless shelters have curfews that require residents to leave at 7:00 a.m. and not to return before 3:00 p.m.

Dr. James O'Connell had very little experience with homeless people when he began his new calling, but as a resident at the Mass General Hospital (MGH), he had a clinic that included alcoholic people living in the area of the Charles River whom he found irascible but fascinating. He had much to learn about how to deal with their health issues, which was difficult, because it required persuading them to change some of their ways. The goal of the program Dr. James O'Connell created involved having people come into a clinic before they ended up in an emergency room.

He remembers when he first took on this job and walked into a nurses' clinic in the Pine Street Inn, thinking he was an excellent physician. The nurses looked at him and told him, "We've been taking care for homeless people here since the late 1960s without doctors and hospitals, thank you very much. If you sit down and watch, we'll teach you how to care for homeless people."[13] What Dr. O'Connell learned there he attributes to Barbara McInnis who was the head nurse and whom he saw as the spiritual guide and the soul of the nurses' clinic. For two months, Nurse McInnis made Dr. O'Connell soak the feet of people who came in. In the waiting room there were yellow buckets of betadine solution. While they soaked their feet of these people, the nurse would talk with them and ask them relevant questions. He saw this as an almost biblical gesture of comfort. As a resident at the MGH, it was impossible to take the time to know the patients or to have a presence, but he had to modify his learning and came to understand that taking care of homeless people requires taking the time to earn their trust and build a relationship.

Soaking feet was also an important way to deal with trench foot, a miserable condition that affected soldiers during World

War I and World War II when they didn't have the proper boots and shoes, and were sleeping outside in the mud or in soggy tents.[14] When feet remain wet for long periods of time, the moisture causes them to swell and to become painful. Homeless people with trench feet need to be able to clean and dry them, then soak them in warm water. They need to change into clean socks and keep their feet elevated when sleeping.

Dr. James O'Connell found that he couldn't use a stethoscope or act like a physician in that clinic. He has an unforgettable memory of a man whose feet he was soaking. He had seen him many times in an emergency room where he was diagnosed with paranoid schizophrenia, yet the man refused any medication to help him. He didn't address a single word to him for the first three or four weeks, but one day he looked at Dr. O'Connell and said, "Hey, I thought you were supposed to be a doctor." When Dr. O'Connell replied that he was a doctor, the man responded, "What the hell are you doing soaking feet?" A week later, while he was having his feet soaked, the man asked Dr. O'Connell if he could give him something to help him sleep. That was the first time Dr. O'Connell wrote a prescription for him and gave him some medicine. A few days later the man said, "Doc, you know that just didn't work long enough. Could you give me a little bit more of that, increase the dose?"[15] After a month the man asked for the same medicine he had resisted taking following a diagnosis in the emergency room. It was a revelation for Dr. O'Connell. He thought that perhaps he had something to do with this man's initial resistance and that he and the other medical staff had a rigid way of looking at things. Within a few weeks, the man, who had been on the streets for twenty-five years, was in a group home where he stayed until his death twenty years later. Dr. O'Connell remembers Barbara McInnis clapping her hands and exclaiming, "That's what it's all about," because he learned that in this field, profound change only happens when you take the time to win somebody's trust. It may take a long time and a lot of patience, but it is crucial in this type of care.[16]

Dr. O'Connell has become an expert on trench foot and many other illnesses that may afflict a homeless person. He practices a new kind of medicine that goes far beyond primary care. As he was soaking feet he learned about the pathology of feet that a person who has been walking around on them for years. These people may also have fungal infections, and neuropathy from diabetes or excess alcohol consumption may prevent them from feeling festering cuts and bruises on their feet. He learned that treating someone's feet is a very important and complicated issue. It's a way of not invading a street person's personal space, a preparation for listening to their heart or lungs. Soaking feet is comforting and a way to start treating the many other illnesses from which a person suffers.

The team Dr. O'Connell worked with included a nurse practitioner, a caseworker, and a physician's assistant. Initially they worked three nights a week at the Pine Street Inn clinic, two nights a week at the clinic, at St. Francis House Shelter, and at Long Island Shelter in Boston. These clinics took place at night when people have a bed, have had a meal, and are in a secure place. Over time, in each of these places the team carved out a space for the clinic in the shelter. At St. Francis House Shelter, they virtually had to work out of the bathroom because it was one of the few places with running water. Now they work there five nights a week. The team practices in these spaces from 6 a.m. to 8:30 p.m. and now works there seven days a week. As the team spread out to all the clinics they were getting to as many access points as possible so that homeless people could see a physician or a nurse at night. They also practice in the motels that house homeless families.

The team then realized that their job was really citywide, and that they needed not only to give care in the shelters, but also to remain tied in with the hospital because some people were so ill. Dr. O'Connell learned that personal connections became an important part of his profession. When people were ill at a shelter and needed to stay at the Boston City Hospital or the MGH, he could take care of them when he was in the hospital and have continuity in their care. That required many hours of work a week, sometimes as much as one hundred. At times it seemed overwhelming because it hadn't been done before, but it was also challenging and invigorating. He remarked, "I'm coming out of seven years training to be a doctor and the medicine was more challenging than anything I had done."[17]

Dr. O'Connell was also encountering cases of scurvy, which he had read about but had never seen before. He was shocked by the high incidence of scurvy among homeless people, as it was a disease that was prominent centuries ago. Scurvy is caused by a diet that lacks vitamin C (ascorbic acid), and causes anemia, exhaustion, and swelling in some parts of the body, and in some cases causes ulceration of the gums and loss of teeth. Scurvy sufferers are lacking nutritious food, such as fruits and vegetables containing vitamin C, which are obviously not available to people who spend their days looking for something to eat and a place to sleep.

In addition to helping people with trench foot, Dr. O'Connell also treats trench fever. Among the homeless, trench fever can cause bloodstream infection (bacteremia) that infects some joints; unfortunately relapses are common.[18] The onset of symptoms is sudden with high fever, severe headache, back pain, leg pain, and a fleeting rash.[19] Once, Dr. O'Connell saw a man in a shelter suffering from schizophrenia who had a new heart murmur, so he made sure that he was hospitalized. There it turned out that the man had an infection on his heart valve caused by the same organism that created trench fever. Lice, he discovered, once regarded, simply as an annoyance, have the potential to be dangerous, as *Bartonella Quintana*, the microorganism causing trench fever, can multiply within the gut of lice and then can be transmitted to humans. That same microorganism has been found to cause a disease in people infected with HIV and infections of the heart and great vessels.[20]

Dr. O'Connell and his team dealt with over a hundred cases of tuberculosis in the first couple of years in one shelter while, at the same time, facing the AIDS epidemic. When he was an intern at the MGH the first cases of AIDS he saw were a new phenomenon to him. The epidemic began to affect the poor community in 1985, and was a very complicated illness to deal with because people with AIDS were living in a shelter where tuberculosis and many infections were rampant. He remarked that "the collision of tuberculosis, AIDS and diseases I had not seen before, all in the context of five or seven hundred people living under the same roof or on the streets became one of those challenges that you just couldn't walk away from."[21] At first, Dr. O'Connell felt overburdened and kept thinking that this would only be a year of work, but in the middle of that first year, he couldn't imagine leaving that challenge. He discovered that the career he thought was thrust upon him was a blessing, a path he respected and loved, that he now refers to as "the best thing that ever happened to me."

Dr. O'Connell had a number of concerns while working day and night, one of them being that he was not financially rewarded for the time he spent. Then he realized that the investment of his time must save hundreds of thousands of dollars in emergency room visits, and that the way physicians and nurses work distorts the way health care needs to be provided with the very vulnerable people suffering with so much trauma. He discovered that "reaching out of the health care system one has to be gentle and take time if it's going to change things."

Another concern that weighed on Dr. O'Connell was that in this new area of work he would be marginalized by members of his own profession, despite all the training that he accomplished. He voiced those concerns to his chief of medicine, who made it clear that the Boston Medical Center and the MGH would embrace his work as part of the mainstream. From the first year and throughout his long career he has been on the staff of both hospitals, and had duties there so that medical students and residents attend the wards with the homeless. Consequently, Dr. O'Connell was in close contact with clinical specialists in these hospitals who would contribute their time to his work with those suffering from AIDS, pneumonia, tuberculosis, and other illnesses. He was proud of the inclusiveness that resulted, and of the incorporation of the care of the homeless in mainstream medicine. He does grand rounds at the MGH on Thursdays and at its clinic for the homeless five days a week, which means that the homeless people that he sees are not separated or labeled.

During that first year Dr. O'Connell's work took him in many directions. He discovered that many homeless people were dying in the streets, and that these people weren't even treated in the clinics. Some of them lived under bridges while most of them moved around. He and his team did their daily rounds on the streets. In his first winter, the Department of Public Health funded the purchase of a van for the Pine Street Inn so that they could reach people who were living on the streets. It would run every night from 10 p.m. to 5 a.m. They discovered that street people are afraid of strangers who might come to make them leave or mistreat them, so it was extremely important to gain their trust. The goal of driving to meet the homeless is not only to bring them health care, but also to take cocoa, soup, sandwiches, dry socks, blankets, and clothing for the homeless, which Dr. O'Connell regards as part of his job. He refers to the people who drive the van as "the unsung heroes of health care."[22] Most of them have experienced homelessness themselves or lived in poverty and are in touch with the people living on the streets. Building up the necessary trust enabled Dr. O'Connell to ask the people he met if they needed health care. Dr O'Connell and his team have been doing this for twenty-seven years and everybody on the street knows that on Mondays and Wednesdays a physician will come by to help them. In the early years, he would stay in the van those long hours. Now, he only stays until midnight or 1 a.m. at the end of the long days he works each week, which he does with pleasure.

In the early nineties, a man and a woman came into Dr. O'Connell's office asking him "Who are the people who are taking care of homeless people in town?" They owned horses at a racetrack and both of them had been trying to help what they called "the back stretch workers."[23] A former businessman, the man had started a program called the Eighth Pole to take care of the workers. He asked Dr. O'Connell to come out to the racetrack to see the workers, and he responded immediately. The man walked Dr. O'Connell around the place and showed him what they were doing there. Many of the workers had migrated from Central and South America and some were poor workers from farms in the South who knew a lot about caring for horses. All of them worked very long days, from morning until late at night, each one hired by the owner of a horse or horses. They would get up very early in the morning to walk with the horses, run them down, train them, and clean out the barns. Dr. O'Connell was stunned at how hard these people worked and realized the difficulties they were encountering with health care, because if those workers left the track to go to a medical appointment they would lose that day's wages. Dr. O'Connell learned that there were no labor laws applying to that isolated world. The employees there were grateful for whatever money they could make, and many of them were sending half of their wages back home to support their families in El Salvador or Ecuador. Most of these people were living in the stables. Dr. O'Connell was horrified by their living conditions and he wanted to advocate for them at the state government level. Even though their living conditions were unimaginable, the workers pleaded with him not to do that because they feared that this would draw attention of the immigration authorities, causing those who were undocumented to lose their jobs and be sent back home. Few people in this country realize that four hundred thousand undocumented people are deported from the United States each year.[24] Those living illegally in this country know very well what could happen to them.

To address this situation, Dr. O'Connell's team brought a trailer to the track where they provide a clinic several times a week, especially during the racing season. On Thursdays, the team's dental clinic is open to these workers because there are no races that day. Dr. O'Connell discovered that the workers suffer from addiction and substance abuse problems, but he found them to be the most wonderful people who are more than grateful for his care and attention. He also found the racetrack to be a very satisfying place for his team because workers there put up with extreme pain and only attend the clinic when it doesn't prevent them from doing their jobs.

I saw a nun who worked with the homeless on television and showed the awful places where these people lived, remarking that "No wonder they take drugs." I think too of so many of our soldiers coming back from Afghanistan with severe combat stress who take drugs to kill their psychological pain. In fact, in 1993, when Barbara McInnis House, a health facility for the homeless was established, it provided an office-based opiate treatment program where trained staff provide treatment that includes counseling and a Suboxone program for the rapid, pain-free, withdrawal from highly addictive drugs.

Dr. O'Connell's clinical practice is part of a team that takes care of street people who will not come to the clinics. The clinics are open at seventy different sites in Boston, and Dr. O'Connell sees this as the most important part of this practice. The team can see those people during a fourteen-hour day. They have a special clinic on Thursdays that is devoted to street people so they are not in a crowded or bureaucratic setting. There is a comfortable waiting room for them, the only such setting in the whole country. They are offered free pastries, coffee, and meal vouchers so that they can go to the cafeteria for breakfast or lunch.

The medical staff sees about a hundred street people there every Thursday morning. This arrangement was created to lure very sick people to the hospital in order to give them the care that cannot be offered on the street, such as x-rays or other procedures needed for proper diagnosis and treatment. These are the people the team sees during the night and that is the best time for engaging them. The clinic at MGH is unique in providing this kind of care. When Dr. O'Connell sees a person about whom he is very worried, he just says, "Come see me tomorrow at the clinic at eight o'clock." They don't care that it's at the MGH, but if he says, "Come to me," it makes a huge difference.[25] They are not going to see a stranger, but someone they have come to know away from the hospital. What Dr. O'Connell has accomplished is to maintain relationships with these people over the years, gain their trust, and care for them in the best way possible.

Now, people on the street head toward the MGH because it's also a place where they can receive help from the social service agencies. There the paperwork is done for them. Because this service is already part of the hospital, Dr. O'Connell and those who work with him don't have to register the people who come in. If these people need to see a heart specialist or any other specialist, the medical staff can arrange it right there and get them in. Dr. O'Connell found that it breaks down all kinds of barriers he used to worry about. Most of the homeless people who are ill wander in because the MGH is only a few blocks from where they live. They do move around a lot, so, if the team is concerned about them, the staff just gives them a cab voucher or public transport card. If they seriously worry about some of them, one of the community health workers will seek them out and bring them in.

The homeless are a very sick population in which severe mental illnesses is rampant. Most are coping with substance abuse and all of them have major medical problems. The combination of these problems has made their lives a nightmare and has forced Dr. O'Connell and his team to rethink and reorganize the way they provide medical care. He works with a psychiatrist and either a nurse practitioner or community health worker during the day and also at the clinics at night. He found that it's not possible to separate mental health care from medicine. He has also realized that it is this traumatized population that has shown him and his team of physicians, nurses, and psychiatrists what they need to do. The team has integrated mental health care and medical care for more than fourteen years. Dr. O'Connell has concluded that "it's the only way I want to practice medicine and it's the best way to do it."

Dr. O'Connell remarked that for many years, his staff had no place of their own and he used to think, "We are kind of a homeless program taking care of homeless people."[26] In 1993 the staff bought an old nursing home that was just what they needed to establish Barbara McInnis House, named after the nurse who supervised Dr. O'Connell in the clinic where he soaked feet, to provide recuperative and rehabilitative care for homeless people who could not be discharged from the hospital onto the streets or to a shelter which they have to leave at 7 a.m. before they recovered.

In 2005, the medical staff worked with the mayor to secure the empty Mallory Pathology Building that is right across from the Boston Medical Center. The mayor let the physicians have it for a dollar a year if they were able to renovate it. For the first time in their careers, Dr. O'Connell's staff had to raise money because, beyond Medicare and Medicaid, they had no access to capital. Dr. O'Connell had spent most of his career making sure the program would survive without having to raise money, but when the building needed to be renovated, the mayor told him $40 million would have to be raised. The team immediately started a capital-raising campaign and created a development department directed by one of the nurses on the street team. She had been a nun who taught in a Boston grammar school that had put her in touch with a variety of people. She raised all of the money that was needed, finishing her capital campaign two months before the stock market crashed in 2008—another case of what Dr. O'Connell likes to refer to as "serendipity."

In the newly renovated multi-clinic facility, which Dr. O'Connell calls the "Step Down" Barbara McInnis House, was expanded to a 104-bed hospital, where the average length of stay for patients with acute medical problems is about two to three weeks. The healthcare system has changed considerably in this country over the last two decades. When Dr. O'Connell was a senior resident at MGH, the basic hospital stay after open-heart surgery was five or six weeks; if a person had a hernia or a gall bladder taken out, that patient stayed from five to seven days. Today, most surgery is done on an outpatient basis, as is chemo-therapy and radiation, but a homeless person can't go back to living under a bridge or on a park bench to recover. The respite center staff sees people who have very complicated chemotherapy regimes, including people with AIDS who need medication for that condition. They admit people a day or two before their scheduled outpatient surgery so they can provide the preoperative and postoperative care that very frail and weak people need. If a homeless person has day surgery, the team brings them to the hospital and also provides transportation to return them to the new recuperation facility they have built.

Now instead of a clinic in the hospital that was getting more and more crowded, the staff's work is in an environment designed to meet their particular needs. Instead of the six clinics they had before, they now have twenty-five, including an integrated clinic for mental and medical health and a dental clinic. Dr. O'Connell discovered that it's not possible to see how two-tiered our healthcare system is until you look inside people's mouths. So many of his patients have broken and missing teeth. Now there are five chairs at the Step Down dental clinic where it is possible to do all the restorative work needed, including fillings, crowns, and more. It has three full-time dentists, as well as fellows from Harvard and Tufts who spend six months there, which means that if Dr. O'Connell sees a street person with terrible dental pain at night, he can have them seen the next morning at the dental clinic.

The Step Down even has its own pharmacy. Instead of having to wait hours for their medications as they would in a hospital pharmacy, they can have their prescriptions filled within minutes of the time they finish their clinical appointment. The building also houses the practice's administrative offices, finance department, development department, and executive offices.

Fortunately, there is also care for homeless people who are suffering from hypothermia as a result of record cold temperatures during the winters of 2014 and 2015 that have exposed them to the condition. It was yet another medical problem of great complexity that Dr. O'Connell had to learn about in his early years. He found that most information about weather-related medical issues came from the military and wilderness literature, and was not sufficiently recorded in medical literature. What he discovered in his research was that 10 percent of the casualties during the Korean War were related to the cold.[27] It is not just the extreme cold that those sleeping on the streets and under bridges experience hypothermia, but also in the period between fall and winter, when the temperature can be in the forties during the day but plummets to twenty degrees at night. They can unwittingly experience extreme hypothermia, especially if they have been drinking alcohol that accelerates the loss of body heat, or using drugs or wearing clothing that has become wet from rain or the ground.[28] Each year at the Barbara McInnis House, the physicians and nurses care for ten to fifteen people suffering from frostbite that threatens digits and limbs. Hands, feet, and tips of noses swell and develop blisters; bloody blisters indicate deep tissue damage and more severe frostbite. Over the course of two to four weeks, the skin turns black and necrotic. Because the staff doesn't know how much viable tissue is below those blackened digits, they are left waiting for one to three months for the fingers and toes auto-amputate as the dead tissue falls off.[29] Dr. O'Connell finds it profoundly unnerving. He refers to frostbite as "an emblematic, avoidable, and disastrous consequence of exposure to the elements."[30] He is deeply concerned about the number of homeless people sleeping on the streets in terrible weather. Many of them refuse to stay at homeless shelters, despite the snowstorms and freezing winds, some would rather be outside on top of a cardboard box with the blankets and soup the Pine Street Inn's Outreach van provides, than squeezed together on the floor of the overcrowded Pine Street Inn shelter. The van's driver knows that with two thousand new rooms the shelters wouldn't be crowded, and that research has shown that "the expensive emergency service numbers go down and that offsets any new housing dollars. So doing nothing for the chronically homeless people costs more money than putting them in supportive housing."[31]

The McInnis House provides many specialized services in addition to care for those addicted to opiates and care for the homeless who have HIV. A team of physicians, nurses, and case managers for homeless people suffering from diabetes, maintaining an active registry of over five hundred homeless patients with diabetes. It also has a Transgender Clinic and a Woman's Health Initiative clinic.

When Dr. O'Connell started, he thought that if he took so much time to develop relationships with people and then deserted them all after one year, he would feel as if he were falling into the same trap that had created this fragmented healthcare system in the first place. At that time there was no career path for caring for very vulnerable people and staying on a recognized professional track. Now the hospital has about eighteen doctors who chose this path as their career. Many of them have been with the staff for ten to twenty years. Like Dr. O'Connell, they are very concerned to provide a continuity of care and an infrastructure for homeless peoples, whose lives are fragmented through their experience of illness and suffering alone. To know that there can be a steady presence of support from a medical team of nurses and doctors has made a huge difference in their lives.

When a patient is nearing death, it feels natural for the staff to say that they will take care of them. The Step Down doesn't technically include a hospice, so the practice had to fill that gap in their system by adding end-of-life and palliative care to the many different things it offers. Dr. O'Connell found that the end-of-life care is a great challenge, as many of the street people have lost contact with their families, and are very much alone. At first, if the medical staff had known a patient for a long time and his or her cancer had become terminal, they tried to put people in traditional hospices in nursing homes, but these patients felt as if they were being abandoned. Dr. O'Connell lives with what he refers to as "that awful fine line between being their medical and healthcare team or their family."[32] As a result, he felt that his medical staff should provide hospice care, an experience Dr. O'Connell found very profound and moving. He discovered that it's very hard to watch people die, especially when they are young and they have no one in the world who cares for them. Beyond the end-of-life care, the staff quite often attends funerals and tries to ensure that their patients will not be buried in a pauper's grave with an anonymous number. The hospice care also includes undocumented immigrants because there has been a steady trickle of undocumented, homeless, dying patients. Because immigrant activists have revealed that it is unlikely that undocumented immigrants, such as those working at the racetrack, will gain access to public health programs soon, patients like Kervin Elleyene say that they feel blessed to have found a place to stay and die.[33]

When I visited Dr. O'Connell at Barbara McInnis House, I saw street people, quietly waiting on chairs in the lobby, nurses coming out with patients and smiling, a woman in a wheel chair who had her lower leg amputated. There is a beautiful quilt hanging from one of the walls. It didn't have the cold anonymity of a hospital. As I watched this group of homeless people waiting to be seen, I wondered as I often had in my life, especially at a time when our economy has been plummeting, why my family has been so fortunate to have a home and companionship even though we have had much illness among us. I have often asked myself "why not me?" and am deeply concerned that too many people live in misery and are marginalized. When I shared this with Dr. O'Connell, he replied, "Life is just a lottery. It's a crap shoot."

Dr. O'Connell is not just an extraordinary physician. He is also a gifted photographer and there are stunning photographs of the people he had cared for on the walls of the second floor of Barbara McInnis House. One is a woman with a wide brimmed hat, smiling at us; another is a homeless person who always dreamed of being a judge and strikes a pose exactly right for the position. The street people have a place where they belong, are respected, and loved. Teams of physicians have visited the Barbara McInnis House from between forty to sixty major cities around the country.

Now that Dr. O'Connell has grown older, he has realized that he needs to cut his working hours to around sixty a week! He feels as if he is on a vacation with his new schedule. It's his passion that drives him as he comments that "I love taking care of the people with my own team, because you realize that you are doing something that people really appreciate. That means the world to lots of us." Another important contribution he has made is to point out the increasing number of vulnerable street people. "I want to bear witness and say this is a disaster—and we're a long way from solving the policy issues."[34]

The list of the many honors and awards that he has received is four pages long. But Dr. O'Connell's true reward is when a homeless person recognizes him and asks to see him in his clinic. He has revealed that what really matters in this life is not fame, but giving, and making connections. It's a work of the heart and of the spirit. It's also a wonderful example of how one person is able to inspire others and create a team that can change the world.

FOUR

Sister Lucille MacDonald and the Emmaus Homeless Shelter

Too many of us do not have a very good opinion or understanding of the vast numbers of people who are poor in the United States. A December 2012 report by the United States Conference of Mayors found that 60 percent of the cities surveyed had seen an increase in homelessness and the same percentage of cities saw homelessness increase in 2013 and in the near future.[1]

According to Susan Fiske, a Princeton professor who has studied people's attitudes toward the poor for more than a decade, "The stereotypes of poor people in the United States are among the most negative prejudices that we have. People basically view homeless people as having no redeeming qualities, having no competence for anything, not having good intentions, and not being trustworthy."[2] In fact, the book by Barbara Ehrenreich, *Nickel and Dimed: On (Not) Getting by in America*, relates the horrific lives of low-wage workers who cannot afford proper food, work under punitive conditions, and often wind up living in a single dingy room without cooking facilities. These workers are not allowed to take sick leave, and often listen to lectures by their employers about getting on with their work despite a serious problem. In some places, they cannot take a break for lunch or eat leftovers quickly, if they are working in a nursing home as a nurse's aide.[3]

In 2012, the City Council of Houston, Texas, passed a law making it illegal to feed the homeless within the city without the permission of property owners. As an example, of Huston's hard line, a nine-year-Navy veteran was issued a citation according to a 2002 law making it illegal "to remove any contents of any bin, bag or other container that has been placed for collection garbage, trash or recyclable materials." The man was just looking for some thrown-out food. His lawyer, a Houston attorney who has fought against the anti-feeding ordinance, took the case and concluded that both laws intended to force the homeless out of Houston and into neighboring municipalities.[4]

There was a similar uproar in California's Silicon Valley where homeowners were outraged that trucks handing out evening meals to the homeless in their neighborhood and sought to have them removed. In Hawaii, a politician was photographed destroying a homeless person's cart with its few possessions.[5]

The 2011 Sequester and budget cuts disproportionately affected the poor and the homeless.[6] Unfortunately these people seem to be invisible to those who are able to pay their rent and have housing and employment. Responses to the cuts are highly partisan, with Senator Rand Paul, a Republican from Kentucky, referring to the Sequester as a "pittance," and President Obama who proclaimed that the cuts will eviscerate our country's domestic spending, as it certainly has done.[7] In 2011, 8.5 million households were spending over half of their income on rent and earning less than half of their area's medium wage.

Rents have gone up, but incomes have not, and poor households are one small financial crisis away from losing their homes. The Sequester hurt programs that deal with homelessness. Housing department budget cuts removed more than one hundred thousand people from shelters. Affordable housing programs closed waiting lists and rescinded rent subsidies. For example, since spring 2012, Massachusetts lost $20 million in federal funding for subsidized housing. The Section 8 program was frozen at twenty thousand vouchers in Massachusetts. There are 95,000 households on the waiting list.[8] An analysis released by the Center on Budget and Policy Priorities showed that, as of December 2013, there were seventy thousand fewer low-income families using vouchers than the previous year. That decline works against the program because Congress generally funds the program based on the number of vouchers in service the previous year. The budget deal that ended sequestration allows housing agencies to replace less than half of the seventy thousand vouchers lost in 2013.[9] Coupled with the cut in food stamps and Medicaid, these changes are making life for the poor even more devastating.[10] Peter Gagliardi, president of a nonprofit housing agency in Springfield, Massachusetts, found that globalization that sends jobs out of the country and a minimum and a long-term stagnant wage has created difficult problems, and commented that "about 200,000 families in the state are spending more than half their income on rent."[11] Chris Norris, executive director of the Metropolitan Boston Housing Partnership quoted a 2012 study that revealed single mothers with a very low average income of $8,727 comprise the majority of homeless families in Massachusetts.[12]

In Maine there are forty-three shelters besides the Emmaus Homeless Shelter run by Sister Lucille MacDonald. On May 30, 2013, the federal Housing and Urban Department announced that the total Emergency Solutions Grants (ESG) program allocation was reduced 25 percent from the previous year by the Sequester. That allocation was affected by a reduction in the Homeless Assistance Grants appropriation to cover both increased renewal demand in the Continuum of Care Program and maintain ESG funding.[13] Homeless people do not have an address, and if they are in shelters their stays are transient so they are unable to vote, much less find proper nourishment. Sister Lucille commented that, "If only they could see that forcing shelters to close will only increase crime, and it costs three times as much to keep a person in jail where no one works with the client that help them better their lives."[14] It also costs taxpayers more when the homeless wind up in emergency rooms and in detox treatment centers. The right wing Tea Party keeps demanding that we cut back on government programs that aid the needy as if the poor and homeless were not part of our country.

Sister Lucille MacDonald is a member of the Sisters of Mercy, a true visionary, and a multitalented woman. She operates the shelter she founded, Emmaus, like a CEO, mothers her "guests" and has become an important member of the community in Ellsworth, Maine. She is also highly gifted at using technological tools to further her cause. She has made numerous contacts with a number of organizations in Ellsworth, as well as with the local people and protestant churches where she is highly regarded.

Sister Lucille joined the Sisters of Mercy when she graduated from high school in New Hampshire. She recalls being a typical teenager, going out on dates and attending parties, but that there was always something in her that drew her to enter the convent. She had an aunt who was a medical missionary in Philadelphia and had been in India and South America. She idolized her and saw how much she was able to do to make the world a better place.

The Sisters of Mercy is a visionary order that was created in Dublin, Ireland, in 1883. Catherine McAuley, who was born at the time of the French and American Revolutions, came to believe in the values of those events as she grew up, especially the call for equality and fraternity, and founded the order. She lived in a hierarchical society where there was great hostility between Catholics and Protestants as well as between the Irish and the Anglo-Irish in a country where there was also extreme wealth and widespread poverty. Unemployment, rapid industrialization, and crop failures caused hundreds of farmers to migrate to urban areas. Social and religious prejudice was rampant.[15] The couple with whom Catherine lived named her in their will and she was determined to use her inheritance to address not only the effects of widespread poverty but also its causes. She was both intensely practical and spiritual. When she was forty-four years old, she built a home with dormitories, schoolrooms, and a prayer room for unprotected working girls and orphans. From there Catherine and her associates visited the poor who were ill in their homes and hospitals. They called their home the House of Mercy. It was strategically located where the poor would be visible to the rich and where young women would find employment. She taught people to value the poor and the poor to value themselves.[16] The people who worked with Catherine developed a routine that resembled a religious institute, praying together morning and evening as well as addressing each other as "sister."[17]

However, Catherine faced disagreement from the Catholic hierarchy who wished to impose a cloistered convent on her group. They were in fierce opposition to women taking leadership in the church. At the age of fifty-three she entered her novitiate, after struggling for years with that decision. The house she built became the first Convent of Mercy. The movement spread throughout Ireland and England. She insisted on freedom from the cloister because for her spirituality was not just the practice of praying, but also of the lived experience of faith in her daily life working for the poor and those in need. Today, Sister Lucille who works long hours at the shelter and with the Ellsworth community, says her rosary on the way to work, continuing Catherine McAuley's heritage.

Sister Lucille received a master's degree in education and for the first twenty-four years of her ministry taught in several New Hampshire schools and was principal of St. John's School in Laconia, New Hampshire. In 1978, her community members traveled to other places to work in the summer. Sister Lucille chose Maine. After that first summer she asked her community if she could work in Maine and, for the next five years kept asking if she could stay one more year. That was thirty-seven years ago.

It is interesting that what motivated Sister Lucille was her suffering. In the early 1970s a drunk driver hit her car and she ended up with major back problems. Ultimately her neck was fused and she had two major surgeries on her lower back. In those days, physical therapy was not available, so she spent a year up flat on her back when she was still young. It gave her time to think and served as a lesson for her. For some people, their suffering is an education; difficult times can change a person's perspective so that they see themselves in people who are in desperate circumstances and in need, start to reconsider the purpose of their lives. Thus, contrary to popular views, suffering can make our personal world much wider. Sister Lucille told me, "It was a great lesson. I wanted to work directly with people that were in need. I didn't know how it was going to evolve when I came to Maine. It just worked its way into something I loved. It was such a gift to me and I am so grateful for it. This would never have happened if I hadn't had that injury."[18]

When she settled in Maine permanently, she and a Franciscan sister who was already there decided to open up a homeless shelter. A property with six acres, including a country store that wasn't functioning, happened to be for sale. They showed the property to their community president and requested the funds to buy it. Then, over ten years, they created a homeless shelter called St. Francis Inn for women, children, and families, reopening the store to give employment to people at the shelter.

During that time, they began to notice that they were getting a lot of referrals from the Ellsworth area, so they decided to look at places that they could purchase for yet another shelter. They wrote a grant application to the state government and in one year opened up the Emmaus Shelter in 1992. The Franciscan sister died of cancer and Sister Lucille continued their mission, which included helping the poor in Ellsworth by offering a wide range of services and referrals to any person in need. The shelter was designed to provide a safe and comfortable environment for people in need of temporary shelter who were willing to work toward ending their homelessness.

Because of her experience with her physical injury, she always has been able to relate to the people who come to the shelter. She tells them that she has been in a difficult situation and she knows what it is to lose a way of life, but also what it is to overcome a problem. She shares the wisdom she gained by saying to each person who arrives, "Now it's all upward. It's not going to happen overnight. Think of it as a puzzle. Right now there is only the border of the puzzle, but you are putting the pieces in there and at some point, who you are is going to be there all together, but right now the pieces are all over and you have to work to put it together. One piece might be to get your birth certificate, another might be getting Medicaid."[19]

Emmaus Shelter is truly a home, unlike some homeless shelters that require their residents to leave at seven o'clock in the morning and return in mid-afternoon. There are twelve people on the staff at Emmaus. During the day there are four and the rest work at night. The shelter has four very well-appointed family rooms, a dormitory for six women and one for five men with beautifully covered beds, and wood panels between the beds for privacy. There is also a comfortably furnished living room, as well as a play area for children. Because the shelter provides three meals a day, there is a kitchen where the guests can prepare their meals. The main meal, in late afternoon is prepared by residents and by volunteers from the Maine Coast Memorial Hospital, the Baptist Church of Blue Hill, the First Congregational Church, and the Church of Our Father of Hulls Cove. Sister Lucille found that the people at the shelter treat each other like a family and often help each other. For example, one man went to the drug store to get the prescriptions filled for another guest and helped him prepare his meals.

The guests at the shelter have come from emergency shelters, permanent supportive housing, a psychiatric hospital, a substance abuse treatment center, jail, prison, or juvenile detention. There are people who are physically and mentally disabled, victims of physical, emotional or sexual abuse, victims of medical catastrophes, unemployed, and individuals and families not earning a livable wage, people forced off disability, and, Sister Lucille added, "People like you and me." Other people were often renting a house, apartment or room, living with their families or friends, or in a hotel, or without shelter. Although the home is able to accommodate only twenty-five people, it frequently overflows with more than thirty people staying there and sleeping in cots, and unfortunately there is always a waiting list. For those on the list, Sister Lucille will make calls to other shelters or give them numbers to call General Assistance that she works with but that has very demanding guidelines when it comes to the income of a waitlisted person.

Sister Lucille is experiencing a rise in the level of homelessness. Vouchers that would help people to find places they can rent are less available because of budget cuts. She also noticed that often people who have vouchers are turned away because of the stereotypes of the poor who are homeless or living on a very low income. Some of the families at the shelter have been evicted because they are unable to pay their rent, or utility bills if they are living on a subsidy. A few years ago, there was a program, Main Street Housing, that was supported by the federal government. It included a reservation program where the shelter was able to put people in a hotel for $500 a week, or find other types of housing. Unfortunately it lost its funding.

People stay in the shelter until they can find housing or until they can get a job. When they find employment, the shelter requires them to give the staff a certain amount of their paycheck, which it keeps it for them so they can earn enough money to pay their first and last month's rent and a security deposit for rental housing. Residents may stay for weeks or months until they can find a job or housing. Sister Lucille found that often landlords do not want to rent to people who have been homeless. She has told them not to mention that they lived in a shelter, but just to give the address of the home, 51 Main Street.

There was an incident when a young woman living at the shelter had found a job. When her employer wrote her first paycheck and realized that she was from the shelter, he fired her. However most of the time, that stigma is pretty rare and people call the shelter asking for someone who could serve as a dishwasher or waiter. Sometimes Sister Lucille gets requests in the spring when there is yard work. An older couple contacted Emmaus once because they needed help to stack wood and get it into their house.

Sister Lucille has set a few rules that make the shelter run smoothly. Children have to go to bed at nine o'clock, which leaves the adults some private time until eleven o'clock, when they are supposed to be in bed. She likes the mixture of children, families, and single people because it brings tenderness out in people. She is very strict about the language they use and how they dress, telling them that they need to show mutual respect. As a result, there are good relationships in Emmaus.

The shelter helps its guests go through the paperwork to receive Medicaid so they can receive health insurance. Most of them are eligible but just haven't pursued it. Unfortunately, that insurance doesn't include dental care. The shelter applies for grants that help them get their teeth cleaned, and often exposes some dental work they may need. Some of the guests haven't had dental work in fifteen or twenty years. Sister Lucille remembers one woman who used to hide her mouth because her teeth were in such bad shape. The shelter was able to get dentures for her and now she can't stop smiling. Once she received her dentures she was able to get a job as a licensed practical nurse in a nursing home. Before that she was just too embarrassed to look for a job. The dentist that serves them charges only 25 percent of the usual price.

One of her guests came from Florida, where her husband went because he had employment opportunities there as well as family. He didn't find the job he hoped for and the living conditions were not good for his wife and their five children, so she returned and lived with her brother. That didn't work out either. She ended up at the shelter with her children. Three of them attended school and there were very young twins. One of the older boys had some emotional problems and the staff was able to get him on a medication that was very helpful. The twins needed speech therapy that the shelter provided for them. This woman was very proactive, completed all the paperwork and as a result received her housing voucher. Since she left, she has been very willing to share her experience to help other people in similar situations. In fact, she was on the stage with her oldest girl and the twins for the Emmaus's twentieth anniversary and spoke eloquently. As always, when sister Lucille is out in the community, someone who spent time in the shelter will stop to speak to her. The woman with the five children ran into her and shared her good news that she found a part-time job where her twins go for therapy.[20]

A number of people who come into the shelter exhibit symptoms of mental illness. Some of them haven't taken their medications, and for some the stigma is so great that they don't inform the staff at the shelter. Others can't afford to get their medications, some have lost their Medicaid and have been unable to renew it, while others have the medicine they need but do not use it properly. Whatever their needs are, Sister Lucille is very upset that they haven't been met. She remembers a plan back in the 1980s to work with the people in two mental health facilities by establishing halfway houses where people would be able to take their medications and start showing that they were in control. They would learn how to cook, take their medications properly and on time, and be prepared to move out into their own apartments. The plan was never realized because of lack of funding. Instead people were discharged with a month's medication when the staff felt that the person was ready to leave. When the people did leave, they stopped taking their medications and people were taking advantage of them. Sister Lucille is very concerned that mental health is an issue that most people don't want to face, and that she sees mental health programs being cut back as well as many other programs that would help people live normal lives. These cutbacks mean that people who are disabled, or in a wheelchair needing one-on-one assistance, can no longer live independently. They may turn to elderly family members who have downsized to a one-bedroom apartment and are unable to care for them. The shutting down of one program ricochets and many other people are affected. Sister Lucille cares very much about people who live on the margins. Emmaus has quite a few people with mental health issues and also a woman who depends on a walker. Because the shelter has had guests on wheelchairs, it is very well equipped for them with a ramp coming into the shelter and a bathroom for the disabled.

As if providing so many services for her guests were not enough, Sister Lucille is concerned about giving hope to people who are marginalized and feel like outsiders, especially when they are alcoholics or drug addicts. Emmaus sheltered one woman who was there six times because she was unable to stay away from alcohol. When Sister Lucille received a desperate telephone call from her, she felt that she just couldn't turn her down. She was torn because she did not want to enable her to stay in that situation, yet she didn't want that woman to think that she is not there for her. The shelter found the woman a thirty-day rehabilitation program. In fact, some people have been able to leave their children with Emmaus, so they can be part of a program, returning to gather their children and move on with their lives.

Sister Lucille has found her guests to be wonderful people and although their stays are short term, they continue to keep in touch once they have found jobs and housing. They are happy to return just to share what is happening in their lives. Often they will come back for the holidays because they might need a little help for their children at Christmas or they might join them for a Thanksgiving meal. They have formed very strong bonds with each other that can be so important for their well-being. In fact, many of the guests return to the shelter just to say hello and share their news with Sister Lucille and the staff. Sometimes they might need just some help like a food box or a gas voucher. Sister Lucille wants them to return for a visit if there is something the staff can do to help them stay in their apartment, or if they need some encouragement about issues they don't feel comfortable discussing somewhere else. For example, the shelter had a family with five children who had resided there for a long time. When they were ready to leave the staff filled the van with furniture and everything they needed and brought them to their new place. The following Monday the doorbell rang; it was the father who needed to pick something up and as he came through the door, he said, "I'm home."

Sister Lucille has found that one of the nice things of a small town, as opposed to Boston or Augusta or the cities where people are numbers and not names, is how many people come back. She received a call from a woman who has mental limitations but had a child that she mothered very well. The shelter helped her move into an apartment, but instead of using fuel she depended on electricity to heat her home and ran up a huge electric bill. Sister Lucille sent a staff member, Brian, to her apartment in order to see what they could do about her electricity bill and to get her some help with fuel. Sister Lucille is more than pleased that despite the fact that the woman has limitations, she knew enough to call and explain what her needs were. As a result, Sister Lucille praised her for getting in touch when she had a problem.

Yet life is not easy in Ellsworth. It serves as a vacation center, but the restaurants and hotels close down in the winter, creating widespread unemployment. The fishing industry has been scaled back. For example, regulators on December 2, 2013, voted to cancel the 2014 shrimp season in the Gulf of Maine. Before the vote, the Atlantic States Marine Fisheries Commission's Northern Shrimp Section cited research that shows that stocks of shrimp are at historic lows because of warming waters.[21] Climate change has affected every part of the world but is especially challenging when people are in dire economic straits. Also, there is no adequate public transportation in Ellsworth; there is only one bus and it goes to Bangor once a day and returns in the afternoon.

Despite the fact that there are some government programs that help the poor, the labor market is responsible for not lifting so many people out of poverty. Unfortunately, government programs for poverty are far more meager than anti-poverty efforts in other advanced nations. According to an article in the *New York Times*, the main reason for this country's persistent poverty is the disappearance of jobs with decent pay that can take workers above the poverty line without government help.[22] Given the number of poor in Ellsworth, the shelter's second mission is to serve them has a regular schedule. Twice a week people come in for food boxes, which contain the only fruit, vegetables, and desserts that they can have. A very large room serves as a food pantry where people come in to get food boxes and its many shelves are filled with different cans. The Shaw's supermarket donates a great deal of food that is transported by the National Association of Letter Carriers that picks up 70,743,973 pounds of nonperishable foods in one month. Three times a week Shaw's and Hannaford stores give Emmaus their old pastries, bread, fruit, and vegetables. The local public schools generally have Thanksgiving food drives for people who come to Emmaus to pick up what they need. The shelter gets cases of food financed by the government three times a year. Then there is the Good Shepherd Food Bank near Lewiston where the shelter can get items for sixteen cents a pound, and also gives two matching grants, matching every dollar the shelter gives them. One of these grants is for the shelter.

A staff member at Emmaus, Brian, takes the van and picks up the food early in the morning and when he returns, the staff sorts what is needed for the shelter. Any overflow is sent to another shelter. On Thursdays and Saturdays, the shelter puts items on the table outside and people come with shopping bags to take what they need until there is nothing left. Sister Lucille found that these people are very solicitous of one another. Each person or family takes a few items and then picks up after everyone has had a least one chance to take food. There are times when Emmaus has an abundance of things people have donated such as toothpaste or diapers that are placed on the table.

There are many donors in Ellsworth. Sister Lucille has the gift of reaching out and inspiring people to donate to the poor and to the shelter. For example, for a period, St. Joseph's Church collected paper products for the shelter every Sunday. Baskets were set along the aisle with the sign "Emmaus Homeless Shelter Paper Collection" and people donated paper towels, toilet paper, and tissues and the shelter wound up with hundreds of dollars' worth of paper. One parishioner called Sister Lucille and told her that she asked the students in her class to donate paper. Some of the paper will be put out on Thursdays or Saturdays when people come in for things they might need. In another month people donated liquids and laundry detergents. The cost of such items for twenty-five people who do their laundry and wash dishes is very high.

Sister Lucille also provides backpacks for children going to school. Parents will come in and sign up, giving the age and grade of the child or children. Little children will need crayons, pencils, and rulers, and high school students will need folders, calculators, and pens. In 2012, Emmaus gave out forty-three backpacks. People in the town are pleased to donate money for this well-known program.

She also provides assistance to people who are in dire need of fuel. The most that she can give them is fifty gallons, worth about $200.00. She has contacts at the oil companies in Ellsworth and they are all willing to donate the fifty gallons so many people need. For example, a woman called Sister Lucille because she could not get any help to receive the fuel she needed until April. Because of the publicity Sister Lucille has received from a yearly auction sponsored by the shelter, and because she is frequently written about in the local newspapers, she receives money from local people and the churches in town. She told me "I never worry about money. If it's meant to happen it will happen. I feel if you are using money to help people, the money will be there."[23]

There is also a room at Emmaus with shoes, boots, and all types of clothing for adults, and children, as well as a large collection of toys. Then there is space for all kinds of kitchenware: plates, coffee pots, toasters, pots and pans, glasses, cutlery, and more. Many shelves are filled with sheets and towels, and there is also an area for personal items such as diapers and lotions. Sister Lucille even thought about helping people without furniture who move into apartments with housing vouchers, so there are storage units, kitchen tables, and chairs, twin and full beds, couches, and small appliances.

Sister Lucille lived at Emmaus for many years before she felt that she needed some privacy and found a small place of her own that is just a fifteen-minute drive away. She is doing the job of five people. She rises at 5:45 in the morning and is at the shelter at 7:15 a.m. and returns to her home in late afternoon. She works until 8 p.m. on various jobs connected with the shelter, such as creating a new website or a PowerPoint presentation, working on her newsletter, meeting with people involved in the yearly auction that raises money for Emmaus, preparing for Thanksgiving, and other holidays, and reaching out to other churches and people in need.

Every year Sister Lucille creates a Thanksgiving Community Meal where the homeless and the well-off mingle so that those who are in the shelter or extremely poor do not need to feel embarrassed about their situations. In 2012, there were 150 people at the meal, for which volunteers cooked, served, prepared the room, and cleaned up. The Jackson Laboratory in Ellsworth, where one of the most important volunteers works, contributed 162 turkeys, fifty hams, and seven fruit baskets.

Then there are Sister Lucille's concerns for the poor at Christmas. Here again, Sister Lucille is so close to members of the community, many of them help her every year. Mark Politte, who owns Stanley Subaru, has a yearly Christmas gift collection for the poor and homeless. Every year in his showroom he has a vehicle that is open where people come in and drop off gifts. He also invites people in the shelter to a Christmas party; after that Brian comes with the van to take all these gifts back. The Bangor Savings Bank and Toys for Tots, local churches, businesses, nonprofit organizations, and restaurants donate gifts for children. A high school and Hancock County Technical Center also contribute. People come in and fill out forms because the shelter is a conduit. People adopt a family and they are asked to buy a gift of at least a thirty-dollar value and also give us a thirty-dollar gift card that helps the recipients buy a meal. Emmaus also ensures that every child gets a scarf, hat, and mittens with their gifts. As a result, 240 families and more than eight hundred children were recipients for Christmas in 2012.

Sister Lucille is working with a number of important organizations that serve the people of Ellsworth. She works very closely with the Next Step Program for people who have suffered from domestic violence, a program that has the means to protect them from perpetrators. Some of the people coming to Emmaus are fleeing domestic violence. The shelter has nine cameras at the front desk that will photograph any perpetrator of domestic violence who attempts to get in. No one can get into the building without ringing the doorbell and being let in by the staff.

As if there were more than twenty-four hours in her day, Sister Lucille works with a pre-release program for people with addictions and alcohol problems in Ellsworth. When someone is ready to be released, they are required to go into stable environment where they can stay in contact with the court. Every day these people, most of them younger, are required to go into the jail for a breathalyzer test. They also work with programs and have a counselor. The shelter works quite closely with them when they live there, but is also working with a committee that is trying to purchase a home to accommodate them, because it is unable to take in all these people.

Sister Lucille is on a committee with hospice, and works with veterans of the Vietnam and Korean wars. In addition, she works with another program, Open Door, a program for drug addicts, to which people who suffer from addiction go every day. If the shelter has room, it will take someone in that program who has dinner with the other guests and spend the night. Sister Lucille also works with the Washington-Hancock Community Service to raise money to provide fuel for the people who have left the shelter and need further help.

She not only is working with a number of organizations in Ellsworth but also helps an alcoholic man she has known for twenty years who lives in a tent city in the woods all year around. Patrick comes into the shelter a couple of times a week. Sometimes the staff will give him soap and towels and a pass to the

YMCA where he can take a shower. They always give him food. He doesn't have his meals at the shelter, but twice a week he goes to the soup kitchen in Ellsworth. He has lost a couple of teeth so the Emmaus staff gives him toothbrushes and toothpaste. A few of the local churches help him and one put him up in a hotel for one bitterly cold week. Usually, when it is freezing, he comes to the shelter and the staff will give him a small amount of money so he can spend time at a twenty-four-hour Denny's restaurant where he can drink coffee. Sister Lucille has given him a tent as well as sleeping bags and provides sweatshirts, boots, and gym shoes in the summer. Sometimes she gives him money for propane for his lantern and she makes sure that the food the shelter provides is something he can eat out of a can, as well as fruit. Ellsworth is very different from an urban environment. Patrick is local so everybody knows him and is more than accepting of his problems.

Emmaus is also working with a group who are ministering to migrant workers who come to the area to rake blueberries. A group came in for food boxes and, shortly after they left, a local business donated a large amount of frozen chicken. Sister Lucille called one of them to pick up the boxes and had the good fortune to see the joy in their faces. The Sisters of Mercy are on the front line about policy reform, making phone calls and writing letters to the Senate and Congress to persuade them to pass the immigration bill.

A wonderful part of Sister Lucille's outreach to the community is her close contact with all of the local churches, regardless of their denominations. She has given sermons at a Lutheran church and also at the Congregational Church during Lent and Advent. During Lent, church members meet once a month in a different church and a minister gives the reflection on the homily. For the last ten or twelve years, they decided that they would have collections in their churches during Lent as well as having collections during their weekly Wednesday night gatherings, contributing $10,000 which Sister Lucille distributes to prevent what she refers to as "double dipping" in the churches. She keeps records of the donations and once a month provides a report on the money that has come in and what has been donated to various people. Once, the local Rotary Club was invited to join the gathering and Sister Lucille developed a PowerPoint presentation for them. The Rotarians were astounded by all that happens in the shelter. She feels that she has to get out and be part of things, and over the years has built up wonderful trust and support from the population so that people can see what is happening at Emmaus, ask if they can volunteer, and also help to fund it.

She is a Sister of Mercy with the skills of a corporate manager. Emmaus received a grant for $12,500 from the Sisters of Mercy in 2013 and two years earlier received a grant of $24,000 from them so that Emmaus was able to send everyone who comes into the shelter to a dentist. Emmaus also receives a Family Birthday Fund of $5,000 a year. Because of their situations, so many people are unable to celebrate their birthdays. The shelter gives each child or adult who qualify a $30 gift certificate. Then once a month all of their birthdays are celebrated with a pizza party.

Sister Lucille remembers that ten years ago there was a man in his fifties whose birthday the shelter celebrated with a gift, and a birthday cake with candles and ice cream. When he blew out the candles, he wept. After he had composed himself, he told her that he couldn't remember the last time that he had a cake or that someone had celebrated his birthday. Then she decided that no one she knows would not have their birthday recognized. People who are homeless lose contact with their families and friends. It was that incident that inspired Sister Lucille to respond to the person who offered her money so that she could establish a birthday fund.

In addition, Sister Lucille manages a Family Fund from quarterly donations. She uses it to help people when they are ready to leave, but do not have money for a security deposit. When she sends it to the landlord, she stipulates that the person who is leaving sign a paper and send it back to her. The money must come back to the shelter, so it is a revolving fund. Sometimes a person may need help with his or her car to get to work. Sister Lucille doesn't like to limit the fund to one particular purpose because these people's needs are unpredictable.

Emmaus also receives $3,000 a year from the Salvation Army. The shelter gives out $50,00 to $100,000 to people in need so they can get clothing, food, and medicine. The annual budget for the shelter is $311,000, with $90,000 coming from the state and the federal government and $221,000 coming from private donations. Like many organizations that care for the poor, Emmaus lost $5,000 because of the Sequester.

The idea for organizing a Spring Fest happened when one of her major volunteers, Renée LaCasse, with whom Sister Lucille is very close, was discussing how to raise money for the shelter. They decided to have a Spring Fest, where they would serve a meal, have items that would be sold at a live auction, and provide entertainment. For the past ten years, the Spring Fest has been incorporated with her spring appeal. It is a tremendous amount of work, not only to prepare for the event, but also to publicize it, create posters and banners, run radio spots, and get in touch with people at the television station. The event takes place at the local mid-level elementary school that has a cafeteria and a stage. A local man donates all the longer tables and tablecloths. Because the event attracts so many people, Emmaus needed to find a place as large as the school.

Renée LaCasse remembers the first year she contacted Sister Lucille about fundraising. She felt called to help and had a background in event planning at Jackson Laboratory where she works. They talked about what they could do and also about Sister Lucille's contact with Masanobu Ikeyima, a noted musician. He heard her on the radio and called her saying, "I must come and play for you." The first year Renée and Sister Lucille did the grocery shopping. Renée did the cooking and they planned the menu together. That year almost 150 people came and they were really packed in a parish hall with buffet tables, an auction item table, and a grand piano that Sister Lucille borrowed from somebody. The fest grew larger each year. In the beginning it was hard to get volunteers. Now Sister Lucille has an amazing couple, who has done the auction year after year and more than fifty volunteers, as it now takes six months to prepare for this occasion.

There is a performance program with speakers and entertainers. After Mr. Ikeyima played for the first two years, there were notable entertainers who donated their time, including Renée's son Gus, who is a violinist. The Reverend Jeremy Stone, a gifted public speaker, supports the fest. Another man who has spoken at the fest is attorney, William Beardsley, whose firm is right across the street from Emmaus. One day he stopped by to see what was happening there and then volunteered to work the night shift during the year, using his skills as an attorney to give the guests legal advice.

The first four years of cooking for three hundred people who attended the fest were more than difficult. Two of the kitchens were no bigger than a small bathroom. Renée had a group of twelve people cooking at her home, which was a trial. Because it was a weeklong endeavor to get ready, she had to take time off from her work Jackson Laboratory. Then after the fest, she was involved in cleanup, dishes, linen, gathering trash, and more. She has gone through three dishwashers as a result.

Now a soup kitchen, The Simmering Pot, cooks for the fest, with food supplied by the shelter, an ice cream place brought the ice cream they make to the fest for dessert. Friends of Sister Lucille from Braintree, Massachusetts, make four hundred biscotti. The event lasts for three hours from 12:30 to 3:30 p.m. At 2:30 p.m., the live auction begins and the entertainment stops. The Bangor Savings Bank tallies the donations.

Sister Lucille also sends out a spring appeal for donations to the Spring Fest when it is out to her mailing list of about three thousand people. At this time of the year, she receives a $25,000 endowment from a family. Between the auction, the ticket sales for the event, and the spring appeal, Sister Lucille receives $50,000 for the shelter.

Among the many volunteers are a number of people who have experienced troubling times, and that has increased their empathy and understanding. The Reverend Jeremy Stone a longtime supporter Sister Lucille, was an orphan, and relates to what people at the shelter are experiencing. One of the women who worked with Renée to do the cooking in the early years of the fest grew up in a one-room home with three siblings and a single mother. She is now a wonderful community leader and runs the Christmas program for Sister Lucille.

Renée LaCasse was very active in helping prepare for the twentieth anniversary of Emmaus. She has remained involved as a volunteer for the shelter for ten years and has spoken at one of the Spring Fests. Renée has an intimate knowledge of what people at the shelter have experienced. Some members of her father's family have been homeless and experienced drug and alcohol problems. The first time she went to the shelter she didn't know Sister Lucille, but responded to a request to buy for a family. She was not only pleased to donate money to a family, but in addition felt as if she were taking care of her father who had grown up in great poverty.

Her son Gus has been helping with the cooking and preparations since he was a small child. His mother has taught him the grace of giving, an important lesson. Even though she has a high position at her work and is very gifted, she told me, "It's good for Gus to know who he is and where he comes from. We are all God's children."[24] Sister Lucille has become part of Renée's family. Renee feels that "God was trying to assign me to do this. Sister Lucille always talks to me, especially about living the Gospels. There is real beauty of the simplicity of that. She feels very connected to her order and her sisters that are trying to ease the world's pain."[25]

The many volunteers are more than pleased to help Emmaus in any way that they can. They experience the joy of taking time out of their personal lives and moving beyond their concerns to help people who are needy in a society that doesn't seem to understand the source of happiness.

Sister Lucille's greatest contribution is one of boundless, unconditional love. It is hard for her to walk down a street in Ellsworth without many people rushing over to talk to her for a few minutes. Sister Lucille's love is based on acceptance of everyone regardless of their problems and their situations, a very rare quality. She has brought out the best in people so that her work is truly the work not only of the Sisters of Mercy but also of the whole community in that town.

$\mathcal{S}am\ \mathcal{P}olk$
and
$\mathcal{G}roceryships$

A young man working on Wall Street, Sam Polk, resigned his job and decided to work with disadvantaged people in the poorer parts of Los Angeles to help them acquire healthy diets. His work has, most importantly, made them socially visible, and helped them to control an important part of their lives. Sam moved from a job where he made millions of dollars and lived a very expensive life that he had yearned for when he was still in college, but found unfulfilling. His efforts have made an important change in disadvantaged people's health and helped them acquire self-respect.

In doing so, he faced an enormous challenge, because we live in a country where the middle class is in decline and the gap between the very rich and the struggling poor has widened considerably. According to NPR,[1] 1 percent of our population accounts for 50 percent of the country's wealth, and many people are not aware of the difficult lives of our poor people or even of their high number.

However, even if a person lives in a comfortable neighborhood with a daily routine that doesn't include poorer areas, opening the newspapers is one way to see the gap. The *New York Times* shows the glaring differences in its advertisements, for example, for huge diamond bracelets and rings from expensive stores piled up. In fact, a study has revealed luxury retail spending is bigger in the United States than in Japan, Italy, France, and China combined.[2] Although there have been efforts to raise the minimum wage, even a high wage such as $10.10 per hour is not enough for a family to enjoy economic security. Although President Obama has called for a rise in the minimum wage to $9.00 in 2010, there have been relatively few results in a number of states. The average wage is $7.26, hardly enough to pay for rent and food. That is just $15,080 a year for a full-time employee, $300 below the poverty line for a family of three.

In fact, in 1995, 33 percent of students in public schools qualified for free or reduced-price lunches, while 51 percent of students in 2015 come from low-income families. According to the National Center for Education Statistics the majority of students in twenty-one states are poor.[3] Some corporate leaders are making many millions of dollars a year, and even presidents of large universities are making up to three million. There have been numerous articles pointing out that higher wages would mean the loss of jobs, but others present contrasting views. Fifty-seven percent of small businesses favor increasing the rise in the minimum wage to $10.10, believing it would lower the pressure to raise taxes.[4]

Low-income families and single people do not eat well because they cannot afford to and because most of them live far from stores where they could purchase nutritious food. Yet on February 2, 2014, legislation was passed that cut $8.7 billion in food stamp benefits over the next ten years, causing 850,000 households to lose an average of $90 per month.[5] When the Republicans originally argued for a cut in the food stamp program (SNAP) of between $20.5 billion and $39 billion, the president threatened to veto both proposals. The bill they proposed also includes billions in crop insurance as well as programs and subsidies for American agriculture.

Given the results of the mid-term elections, with the new majority favoring tax cuts, the outlook for working poor is not favorable. In fact, low-income families pay more taxes than the wealthy. According to a new analysis by the Institute on Taxation and Economic Policy, in 2015, the poorest fifth of Americans will pay on average 10.9 percent of their income in state and local taxes, the middle fifth will pay 9.4 percent and the top 1 percent will average 5.4 percent.[6] Economist Lawrence Summers commented that a substantial part of our success or failure in raising middle-class living standards is not only the result of overall economic performance, but also the distribution of income.[7] Mr. Summers is part of a commission of economists and policy experts from several countries that is publishing a detailed analysis of the wage slowdown, defining it as the challenge of our time. It is not difficult to see that this overwhelming economic problem can threaten to become a problem for our political system and democracy. Imagine people working two jobs in order to survive, without time to vote or to become engaged in considering the policies that are affecting their lives.

Some years ago, Sam Polk was unsure of his working life, asking himself if he should continue on his path as a member of the 1 percent elite in this country or follow his heart and walk away from his prestigious job. At thirty years old he was a senior trader for one of the largest hedge funds in the world, but he was wracked with conflict because, after eight years on Wall Street, he came to see the world in an entirely different way, and no longer felt comfortable with his lifestyle or employment. He was internally distressed.

When he was young, he dreamed about becoming rich and successful. His first step was to be accepted in Columbia University. In his junior year he received a summer internship at Credit Suisse First Boston, one of the most prestigious investment banks in the world. He felt it was a miracle that he got that internship, because, looking back, his first few years of college were a disaster. He was drinking and taking drugs, was arrested twice for fist fighting, and suspended from college for burglarizing the room of a campus drug-dealer. After the internship, he quit taking drugs, returned to Columbia, and buckled down to work, thinking that his life was back on track.

But there were still issues that were upsetting him. He reached out to a counselor who referred to herself as a spiritual teacher. She explained that her teachings were grounded in Native American belief systems and used words such as "spiritual disconnection" that didn't make sense to Sam. In their first session she explained that his problem with drinking and drugs was actually a symptom of a deeper problem, a spiritual disconnection. If he were going to regain wholeness or connect with his heart he would have to start becoming sober, so Sam stopped drinking.

When Sam got the job on Wall Street, he met with his counselor twice a week, and did the spiritual work that she suggested—meditating, writing in a journal, and reading spiritual books. He wasn't sure about doing this, but felt it was helping him with his job. Then one day, she returned to the subject of spiritual disconnection, and told Sam that he had lost touch with his own inherent value, a condition that is pervasive in the Western world. She added that perhaps that was not only because of his past drinking and drug abuse, but also because his need to become rich and successful was a way for him to prove to the world and himself that he was valuable. She then introduced a Native American concept called circle of consciousness that held that from the moment a person is born, they are inherently valuable, and that one life is not more important than another. This is a concept that differs from the widespread but unspoken belief and some people matter more than others. The counselor then told him that it is possible for him to connect with his inherent goodness, and when that happens, his life will bloom like flowers.

Sam began to look forward to his time with his counselor because she listened very carefully to his thoughts and ideas. For the first time in his life he felt that he was being valued for just being himself, and that he had nothing to prove. He was living a double life. During the day he was a fierce trading-floor warrior. At night he was meditating and writing in a journal to connect with his inner voice. He felt very lonely despite the fact that his counselor's work helped him up the corporate ladder. He ate in the most upscale restaurants, wore expensive suits, took lavish vacations, and lived in a $6,500 a month apartment. With each passing year, his counselor's words would come back to him, that he was seeking value through money and his achievements in his job. Sam began to feel hollow.

Fortunately, he was very close to his twin brother who recommended a book to him that he had just finished, *Tattoos on the Heart*, by Father Gregory Boyle, a priest who started Homeboy Industries to create jobs for young people who led deprived lives in a poor and violent neighborhood of Los Angeles. Father Boyle referred to the gang members and the work he had done with them as the greatest privilege of his life. Then Sam understood the meaning of the circle of life.

A few weeks after he finished the book, the stock market plummeted and millions of people lost their jobs, retirements, and homes, while the people on Wall Street actually made more money. One day, when Sam was in a meeting with his cohorts discussing hedge fund regulations, he blurted out that the regulations would be better for the system as a whole. His boss leaned across the table and told him, "I don't have the capacity to think about the system as a whole. I can only think about what is good for our business."[8] Sam felt sad and realized that this was the example of the Western belief system, that some lives matter more than others. He recognized that he also had believed it and had spent every day of his eight years on his job struggling to reach the top. For the first time he saw what he regarded as the destructiveness of that system, and how oblivious to the damage that belief system was causing.

He wrestled with his dual outlook. One part of him wondered if he was crazy to be walking away from million-dollar bonuses, but another part felt that there had to be more to life than endless accumulation of money, jockeying for position and power. At the end of the year, 2010, he left Wall Street and decided to move to Los Angeles. His fiancée, Kristen, who graduated from medical school arranged to transfer her work and accompany him.

When Sam arrived he had no idea of how he would lead his new life and began volunteering. He worked with homeless teens in a drop-in center and taught writing to girls in the foster care system. He even started to go into juvenile jails and found that it was very difficult to see such young children wearing uniforms. He felt that these youngsters needed to be valued, and brought back into the community rather than being ostracized. He also believed that many young people who committed violence experienced it themselves. He used to start off with these youngsters by listing the drugs he once took, because they are so anxious and upset that it was hard to get their attention. Just listing the drugs was a way of getting them to listen. Sam would also talk to them about what it meant to wear a mask, covering his own feelings that inside he felt powerless, fearful, and worthless, and that he tried to create an exterior that was successful and powerful. He even told them that if their teachers knew that they had become experts on the understanding and analysis of drugs, they would stop characterizing them as poor students.

Three years later, Sam talked to his wife, Kristen, about his volunteer work and they decided to watch a documentary, *A Place at the Table*. It focused on hunger, and how in the richest country in the world, millions of people don't know where they will be able to have the next meal, fifty million people rely on food stamps. What stunned them is that one-sixth of the population survive on the cheapest and unhealthiest food. They watched more documentaries that corroborated what Sam had experienced, such as oil companies that are more interested in profit than clean water, and of other industries, nearly all of which echoed the sentiments of his former boss. As they watched these documentaries, they saw that industries are making decisions benefiting themselves financially, with consequences for poor families who have freeways that partition their neighborhoods and waste dumped near their homes, children in underfunded and inadequate schools. Further, Sam and Kristen found that people who live in poverty are disproportionately targeted by food company advertisements and receive no education about nutrition. Children especially are targeted with advertisements about chips, soda, and candy. Too many of their parents are working two or three jobs and have no time to cook, and no fresh produce in the neighborhoods, but there are fast-food outlets on nearly every corner. Sam concluded that poor people have been told in so many ways that they are not as valuable as rich people, that people weren't just hungry and obese because of what he saw as a toxic food culture, but that they were stressed from growing up in a culture that told them that they were worthless.

In her 2014 book, *Hand to Mouth; Living in Bootstrap America*, Linda Tiradoe writes,

> We have learned not to try to be middle class. It never works out well and always makes you feel worse for having tried and failed again. It makes more sense to get food that will be palatable and cheap and that keeps well. Junk food is a pleasure that we are allowed to have; why would we give that up? There are very few of them.[9]

At the other end of the spectrum is a very expensive website called "Nutrition Action," that has a weekly newspaper, books, and DVDs that only the wealthy can afford. And now a restaurant chain has opened up with healthy food for the super rich.

Sam had struggled with obesity and food most of his life. He was overweight as a child when the emotional side of obesity was very difficult, and included feelings of shame, and self-blame. Although he was very close to his siblings, his parents were not good at parenting. He knew what it was to be hungry. Although he grew up in a middle-class suburb, his father was tight with money. He would order a pizza, just one for six people. He found that he had to wolf down one slice in case he wanted another. He once took a slice in his bedroom and hid it. The movie he and his wife watched struck him with the confluence of hunger and obesity. The discovery that five miles away there were children who were overweight, but also were wondering about the possibility of their next meal, made Sam put his own childhood situation in perspective. He became concerned about these children and their parents, who want them to be healthy despite their difficult situations.

A practice that makes life even more difficult for people who live in poverty is that many low-income people are unable to use banks. As the St. Louis Federal Reserve has pointed out, "unbanked" consumers spend about 2.5 to 3 percent of a government benefit check and between 4 and 5 percent of a pay-roll check just to cash them. Because they don't have checking accounts, they must pay for money orders. Considering the cost for cashing a biweekly payroll check, and buying about six money orders each month, a household with a net income of $20,000 may pay as much as $1,200 annually for alternative service fees, more than the expense of a monthly checking account.[10]

After Sam and Kristen had talked about these documen-taries, Sam decided to start an organization to help struggling families. They not only wanted to buy healthy groceries for poor families, but also educate people about nutrition, thus helping them to navigate what he and Kristen saw as a toxic food envi-ronment by reading labels, cooking food, and navigating grocery stores. They contacted the head of Vitamix's corporation who was pleased to donate a number of blenders and found corporate sponsorships for the families who will participate. Then they contacted filmmakers who donated DVDs such as *Forks over Knives*, *A Place at the Table*, and *Hungry for Change*. Sam knew that providing education and resources was only the begin-ning, and that the organization also needed to focus on mental, emotional, and spiritual aspects as well.[11]

He contacted Father Boyle at Homeboy Industries, who responded immediately and became very important to Sam not only as a mentor, but also as someone, who cared deeply for him. When Sam visited Homeboy Industries, he found that it took up an entire city block. Instead of hedge fund managers and traders, Sam encountered gang members with tattoos. Father Boyle was surrounded by important-looking men in suits when a scrawny twelve-year-old child came in, and Father Boyle left the men and gave the child a big hug. While everyone waited, he put his hands on the child's shoulder, and gave him his undivided attention. When they finished he gave him another hug and sent him on his way. When Sam saw the joy on that child's face, he realized how much his life had changed; his billionaire boss was no longer his idol, Father Boyle was. He discovered that Father Boyle, whom many of the youngsters he serves lovingly call him, "Dog" in their own lingo, asked to be assigned to the poorest parish in America, an area overrun with gang problems. His work reveals that children who engage in violence are marginalized and not valued, so they turn to whatever support system they can find. Homeboy Industries has become the largest gang intervention program in the world, and Father Boyle serves as a father figure to thousands of emotionally needy youngsters. He not only became a mentor to Sam, but also offered to partner with him in Groceryships, the organization that Sam was envisioning.

Sam left his first meeting with Father Boyle determined to create an organization, and spent the next few months creating a logo and a website and finding lawyers, one of whom is his twin brother, a Harvard educated lawyer, who draws a low income working for worthy causes. Sam also hired interns, launched a website, and established a board of directors. Sam and Kristen also met with many different people: nutritionists, doctors, social workers, professors, world-renowned diabetes physicians, and directors of major nonprofits, community organizers, and local celebrity chefs. In 2013, the American Medical Association declared obesity a disease, describing it as a long-term illness.[12] Then he watched healthy eating documentaries, and read a dozen books on nutrition. After that he wrote a nutrition curriculum that distilled everything he had learned and approached it from a different perspective. Sam knew from his own experience that people who have issues with food in their lives have one thing in common—they blame themselves.

Sam also saw the connection between the rampant obesity in the United States and the type of food we consume as well as the connection between obesity with race, ethnicity, and poverty. African American and Hispanics have a 50 percent chance of developing diabetes over their lifetime; Americans in general have a 40 percent chance.[13] The lead author of the study, Dr. Edward Gregg, has concluded that socioeconomic status is more important than race. The economic divide reveals that people in the lowest income brackets have disproportionately high rates of diabetes. He pointed out that lowering people's risk of developing diabetes required the availability of healthier food options, more information about what we eat, and what sorts of foods are healthy.[14] As Sam discovered, our country is saturated with cheap, convenient, readily available high-calorie, and nutritionally poor food whose consumption is encouraged by advertising, poor labeling, subsidies, and the lobbying efforts of powerful corporations. Twenty percent of children and 23 percent of adolescents consume pizza every day, which is high in salt and saturated fat. Eating pizza as a snack or in a fast-food restaurant increases the calories young people consume. Lobbies such as Dairy Management Inc., which helps companies create and promote menus that contain dairy products that are far from healthy, support these diets regularly. For example, in 2013, it helped Domino's Pizza introduce a United States Department of Agriculture–approved school lunch pizza called Smart Slice in 450 districts across thirty-nine states, helped Pizza Hut create the Three Cheese Stuffed Crust Pizza, and Starbucks launch its high-calorie smoothies.[15] Healthier food such as fruit and vegetables are more expensive, poorly advertised, and not backed by a robust lobbying effort.

Sam started the curriculum by explaining how our food system has changed in the past fifty years, with the rise in processed food. At first he included five important food groups—fruits, vegetables, protein, grains, and dairy—that he felt were antiquated. But, in order to give people a useful framework for thinking about the modern food environment he came up with three groups: processed food, less healthy food, and healthy food. Even though processed food is touted as healthy, it has high amounts of sugar, salt, and fat, and there are strong lobby groups defending the inclusion of these additives. For example, a public relations company that defended the International Dairy Foods Association's right to put artificial sweeteners in milk without additional labeling runs the Calorie Control Council, a trade group for manufacturers of artificial sweeteners. It also led a petition to remove saccharin from the Food and Drug Administration (FDA) list of carcinogens.[16] Sam's project was not an easy one.

Next he focused on the structure of his organization so that everyone who participated—nutrition educators, Groceryships staff, and people who joined the program—would sit in a circle to emphasize that they are all equal. About seven months later, he put together a staff of volunteers who met at his house on Sundays to create the curriculum. It was then that Sam discovered that the obesity crisis wasn't just about poor people, but about everyone who had a tortured relationship with their own bodies.

In the next few months he raised $50,000 to support the program. Sam knows many people on Wall Street, such as his first boss who was a very generous man who mentored him and cared for him as Father Boyle did. When Sam called and asked him to buy only one Groceryships his former boss replied that he would take ten. Groceryships provide families the money to buy fruits, vegetables, grains, beans, and seeds for six months, together with a comprehensive program of education and support to empower them to increase their health by including more of these healthful foods into their diets. For those six months, families receive gift cards allowing them to buy healthy food.

Its clinic partners monitor the families' health and progress by examining changes in weight, cholesterol, and glucose levels during the six months. Nutritionists are on call during the week to provide nutrition counseling and recipe suggestions. The participating families receive DVDs including *Forks over Knives* and *Hungry for Change*, blenders and other kitchen appliances, *Food Feelings* journals, copies of *SuperSprowtz* children's nutrition books, and copies of *Chop, Chop* magazines.[17]

After a few months, the group was ready to start applications process and interview people for the eight spots in the pilot program. Sam and his staff found partnerships with people in low-income communities. People who wanted to take part include in their applications information about their monthly salary, and their rent. Almost half of the families were paying half of their monthly income on rent. Then there is the issue of partnering with an organization, or with hubs for low-income support, in order to find a location for the program. Their first program was held at Father Greg's Homeboy Industries, and then they partnered with Los Angeles' Promise, and with St. John's Wellness.

One of the first people they interviewed was Helen, a woman who was in her fifties. Helen cared for six boys and girls, who are the children of her drug-addicted siblings living on the same street. Her siblings were allowed into her house only twice a year, on Thanksgiving and Christmas, when they came to eat a meal with their children, but were then required to leave. Every time, the children would seek reassurance and ask Helen whether they were going to become like their parents.[18] Helen entered the program because she wanted to teach them how to eat well and be healthy. Then Sam realized that he had spent so much time thinking about nutrition information and program structure, that he had no idea what it was like to live in Los Angeles' South Central neighborhood or walk in that woman's shoes. He wondered if he would be able to help Helen, given his very different, and, in his opinion, limited experience in life. He called his counselor who told him, "Just tell your story, speak from your heart, and be humble."[19]

One month later the pilot program began and three people from Groceryships sat in a circle with eight women from South Central Los Angeles. The women stared at Sam with doubt and skepticism. Sam described the structure of the program, with the first hour focused on education, and the second a sharing circle to talk about emotions. He then said that until that moment he didn't know if Groceryships could work, but he thought it would and if it did, it would help a lot of people. He invited these women to help co-create this program that would help their communities and many of other communities as well. Some women looked at Sam and nodded; a few remained silent. After that people introduced themselves and spoke about why they attended. Women shared their experiences: how their obesity crisis impacted them; how family members had died of that illness; how their children were teased for their weight. Then Sam talked about his own family's history of obesity: his father was overweight and had Type 2 diabetes; his mother and his younger brother were also overweight and had bariatric surgery. Then he revealed his personal struggles, including his current one, that one day the previous week he had eaten six doughnuts. The women looked at him with some doubt as if to say, this person is going to teach us to get healthy? Sam continued that he had struggled with food everyday of his life, was a heavy child, and was constantly teased. As an adult he admitted that he had been on a diet for twenty years trying to lose the same twenty pounds, but it hadn't worked out yet, although he was hopeful. When the meeting ended, he was discouraged because the women had asked only a few questions, and there had been very little participation. During the sharing circle, the women gave one- or two-word answers and the meeting ended early because there was so little participation.[20]

For the second meeting Sam and his staff arrived early, put out eight new vitamixes to give away, and waited for people to arrive. When the door opened every family walked in. For the nutrition education, his partner talked about vegetable smoothies, although he wasn't sure how kale smoothies would be accepted in South Central Los Angeles. But when the smoothies were prepared, the women loved them. During the sharing circle afterward, the women were reserved and only gave one-word answers. When it was Sam's turn, he told them how difficult it was to be a kid growing up overweight in this world. His identical twin and he were called "the pork brothers" instead of the Polk brothers.[21]

The following week, the meeting was started as usual, by reading a few passages about the principles of Groceryships, and later held the sharing circle with the question, "How are you doing?" Again the replies were only one or two words. When it was Helen's turn, she looked at Sam and said, "It's been twenty years since someone asked me how I was doing," and tears rolled down her face.[22] She said that she had taken care of people her whole life and that the program made her realize that she was important too and worth taking care of. She realized that the program was not just about food, but also about the value of her soul. After Helen, the next woman shared her story about an abusive marriage and wept. She also spoke about losing fifty pounds and than gaining them back and wept again. The emotional wall between the staff and the women crumbled. One woman told the group that she was getting negative feedback from her husband who made fun of the program and wouldn't eat her new meals. Thirteen weeks later he attended his first meeting and is now very supportive of her. The participants talk about the hard times in their lives, such as working the overnight shift at Target, how to react when a mother's two boys have their phones stolen at gunpoint, and what it feels like when their children say that their classmates are calling their mother fat.[23]

Three months into the program, Helen shared with the circle that she was inspired by everything she was learning, and that she wanted to bring it to the rest of South Central Los Angeles. She started the process of making community film screening of movies like *Food Inc.* and *Fed Up*. She is already showing signs of becoming a great community leader and has the potential to change the way people eat in South Central. She has learned that with the community behind you, anything is possible.

Over the next few meetings Sam had to put a box of Kleenex in the middle of the circle because if one person wept, they all did. Because the program is funded so that the participants can purchase healthy food, he began hearing reports of how wonderful the produce is, and that their children were making kale shakes with their friends. The participants started eating better and sleeping more, exercising, and losing weight. For Sam, the most touching part were the emotional and spiritual changes. The women started referring to the meetings as their safe place. Helen would say that when she walked in she would unzip herself, and two hours later she would zip herself back up to face the world.[24] For twelve weeks not a single person missed a meeting. A young mom said, "I love this group because it reminds me that I exist."[25] These people actually found that eating nutritious food was cheaper than eating junk food. Brown rice, dried beans, and frozen vegetables are less expensive to eat at home than eating at McDonald's. While feeding a family of four costs $20 at McDonald's, cooking meals with rice and dried beans is far less than that. The participants may be working two jobs, and have little time to cook a substantial meal, but they have learned a good way to prepare meals. Then there is the issue of exercise. Sam found a yoga teacher who volunteered her time for a year, raised money for space, and the group practiced once a week.[26]

Sam also wanted the media to carry his message, and soon enough reporters started asking to attend and with the permission of the families, Groceryships had a *Los Angeles Times* reporter sit in on their meetings to profile to what was happening, and ABC7 had a wonderful section celebrating Groceryships. Sam believes that the reason there is so much interest in the program is because he and his staff have created a safe, sacred space, which is an emotional oasis in the modern world. What has grown in that space is connection that includes bearing witness to each other's struggles, and helping each participant discover that he or she is someone who really matters. At every meeting Helen talks about how grateful she is that Groceryships was brought to South Central Los Angeles. Sam has been eating better and losing weight. Now Sam feels that everyone belongs to a community, and after these meetings he is returned to wholeness, empathy, and love.[27] The space where participants meet is not about a service provider and service recipients, but about everyone coming together. Sam has remarked that the meetings are not about poor people and rich people, but about everyone, that the poverty and inequality of our world are symptoms of a spiritual disconnection at the cultural level.[28]

Groceryships worked with eight families in the spring of 2014, ten in August, and ten in October. In the spring of 2015, a member of a Groceryships group, Ana Guzman, arranged a meeting between Sam and the principal of the elementary school her children attends because she wanted to start a Groceryships group at the school. She recruited ten new participants and launched the first Spanish-speaking Groceryships group. Ana also agreed to co-lead the group with Brenda Lomeli, a volunteer health coach. Groceryships launched four new groups in the first quarter of 2015: Normandie Elementary, John Muir Middle School, L.A. Job Corps, and Manual Arts High School.

Sam also designed a Corporate Wellness Program in September in which a health coach works with employees on nutrition and emotional health. It includes stress reduction, meditation, understanding emotional eating, and the development of good habits. The corporation is funding it, and Grocery-ships uses the profits from that program to bring its program to low-income families in surrounding areas.

The program has acquired such a good reputation that it acquired new partnerships in 2015. Farm Fresh Food to You now brings local organic produce directly to the participating families at a very generous discount. Luvo Foods donates healthy frozen meals, and Food Forward coordinates the donation of fresh, farmer's market produce to the families. These partnerships are bringing healthy food into South L.A. either free of charge or at affordable prices.

At the end of the six months of every program, there is a graduation ceremony. Sam gives a diploma to each family, and a photographer takes a photo of each one. The results of the first program were impressive. The participants lost an average of six pounds and the consumption of fruits and vegetables rose, while consumption of processed food declined. There was also a marked decrease in eating at restaurants or fast-food places. The first graduation was held at Manual Arts High School, in a room decorated with flowers, streamers, and framed portraits of each participant. Instead of the leggings and T-shirts they wore to meetings, the graduates wore dresses, curled their hair, and did their nails. About seventy-five friends and family came. Congresswoman Karen Bass was the keynote speaker and brought each of them certificates from Congress marking their achievements.[29] By then, the project had gained a lot of media attention.

Groceryships keeps in touch with all of its graduates. It has a quarterly alumnae meeting where families come together with speakers who have graduated and remained healthy. These events show that although the program lasts only six months, most of the families involved now have food budgets and their expenses have gone down since they changed their diets over the long term. For example, one of the classes focused on how oatmeal is cheaper than boxed cereal, and even suggested the idea of serving brown rice with fruit and nuts in the morning. It became a breakfast favorite for many of the participating families. In fact, many of the families have made changes in their own environments helping the goal of Groceryships. One participant took over breakfast duty at her church, replacing pancakes and bacon with brown rice, cereal, and fruit. Another started teaching a nutrition class at her child's elementary school. The teenage sons of another participant started hosting fruit and vegetable smoothie parties for his friends.[30]

Angela Carrasco, the director of Groceryships has written a most touching blog about her life experience, and her appointment as director by Sam Polk.

> For as long as I can remember I had always been fat. In the Dominican Republic where I was raised on a farm until I was 9, I was given the endearing nickname of La Vaquita (little cow). But as an adult I realized that there was a specific moment when the weight started piling on like the Oreo cookies I'd stack by my nightstand. It was when I was five years old and my mother left me. I was left to the care of my sweet grandmother who know how to love via feeding and my aunt, the town's social butterfly and who had three boys of her own to raise. I wasn't an orphan and had a roof over my head, but I understood on a deep level that my Mom has chosen to leave me behind. I subconsciously connected my

mother's abandonment with being unworthy of love, pushing me to food to fill the void that she had left. The initial
abandonment was only the beginning. My childhood was
plagued with sexual, physical, and emotional abuse. Before
she left, Mother was everything but a mom to me. She was
violent to her five children and a wordsmith in emotionally
abusive language. Her repertoire included "You ruined my
life, I should have aborted you all." I was sexually abused
by a cousin 10 years my senior when I was in the care of my
grandma and aunt. That permanently scarred me and caused
the selective memory I am trying to awaken from. I lived on
autopilot, going through the motions, and with too many
responsibilities to grow up like a kid should. I gained com-
pulsive, emotional eating, and bulimia nervosa. It was a way
of self-mutilation when I again became the object of sexual
and emotional abuse from another man. My stepfather's
love for me grew darker and more twisted with time. He was
obsessed and would fabricate stories in his mind that fueled
his jealous rages and would make me plead for him to stop. I
started binging and the fear of gaining back the weight pushed
me into purging. My battle with my eating disorder has been
a long and arduous one. Some days it makes me drop to my
knees pleading for mercy and on other days, I kick it straight
in the face. I think we can now call it a draw. No, I'm going to
give myself the credit due and declare a win. Food has been
both an escape from all the pain, filler for the voids and a tick-
ing bomb in a life filled with landmines. I moved from New
York City to Los Angeles in 2009. LA and the universe saved
me by placing amazing people in my path, instrumental to my
healing and my newfound genuine smile. I enrolled in The
Institute for Integrative Nutrition to get a degree as a holistic
health coach. I kept my full-time and high-paying PR job, but
I secretly hoped that health coaching would turn into a full
time career, because I wanted to help people who struggled

with food the way I did. One day I went to lunch with a fellow student, Jeff, who wanted to introduce me to the founder of a startup non-profit called Groceryships, and over the next 24 hours my life changed completely. Sam Polk was looking for a Spanish-speaking health coach. When Sam sat down across from me, he looked like every other yuppie I'd ever spoken to. But when he started talking about the correlation between eating and emotional trauma, and his deep desire to help everyone struggling with food, especially people more in need. I was hooked.[31]

Because of the success of the program's groups in 2014, the program launched ten new groups in South Los Angeles in 2015. It also received new funding from a number of foundations. It hired David Foster, a private equity manager, as Director of Operations, and Kip Stringfellow, formerly of Singularity University in Silicon Valley, as Director of Business Development. Dana Rizer has contributed her time to help build Groceryships curriculum, and managing its partnership with the L.A. Job Corps. Raheem Parpia has contributed her efforts to help with event planning, marketing, and conference-booking. In addition, Groceryships is working on a social enterprise to sell healthy, plant-based meals at SNAP-affordable prices ($2.00–$2.50 per meal).

Membership of the Board of Directors of Groceryships reflects Sam's close family ties and also his contacts with companies he fled a few years ago. His wife, Dr. Kristen Thompson, has joined Sam in his work. She spent two years as a resident in General Surgery and is now a psychiatric resident at University of California, Los Angeles. She is interested in the psychosocial and emotional issues surrounding obesity. Benjamin Polk, Sam's brother, is Staff Attorney and Skadden Fellow at the Legal Aid Foundation of Los Angeles where he provides transactional legal support to South Los Angeles community-based organizations and nonprofits that are launching social enterprises in low-income communities. Michael Meyer is the Head of Sales and Trading, The Seaport global, having held senior level positions for Merrill Lynch and UBS Securities. Jerry Cudzil, the Head of U.S. Credit Trading at TCW, and Kurt Halvorson, a Portfolio Manager at Western Asset Management, in Pasadena, are also on the board. Joe Spiccia is an associate in litigation at a statewide insurance defense law firm in El Secundo, California. He has represented workers suffering discrimination, harassment, and wrongful terminations at work. When he earned his law degree at Case Western Reserve University, he was the director of a joint program between the school and Big Brothers, Big Sisters, providing mentorship with children within the community. He brings a lifelong interest in the emotional and physical affects of food to Groceryships. Jeff Taraday, a nutrition advisor, is a reformed junk food addict who discovered the healing and transforming power of a plant-based diet in 2010. He is a certified Nutritional Education Trainer through the Nutritional Education Institute and has completed a certification in plant-based nutrition from the T. Colin Campbell Foundation. He coaches individuals and families throughout the country to smoothly transition to plant-based diets and achieve optimal health.

Sam has used his unusual skills in new ways to create change through comradeship across cultures, economic, and social divides as a basis for a healthy life both in diet, and self-confidence. He has made the people we have made invisible feel cared for, and created a community that has no boundaries. He is a visionary and a wounded healer, showing us that one person can make a difference in this world.

SIX

*Wendy Young
and
Kids in Need of
Defense*

Wendy Young, a lawyer, founded Kids in Need of Defense (KIND), an organization of pro bono lawyers who are taking on very complex and politically sensitive cases of child migrants who are brought to court without a lawyer to defend them. She became interested in the fate of refugees when she was a teenager because the Immigration and Naturalization Service (INS)was detaining Haitian asylum seekers and were holding them in the jails surrounding her community. Her town was one of those classic small towns where the prison industry was a big source of support in the community. She discovered that refugees from the Caribbean were filling these prisons, and, with her French teacher going into the facilities to teach the detainees English, Wendy's interest was sparked.

When Wendy attended college she became very interested in international affairs and spent her junior year in Vienna where she had an internship with the United Nation's Relief and Works Agency (UNRWA) for Palestinian refugees. There she had another introduction to some of the challenges faced by displaced communities and the kinds of protection they needed. After college Wendy spent two years teaching English in Japan and at the time decided that she would attend law school and focus on human rights issues. She was accepted at the Washington College of Law at the American University in Washington, D.C., which has strengths in human rights law. She was also excited about being in Washington, D.C., where there was so much to do with the issues which she was interested in.[1]

Once Wendy graduated from law school she worked briefly with a think tank, the Refugee Policy, which no longer exists. She decided that she was more interested in working on policy and advocacy rather that doing research. She then had a two-year fellowship with a Latino Civil Rights Organization, called the National Council of La Raza (NCR). It is the largest national Hispanic civil rights and advocacy organization in the United States and works to improve opportunities for Hispanic Americans. It conducts applied research, policy analysis, and advocacy in five key areas including civil rights and immigration. Wendy spent almost twenty years with that organization and then eleven years with a group called the Women's Refugee Commission, founded in 1989 and affiliated with the International Rescue Committee. That organization works to improve the lives of women and children displaced by conflict and crises around the world. It sends fact-finding delegations of professionals to meet with refugee women and children in order to learn about their needs and conditions. Recent delegations traveled to Jordan, South Sudan, Colombia, Liberia, and Thailand. The staff includes women working at senior levels in human rights, as well as education, law, government relations, and communications.[2] Throughout this time, Wendy pursued a constant goal, regardless of where she was working, which was to focus on how children arriving alone in the United States are treated in its system. It was an issue she started working on in 1989 and that was receiving very little attention because the number of children arriving alone at that time was not very high. Those who did arrive were being held in juvenile jails, and often deported without consideration of their immigration cases. She considered these children as an overlooked and neglected part of the population.[3]

She then worked at the United Nations High Commission for Refugees (UNHCR), representing them in her Washington work for about three and a half years. Her work at UNHCR and the Women's Commission gave her great exposure to refugees overseas. In 2008, Wendy received a call from Senator Ted Kennedy's office from a close friend and colleague who had been his chief counsel on immigration policy. She told Wendy that she was leaving and asked her if she would be interested in applying for her job. She was only there for a year when Senator Ted Kennedy became ill and he stepped down from the Judiciary Committee where she was part of his staff. While at the UNHCR she had the opportunity to work with actress and director Angelina Jolie, and was involved in early discussions about joining with Microsoft to create a new organization that would provide legal services for children who arrive in the United States unaccompanied.

After a couple of years of planning, KIND was created. Wendy became the president of that important organization.[4] In that position she returned to the center of the issue she had worked on for her entire career and which she was passionate about. She felt that it was a nongovernmental organization (NGO) that was strategic, innovative, and very mission-oriented, and was attracted by the idea of an NGO with corporate thinking behind it. UNHCR Special Envoy, Angelina Jolie, is cofounder and patron of KIND; Brad Smith, President and Chief Legal

Counsel at Microsoft, is the other cofounder, and Chairman of the Board.

KIND is trying to help an increasing number of refugees, as the number of child migrants crossed our borders has surged. A quarter of them were coming from Honduras in 2014.[5] These children could aptly be named as refugees rather than illegal immigrants since they are fleeing horrific violence. According to *The Economist*, Honduras has the highest murder rate in the world after Syria, and the killings and tortures are of young children, their siblings, and their parents. The United Nations has consistently listed Honduras as having the highest murder rate in the world, 90.4 killings per one hundred thousand residents, nearly three times the rate a decade ago.[6] The majority of the children who attempt to cross our borders, after walking for days and hundreds of miles, come through Mexico from Honduras, El Salvador, and Guatemala. Many of their families have given money they could ill afford to "coyotes" (smugglers), most of whom are connected with organized crime, who charge high prices to take them to the border, and kidnap some of them for sex trafficking.

One eleven-year-old boy's father was robbed and murdered by gangs at his job. His mother used their life insurance to hire a smuggler to take her to Florida, promising to send for him quickly, but that never happened. Three people he knows were killed in 2014, and four others were gunned down at a nearby corner in two weeks. When a girl his age resisted being robbed, she was clubbed on her head, dragged off by two men who cut a hole in her throat, and left her in a ravine across from the boy's house.[7] Although homicides had dropped in 2012 after a gang truce, in 2014, murders of children aged seventeen were up 77 percent over the previous year. As a result, between January and May 2014, 2,200 children from San Pedro Sula, the city with the highest homicide rate, fled to the United States.[8]

The children of El Salvador are also fleeing from gangs and violence. Children who do not agree to join gangs may be killed. Although El Salvador has moved from a military dictatorship, the civil war that took place between 1980 and 1992 was caused by gross inequality between a small and wealthy elite that dominated the government, the economy, and the majority of the population who live in abject poverty. In 1992, a United Nations sponsored peace agreement ended the civil war. However, no sooner had that country begun to recover when it was hit by a series of natural disasters—a hurricane in 1998 and earthquakes in 2001—leaving more than a million homeless. The economy depends heavily on the money sent home by Salvadorians living in the United States. Poverty, natural disasters, and their consequent dislocations have left their mark on El Salvador's society, which is the most crime-ridden in the Americas. Although the country has returned to democracy, criminal gangs and the drug trade are serious challenges to its security. According to UNICEF report, El Salvador has the world's highest rate of homicide for children and adolescents.[9] Karla Castillo, who helped interview six hundred Salvadoran children after they were caught in Mexico and sent back home, found that 58 percent of children are fleeing from violent gangs.[10] Some of them are seven; most of them are between twelve and seventeen. Traveling alone they risk murder, kidnapping, rape, beatings, and the danger of falling from the top of the Mexican freight train knows as "La Bestia" (the Beast). The United Nations estimates that seventy thousand gang members operate in Honduras, El Salvador, and Guatemala.[11]

A military dictatorship, supported by the United States for thirty-six years, Guatemala now has an elected president. However, the high rate of crime and violence against women is still a serious problem. The first female attorney general, Claudia Paz y Paz, took on the recurring violence in ways that made a huge difference in the murder rate. She became well known for her prosecutions of organized criminals, drug traffickers, and retired military officers including the former dictator, General Efrain Rios Montt. But in January 2014, the Constitutional Court ruled that Claudia Paz y Paz should step down in May, seven months before the end of her four-year term. She had been helped by a special UN commission of international prosecutors, and the former President Otto Perez Molina had increased her budget, and allowed her to work unimpeded.[12] As in every authoritarian or military regime, changes to a democratic system do not happen quickly, because many of the people responsible for the ousted regime are still prominent.

Indigenous peoples live throughout Central America, but the Mayans of Guatemala are the only indigenous culture that constitutes a majority of the population in a Central American republic, constituting 51 percent of the national population. Twenty-six indigenous Mayan languages, including Quiche, are still spoken.[13] Guatemala's indigenous people were terribly oppressed during military rule. Rigoberta Menchu became involved in social reforms and was prominent in the women's rights movement. In 1979, she joined the Committee of the Peasant Union. That year her brother was arrested, tortured, and killed by the army. In 1983 she told her story to Elizabeth Burgos Debray who was able to understand Quiche, so she could capture the story of Rigoberta who couldn't speak Spanish. The resulting book *I, Rigoberta*, published in English, attracted considerable international attention around the world. In 1993, she received the Nobel Prize for Peace. Since the end of military rule in 1996, there have been some gradual and important changes for Guatemala's population, but protection, redistribution and access to land, improved wages, and working conditions are still big issues. Less than 1 percent of export-oriented agricultural producers still control 75 percent of the best land, leaving indigenous people to continue to seek wage labor through internal and external migration.[14] Many of the Mayan people have moved to the cities and they too are subject to violence. However, despite the many problems faced by Guatemala, the former president has welcomed an important group that works on behalf of migrant children to his country for talks on his country's problems.

Although there are immigrants from around the world entering the United States, most arrive from Mexico and Central America. There are two stories about the treatment of the young children crossing our borders. One is that, according to the Office of Refugee Resettlement (ORR) that oversees the care of children after they are turned over by the Customs and Border Protection, a vast number of unaccompanied migrant children have been released to relatives in states with large established Central American populations. Among these states are Texas, New York, Florida, California, Maryland, Virginia, and Massachusetts. Sponsors must be vetted by social workers, a process that includes criminal background checks, and must also promise to have the child appear at required immigrant court procedures.[15]

The other story of the fate of these children is the shelters where they reside for a few weeks or too many months until they find a sponsor or are placed in deportation proceedings. Their treatment in these shelters is often horrific, and the outrage of people who live near these shelters considerable. People complain that their taxes are being used for these shelters, and there have been many public protests. A few of the protesters who marched against a proposed shelter in a town in Michigan were armed with semiautomatic rifles and handguns. Someone spray painted anti-immigrant graffiti on a wall at a former Army Reserve facility in Maryland that was being considered as a shelter site.

Protesters in Riverside County, California, turned away busloads of migrant children and terminated a proposal to open a shelter nearby. Residents often believe the shelters are tremendously costly, without knowing that the federal government pay contractors to run them.[16] Catholic churches in Texas have set up a refuge for hundreds of women and children released by the border patrol, and other churches such as the Baptist Church have made their wishes known for children's health and safety, but they seem to be drowned out by the misunderstanding, and anger of people who don't want to have shelters established in their communities.

Yet there are states that welcome immigrants, and Massachusetts is one of them. Former Governor Deval Patrick offered temporary shelter to one thousand young immigrants. Nearly as many have arrived since January 2014 and are thriving in towns like New Bedford and Chelsea.[17]

In October 2014, President Obama approved a plan to allow several thousand young children from Central American countries apply for refugee status in their own countries, providing a legal path for some of them to join families already living in the United States. The program is aimed at helping to discourage many children from taking a long dangerous trek across Mexico in an attempt to enter the United States, but rather to join their parents after a safe and legal journey. The program is not, however, for children to join undocumented relatives in the United States. To counter the strong anti-immigrant sentiment, such as that expressed by the executive director of the Center for Immigration Studies, the president responded that four thousand of the seventy thousand refugee visas would be allocated to these children.[18] It will take much time for the program to be implemented and, unsurprisingly, is opposed by anti-immigrant groups. Researchers for Human Rights Watch have noted that children who are fleeing violence don't have the luxury of waiting for the government to review and assess their claims in what surely will become an overloaded system with a backlog.

Then there is the issue of the abuse of children crossing the border by the Customs and Border Protection, an agency within the Department of Homeland Security. The agency arrested more than eighty-six thousand alien young people at the border every year from 2001 to 2006 the majority of them from Mexico and were deported almost immediately.[19] Some of the children crossing the border say they have been subjected to physical, sexual, and mental abuse in U.S. Border Patrol Stations. This includes being held in crowded, frigid holding rooms, sleep deprivation, verbal and psychological abuse, inadequate food and water, and denial of medical care. One twelve-year-old girl was so mistreated in a children's shelter that she hanged herself from a shower curtain rod in a bathroom.[20] According to new data obtained through public records requests by a Washington-based immigrant advocacy group, of 809 abuse complaints made between January 2009 and January 2012, only thirteen cases led to disciplinary action, which was nothing more than counseling for the accused.[21] Unchecked power, an overload of cases, and unprepared exposure to different languages and cultures is not a recipe for decent conduct.

Between 2013 and 2014, there has been widespread reporting of the improper and cruel treatment of these children in many newspapers, such as the *Huffington Post*, *Tucson Sentinel*, and *New York Times*, and on National Public Radio, and even in a speech at the United Nations by the new Human Rights chief Zeid Ra'ad Zeid. In a strongly worded statement on civil rights abuses around the world he expressed concern about the U.S. detention of unaccompanied minors who have crossed the border.[22] Human rights groups in the United States, like the American

Civil Liberties Union (ACLU), as well as a number of churches, have also spoken out on behalf of unaccompanied refugees. "There's a culture of abuse and impunity in the Agency," said ACLU staff attorney for the Border Litigation project.[23] A man who left the Border Patrol five years ago as the agency's chief of staff has told NPR that he had wrestled with several different challenges: a legacy of secrecy; an unclear process to investigate field complaints; and the difficulties of expanding the agency so fast, from ten thousand to twenty thousand agents in just three years.[24]

The major issue is not just the treatment of these unaccompanied children, but also how to prevent them from being deported to dangerous situations where they may be murdered. In the immigration courts the Department of Homeland Security is represented by a trained lawyer who acts as a prosecutor, and argues that the child should be deported. The child, however, has no legal representation and may even be as young as three years old. KIND is dealing with this maelstrom of politics and social problems and the pressing need for attention to the human rights of children seeking asylum.

Wendy is more than upset about the stereotyping of immigrants, and the belief that they are a danger to our society. Sometime in 2012, a "60 Minutes Program" profiled a father who was a member of a neo-Nazi group and went after immigrants at the border with guns, as if they were criminals. The way immigrant children live in detention was another terrible problem Wendy saw and had been discussing for many years, especially in the Women's Refugee Commission. She found that what really brought attention to these children was the situation of Elián González, who became the focus of an international uproar in late 1999 and early 2000 after he was rescued from a boat accident that killed his mother, and ten other refugees trying to reach Florida.[25] After two Florida fishermen found him stranded on a raft floating offshore, members of his extended family took him into custody. Fidel Castro, the boy's family in Cuba, and eventually the U.S. government supported the child's father who wanted his son back. After months of legal squabbling, endless press coverage, and heated demonstrations in Miami and Cuba, Elián was returned to Cuba by the U.S. Attorney General, Janet Reno, in a very dramatic way.[26] Although this was a difficult and heart-breaking episode, it gave people like Wendy Young and her colleagues an opportunity for awareness-raising and advocacy. She wrote a series of articles about this in the *Los Angeles Times* that won the Pulitzer Prize.

After 9/11 Wendy found that attention to immigration came to a grinding halt. When the Homeland Security Act was created, KIND immediately began to work on removing the care, custody, and placement of children who cross our borders from the INS because it did not treat them well. Before the creation of the Department of Health and Human Services (HHS) in 2002, children were often detained in criminal facilities with juvenile delinquents. Even if children were held in one of INS special children's centers, they were put in conditions that resembled detention, and that did not respond to their needs.[27] The aim was to move this function from that agency to the HHS. Just before legislation on that issue went to the floor, KIND gained both Democratic and Republican support and the program was indeed moved to the HHS, which also funded the Vera Institute of Justice to enter into contracts with seventeen organizations including KIND, to help find pro bono assistance for the children in legal immigration proceedings Most of these organizations work with the children while they are still in a detention center. These organizations inform the children about their rights, and then do a one-on-one screening in most cases so that they can present a summary of the child's case and their possible eligibility for immigration release.[28] If a child is released from custody, he or she is referred to KIND, the only national organization that matches the children with volunteer lawyers so that they actually have representation during the proceedings. Unfortunately, over half of these youngsters go through the proceedings without legal counsel, either because they are not being referred to attorneys or because they are released to a site where the services of KIND or any other organization are not available.

Wendy finds that given the high rate of unaccompanied children crossing our border, their needs are greater than KIND can provide. She found that one of the shocking parts of KIND's work takes place with children as young as two years old who are in deportation proceedings. In fact, when Wendy was still with the Women's Refugee Commission they were following the case of a toddler who appeared in court in Florida where the child was held in a detention center. An INS official had to carry the child into the courtroom, and the judge actually asked the deportation office to represent her in court because the child had no lawyer. The officer who brought in the child responded, "I think that there is a conflict of interest," and the child was deported back to family members.[29] One of the challenges in Wendy's work is that there is so little information about these children, especially at that young age. There is an assumption that there has got to be someone in their home country who will care for them, an issue that KIND is working on.

KIND is dealing with a number of major problems: children that are released in custody; language barriers with children; traumatized children; and the number of government organizations that are involved in child immigrants. The ORR, which has long experience in caring for resettled refugees, worked to develop a list of placement options for the children in its care. But Wendy has found that among the problems with ORR programs for these children include excessively long detention, the overuse of secure facilities, and the lack of spaces for children in need of therapeutic care.[30] Wendy also noted that the ORR continues to use shelters in remote locations to keep children close to the border and ready for deportation if that decision is made. As a result, she is planning to open up offices to give legal help to these youngsters in Texas and other similar border locations. So many different government agencies have a role in these children's lives that Wendy has concluded that spreading responsibilities is a recipe for getting nothing accomplished in Washington. The agencies, for example, the HHS, ORR, and the Department of Justice don't work well together. Although the different federal agencies are now starting to have meetings about unaccompanied children, Wendy found that making progress in this area is very difficult.[31] Other issues are the questions of the immigration budget. Anti-immigrant groups apply pressure on the government, complaining that their taxes should be used for people in the United States. Another significant obstacle to appropriate treatment is that immigration programs treat immigrant children and adults identically under U.S. law.[32] Children who do not speak English, are often traumatized, and whose average age is fifteen, face trained government attorneys before administrative justice.[33]

While there have been successes in reuniting these children with their families in various states, there are also difficult issues for the children who are allowed to remain in the United States in foster homes, with distant relatives, or with a family friend. Some have been released to an older sibling who is only nineteen years old. Wendy has seen many difficulties in these situations. While some of the federal foster care for children who have been accepted into the United States is working, state foster care is not always successful. Giving these children the support they need is the next frontier that Wendy looks forward to tackling.[34]

She has found that the young people she has worked with are amazing and have experienced more in their young lives than most of us. They believe in the American dream, are eager to attend school, and do well in their lives, including supporting their families. In KIND's annual reports there are always stories of children who have been accepted as immigrants and have done extremely well. Jeannette's story is a perfect example of their resilience and a reminder of the good fortune we all experience when someone does well in this country.

Not very long ago, Jeannette, seventeen, who was born in Guinea and came to the United States as a young teenager, was living in deep despair. She was not eating, not going to school, and rarely leaving the house where she was living. In immigration proceedings, she was terrified of being forced to return to her abusive parents, who hadn't cared for her in years, and to an unstable country where she had no one to take her in. Her numerous attempts to find a pro bono attorney had been unsuccessful. She was sure she was going to have to go back; she had so few resources that she didn't even have the money to return to her home country. Now Jeannette is a vibrant young woman about to graduate from high school. She was accepted as an immigrant and applied for college so that she can become a nurse and fulfill her passion for helping people. She has a strong sense of herself and knows what she wants to do with her life. She's already been accepted to one college. She's on her way.[35]

Jeannette would be far from this path if she did not have a dedicated pro bono attorney. In an interview with KIND in May 2011, Jeannette described her struggle to find a pro bono attorney, highlighting the plight of thousands of unaccompanied children in the United States, and how having a pro bono attorney quite literally changed her life.[36]

When I began living with my aunt who was my sponsor in the United States, I started going to school. I was also going to immigration court with my aunt, but we did not find a lawyer to help me because every lawyer that we went to was either too expensive or they said my case was too hard and that they couldn't help me. I was really desperate. My aunt and I went to the court three or four times and every time we went, I prayed to God that everything would go well. I was really scared that the judge was going to say, "Okay, you have to go back home." Every time I would go up there, the judge would ask me if I had a lawyer. When I told him no, he asked if I wanted to extend the time. I would say yes, and then we would come back again.

We went to some free lawyers and they said, "Your case is too difficult" and some wanted to charge us $5,000 to start. Where were we going to get that money? We went to about six lawyers, and they couldn't help me. I was feeling completely hopeless.

And then my aunt, she told me, "Okay Jeannette, we don't have any lawyers so you have to go back home, there is no choice." I knew that going home was going to be horrible. I wasn't going to go back to school. I was going to be desperate, probably like hurting myself and running away. The next time we went to court, the judge told me I had to voluntarily go back home because I didn't have a lawyer. So I really had no choice.

My aunt and I were preparing for me to go back, for my departure, but we didn't have any money to buy my ticket so I had to stay at home for about three months instead of going to school. My aunt was scared that the police would come to her door and ask her, "Where is Jeannette?" and that she would be in trouble. She was scared that the police would arrest her because she didn't want me to overstay the time that they gave me for my departure. She was really scared and was fussing at me every day. We were not getting along. I didn't eat. I was starving myself. She wouldn't let me see my friends. I was wondering, "What am I doing in this world?"

I had a friend who came to my home when my aunt was at work and said, "Jeannette, I am really worried, what is happening with you? You are not coming to school. You should tell your aunt that you should come to school." I told her that she didn't understand my situation, and that I couldn't come to school right now because I am in departure and my aunt kept me at home for three months without doing anything. Sometimes I would go three days without eating. I was hopeless. My friend asked me if I needed help and to call her if I did.

The next day I called her and said, "Okay, I thought about what you told me and I think I need help because I don't think anyone will help me." She gave me her social worker's number [the friend is in a foster care home] and I called the social worker and I told her my problem. I scheduled an appointment with her and she came to see me at home while my aunt was at work. She asked me what was happening and I told her everything. She was going to see if the agency where she worked could help me, and unfortunately they couldn't. When she told me that she couldn't help me, I was thinking, "What is happening to me again?" So I had to give up everything. There was nothing, I didn't have any hope. I called the police and told them that my aunt was not treating me fairly and that I didn't know if I wanted to stay with her for the rest of the time I had to spend in the United States. The police couldn't do anything either; the only thing they could do was give me a shelter number. So I called the shelter but nothing happened.

It was one week before I was supposed to leave. I didn't have a ticket but I was hoping to get one because if I didn't leave, immigration was going to come and get me and I didn't want that to happen. The social worker called and told me, "Jeannette, I have good news. I found somebody for you!" I couldn't believe it. She told me that his name was Paul and that he worked for an organization called KIND. She gave me Paul's number and I talked to him.

That day I was happy, I was really happy that I met Paul Lee (a KIND pro bono coordinator) and he was really nice to me. He asked me if I needed to get out of my aunt's house that same day. The social worker took me to a group home. I was finally happy, and that was the beginning of my life. From that day I started having hope because I was actually having somebody care about me. For the first time, in a really long time I felt like somebody was really willing to help me.

Paul explained that he couldn't be my lawyer but that he was going to give me the number of a pro bono lawyer he had found for me. Then Bill started going to the court with me. And I felt that it was really great." (Jeannette's pro bono attorney was Bill Ecenberger.)

I didn't share that story with very many people, but it felt great to share my story with Bill. It felt like I was reliving everything that I had inside of me since I couldn't talk to anybody. He was really great to me when I first met him. He was kind; he was willing to help me.

When I went into the courtroom with a lawyer it was kind of like my dream was becoming true and I finally have a lawyer because I always dreamed of that. Bill was the reason for this, he helped me find a shelter, and he is helping me with the process of getting my papers.

I live in an independent living facility. It is really great because everybody is nice to me, they comfort me, and they encourage me to do well. I motivate myself to do good in school because I know that my parents are not here to encourage me to do that, and I know where I came from, where I am, and where I am headed. I think about my future and who I want to be, so I take everything seriously.

To other people in my situation I would say that if a young person like me experiences this type of thing they should be patient and they should have hope and believe in themselves. They should encourage themselves and not be discouraged.

I used to be really sad when I would talk about what was happening with me because it reminded me of everything. But now I can talk about it because what I have dreamed of is coming true. I've dreamed that one day I am going to be living independently, and I will become successful. That is happening right now because I am about to graduate from high school. I am living independently and I am taking really good care of myself, so it's a really big accomplishment for me.

I would also say that Bill, Paul, and KIND were like angels that came to me, because I am really grateful and I don't know how to thank them for helping me. Even now, I really don't know how to thank them.[37]

Laura was twelve years old when her parents sent her away from China with human smugglers, also known as "snakeheads," against her will. After a long and frightening journey to the United States, the snakeheads gave her to the uncle who paid them about $10,000. For the next year, Laura lived with her uncle's family in a basement storage room without access to the rest of the house. The basement had a door to the street, but Laura did not know where she could go. She did not have any travel documents, and she knew no one. On occasion, she would be permitted to eat with the family; other times, she ate whatever food was given to her afterward. A family friend convinced her uncle to enroll her in junior high school. She began to work for another family friend, an "auntie" at a flea market who paid her a small amount of money, and told her to lie about her age. Laura spent the money buying food so she would not be hungry. Then, Laura was moved to another relative's house, a supposed aunt and another uncle. She lived in the family's living room, and was allowed to continue going to school. Laura's uncle yelled at her often, and she was told that she had to get a job. She worked long hours at a salon, sometimes without any breaks, including for food. She eventually met someone who told her about a lawyer who could help her. She was hesitant for many months but finally contacted the lawyer. Laura was moved into a federal program to help trafficking victims and was then referred to KIND. An attorney from Holland & Knight took her case and helped her gain status. Laura lives with her foster parents in California, and would like to go to college to study accounting.[38]

There are many stories like these. Wilmer Villalobos Ortiz was orphaned in Honduras when he was eight years old. He was left with an abusive aunt who whipped him with an electrical cord and forced him to quit school in the seventh grade. His aunt made him work seventeen hours a day at her pool hall and bar where patrons included gang members who targeted him for recruitment. When he was fourteen the gang asked him to join and threatened to kill him if he refused, holding a knife pointed to his stomach. They did worse things to him that Wilmer refuses to discuss. When he was fifteen, Wilmer escaped and headed for the United States. He spent six weeks riding on top of freight trains with fleeing children to get through Mexico. He saw members of the Zeta drug-traffickers stop his train, club a woman unconscious, and snatch her young son from her arms. Another time, he saw a boy his age stumble while trying to get on a moving train, only to hear his screams as the boy's legs where cut off by the wheels. The Border Patrol caught Wilmer after crossing the Rio Grande into Texas. He spent a year in two detention centers for children before landing in a foster home in Arlington, Massachusetts, where he attended high school while his deportation case was taking place.[39]

Daniel White of Goodwin, Procter, who normally handles transactional corporate law but volunteers with KIND, took his case. He told Wilmer what would happen in court, what questions would be asked and how to respond. Wilmer received his green card after winning the right to stay in the United States. Without a lawyer he would have been deported like so many others.[40]

Given the number of pro bono lawyers who work tirelessly for these children, KIND has created a Pro Bono Attorney of the Month on its website, and their stories reveal the difference an attorney can make. When questioned about her personal growth as a result of working with unaccompanied children during their legal case, Alexandra Hess replied, "The most humbling and profound lesson learned has been how little effort it takes to make an enormous impact on unaccompanied children. In my very first meeting with my first client, I explained who I was, the role of the lawyer, the process of a Special Immigrant Juvenile Status case, where he was in that process, what legal permanent residency could mean for his future. At the end, he looked up at me and said, 'you mean, you will walk in first, in front of me, when we have to go to court? You will tell me where to stand.'" That moment moved her so much that it continues to drive her to take on as many cases as possible and encourage others to do the same.[41] Beyond her legal work with youngsters fleeing death in El Salvador, she often keeps in touch with the youngsters she helped and even teaches them English so that they can take their residency exam. Further she spends the time needed to build a close relationship with a child to tell their story, which is time consuming, given the trauma they experience and find difficult to reveal.

Children are referred to KIND by numerous sources including the government and NGOs. Its online referral form ensures that it can work efficiently to try to find pro bono attorneys for these youngsters. And then there is the ubiquitous word of mouth like Jeannette's friend and a social worker. KIND's caseload is always too high for the number of lawyers who work on its behalf.

When a KIND client needs counsel urgently because of approaching deadlines or when a case is especially complex, KIND hosts Fellows at the American Friends Service Committee, New Jersey; Ayuda, Washington D.C.; Cabrini Center in Houston, Texas; the Door; the Legal Aid Society in New York City; Greater Boston Legal Services; Esperanza Immigrant Rights Projects; and Catholic Charities, Los Angeles.

There are two opposing positions on immigrants. One is held by a large group of vocally anti-immigrant people who are represented by Republicans who hold a majority of seats in Congress. The other is the position of our very large Latino population as well as a number of national charities. One of the representations of one of the Catholic social services testified before Congress in 2014. One of the Republicans asked the nun who was testifying, "What's wrong with the Catholic church that you have to turn to the federal government to support your programs? Can't you do it on your own?" She responded saying that to alleviate poverty we have to start with social justice. If we are working for social justice, we have to start with the government that provides over half of our budget.[42] Given the Sequester policy that made major spending cuts including cuts for shelters of children crossing our borders, the need for public support is greater than ever. In 2013, two hundred House lawmakers voted to halt an Obama administration program that provides reprieve from deportation for some children who are here illegally. Representative Steve King of Iowa said "many young immigrants have calves the size of cantaloupes" from running drugs across the Southwest border.[43]

In 2015, Donald Trump has presented himself as a candidate for the next presidential election. He traveled throughout the country giving angry anti-immigrant speeches about how they take away work from our citizens, cost us too much money, and more. Like many people in this country, Trump doesn't seem to realize that undocumented immigrants pay taxes that support our programs such as social security, but are unable to benefit from them. Unfortunately, Trump's unfounded bombast received high ratings in public opinion polls. Other candidates used the words "terrorism and immigrants" in the same sentence. The very concept of immigration stokes emotions about national security.

Yet there are other views on immigrants and how much they have contributed to our society. A report published in 2015 by the National Academy of Sciences, Engineering and Medicine found that the latest generation of immigrants assimilate quickly and broadly, with their integration increasing over time "across all measurable outcomes."[44] Also a panel of immigration scholars wrote a report that covered forty-one million foreign-born people and 11.3 million undocumented immigrants and their children born in the United States. A professor of sociology at Harvard said that the report should allay fears that recent immigrants commit crimes more frequently, burden health care systems or fail to learn English.[45] One has only to think of Jeannette's strength and her pursuit of education. Buried in the political dispute of immigration is that the bipartisan supported act in 1965, which opened the floodgates to people from parts of the world who had been excluded in the past, has made the United States younger and more diverse. It has also made it more secure, since a high number of immigrants and their children joined the military after the act, making it more ethnically diverse.[46]

Too many people forget that the United States is a country of immigrants and has wide diversity in its population. One woman who gave a presentation on her book about veterans finished by talking to people in the audience at the Massachusetts venue. She was startled when one woman burst out in anger "It's all those immigrants!" She felt it was useless to explain to her that she and her husband were immigrants, had graduate degrees from Harvard, and had done much for the community.

Leaders of forty-one groups are supporting an overhaul of the immigration system, among them labor leaders who favor immigration, the Communications Workers of America, the Service Employees International Union, and the Dreamers, the United We Dream network, an active group of Latinos advocating immigration reform.

What helps Wendy deal with what she calls, "the uncharitable attitude that people have," are the other NGOs and volunteers which KIND works with. Faith-based organizations that help her are the U.S. Conference of Catholic bishops, the Lutheran Immigration Refugee Service, and several Jewish-based agencies.[47] Also, an organization that has support throughout the country, MoveOn Civic Action, sent a check of more than $100,000 dollars to ensure that children have the legal representation, and the support they need for the immigration hearings that their lives may depend on. Wendy replied that every dollar equals four for pro bono lawyers. While right-wing billionaires are working against help for migrant children, their overwhelming wealth can never prevent people from caring or KIND from continuing its amazing work.

Wendy is a visionary. She has created a new program in Guatemala to work with children before they are sent home to help them reunite with their families and provide them with appropriate service for their safe reintegration. KIND's program works in partnership with local Guatemalan NGOs. She has done so because returning children will be accompanied by a deportation officer to the plane that will return them to their home country, but when they arrive they are literally lost. These children have come from countries that are poor and have little or no child welfare services. Most of the Guatemalan children KIND works with are from indigenous communities which are discriminated against. Yet the organization has found that most of the Guatemalan children whom they have worked with have a person that they can go back to—often a parent, sometimes a grandparent, an aunt or uncle. KIND ensures that the family member comes to the airport to welcome the child together with one of their partners in the Guatemalan NGO. KIND has set up youth support groups in Guatemala so the young people can talk with each other about their experiences.[48]

The wife of the former Guatemalan president Otto Perez Fernando Molina once convened a large forum with countries throughout the region, including the United States, El Salvador, Mexico, and Canada.[49] It was the beginning of a dialogue for creating a regional framework for the protection of child immigrants. Besides presentations from the various governments there was a round table with the NGOs who shared the experiences of their work. The following day there was a working session for representatives from governments and NGOs to discuss what is happening within their countries, what trends they are experiencing with child migration, and what kind of national initiatives they have created to increase protection of their children. Wendy found this very constructive since the countries involved felt that this was a growing phenomenon that they needed to address. There was also concern about educating children about the dangers of migration. She sees a big need for greater awareness and to get people to talk about the root causes of migration, such gang violence, drug trafficking, poverty, and lack of educational opportunities.[50] Many of the young migrants crossing our borders are hoping to reunite their parent or parents who are in the United States. Wendy found that government representatives from Guatemala and El Salvador demonstrated leadership during the meeting. She also realized that the U.S. representatives would not have attended if the former First Lady of Guatemala hadn't convened it. She feels that our government needs to demonstrate more leadership and not only focus on child migrants, but also participate as a regional actor because we need to support countries in their efforts to try and address child migration.[51]

Wendy also had conversations with the American embassy in Guatemala about the fact that many of the child migrants are indigenous and face language and discrimination issues. She feels that whether this will result in anything to improve these communities is an open question.[52] According to Minority Rights International, while constitutional law permits universal suffrage, indigenous people's voting rights are still limited by exclusionary social practices, such as the scheduling of elections during the harvest season and inadequate transportation. After achieving an alliance between her movement and the one of Guatemala's political parties, Rigoberta Menchu ran for the presidency in 2007, promising that if she won, she would foster a plural and inclusive government where indigenous and Spanish-speaking indigenous people would all have the same rights.[53] Wendy feels that a large part of the challenge in working on child migration is that some of the issues KIND is working on are very complex and difficult.

One of KIND's board members with experience in the region wanted to engage in this regional effort more systematically and hire staff to help. That member asked her "Do you think you are really going to fix these problems in Central America?" Wendy replied, "No, but if you don't start fixing it, nothing is going to happen."[54] She understands the importance of one step at a time, and that to make sweeping changes one needs an authoritarian government that would openly undermine the rights of children.

KIND is pleased that, in the fifth year of its Guatemalan Child Return and Reintegration Project (GCRRP), it is operating in partnership with the Global Fund for Children, which has helped hundreds of children return safely and reintegrate into their communities by providing them with access to services that will help them support themselves and give them a hopeful future for them in their countries. The services include assistance with family reunification, education, vocational training, and access to health care, including psychological counseling. Most of the children in GCRRP are from the Western Highlands where poverty is rampant, and families depend upon low-wage agricultural work for their livelihood. The majority are Mayan children between fifteen and seventeen years old, who speak a Mayan language, but not Spanish and have little formal education. With its local NGO partners, El Refugio de Ninez (Refuge for Children), Fundación Castillo de Amor para la Niñez (Castillo Foundation of Love for the Child), Desarrrollo Sostenibile para Guatemala (Sustainable Development for Guatemala), and Asociacion Pop No'J, the project has helped children and their families in a number of ways, including finding scholarships to cover school fees, vocational and entrepreneurial training, referrals to medical services, as well as peer and psychological support, especially for female victims of sexual abuse. GCRRP also helps families that lack adequate food and clothing. KIND is planning on expanding its program to help more children in Guatemala and the region who need assistance when they return from the United States. The program has grown through a partnership KIND established with the Office of Refugee Resettlement Division of Children's Services (ORR DCS). KIND's GCRRP staff trained case managers, clinicians, and program directors in more than fifteen care provider centers funded by ORR DCS in Arizona and Texas to help them identify and assist Guatemalan children in their care who may be interested in the program.[55]

What KIND has accomplished is extraordinary. It has helped more than 7,500 unaccompanied minors who were referred to them. It has partnered with more than 250 law firms, corporations, and law schools that agreed to represent unaccompanied children in their immigration proceedings. Pro bono attorneys working with KIND practice in many different fields, so KIND provides comprehensive training for them and mentors attorneys throughout every stage of their clients' cases. Besides helping these children in their court proceedings, these attorneys have become zealous advocates for their clients, and also show these children compassion and care that many of these youngsters have never experienced in their lives. In addition, law firms house nearly all of KIND field staff in site cities such as New York City, Los Angeles, Newark and Roseland, New Jersey, Boston, Baltimore, and Houston.[56]

The National Association of Women Lawyers (NAWL) launched a new bro bono project with KIND and the American Bar Association Children's Rights Litigation Committee to identify opportunities for NAWL members to help protect the rights of children and families. "The lack of legal services particularly for women and families has reached a crisis point nationwide," said Beth Kaufman, partner, Shoeman Updike & Kaufman, LLP, and NAWL President.[57]

KIND has represented children who have fled from sixty-six countries and has trained more than 9,500 attorneys throughout the country. Since 2009 the organization has worked with 150 law firms, corporate and law school partners, and has received more than $50 million in pro bono assistance. It is supported by numerous corporate partners including Credit Suisse, JP Morgan/Investment, Global Emerging Markets, Oppenheimer Funds, Walt Disney Company, Viacom, and Warner Brothers, to name just a few.[58] It was awarded a grant from the John D. and Catherine T. MacArthur Foundation to create a comprehensive training program on representing unaccompanied children for pro bono attorneys throughout the country with the Catholic Legal Immigration Network, and the Center for Refugee and Gender Studies.[59]

Then there have been the politics of the 2014 mid-term elections and the selection process for the 2016 presidential candidates, during which both Democrats and Republicans are trying to distance themselves from supporting immigration reform. This is going to have long-term consequences because Latino voters are going to withdraw from participating in elections, and no longer trust our government. Yet the National Council of La Raza presented KIND with its Annual Public Service Award in 2012, and KIND's Chairman of the Board Brad Smith accepted the award before more than 750 government officials, business leaders, and community activists at a ceremony hosted by a news anchor for NBC's *Today Show*. In the spring of 2014, KIND met with Vice President Joe Biden and the National Security Council, led a briefing with former Speaker John Boehner's Working Group on Unaccompanied Children, and presented at numerous other Congressional staff meetings throughout the summer.[60] KIND's office is in Washington, and Wendy meets with members of Congress and the Secretary of HHS. She has also met with former Attorney General Eric Holder who expressed his desire to work toward a solution that would ensure that children do not have to face a courtroom alone.

As already noted, there are two opposing views of immigration in this country. Those who hold one are loudly objecting to immigrants; those who hold the other are quietly making a tremendous difference. Wendy is among those making a difference. She is not only highly intelligent and knowledgeable about making important connections, but is also tackling the most difficult challenges. She has shown this country the value of children in distress, and how when they are treated well, they become important members of our society. She has also shown us that we are not powerless and that a person who cares deeply about people in distress can make an important difference in their lives.

SEVEN

David Crump
and
Trauma Love

In this country's Pledge of Allegiance to the Flag, the line "one nation indivisible, with freedom and justice for all," belies the divisions that separate us: race, ethnicity, and socioeconomic factors. Besides the country where so many of us live, oblivious to differences, there is another country where the poor live in housing projects, and dangerous neighborhoods. The young people in that country do not experience freedom of choice or justice.

Neighborhoods and streets have their own structure where neither police nor parents are able to provide order, a society where age, blocks, and status establish the parameters, and where their safety is created by violence. In many cases, the parents are single mothers trying to make ends meet, encouraging their youngsters not to let themselves be bullied, but "to fight back." In some cases there is neglect or abuse in homes. In some of the dangerous parts of Boston, families are doing everything possible to protect their children from the violence in their neighborhood. They make certain their children do their homework, stay away from drugs, and they even go to church together. Yet, one of those children watched his brother being shot while he was riding his scooter. After his brother died, the youngster purchased a gun because he was afraid, and felt that he needed to protect himself.[1]

In Chicago's Cook County Hospital, which has one of the busiest trauma centers in the United States, researchers started screening patients for PTSD as a result of gunshot wounds, stabbings, and other violent injuries. The constant pressure of living in a neighborhood that may be like a warzone also leads to PTSD. Just like veterans of Iraq and Afghanistan these people can suffer flashbacks, nightmares, inability to sleep, paranoia, and social withdrawal.[2] People with these symptoms like the young man in Boston watching his brother being shot, will be more likely to carry a weapon in order to restore feelings of safety. Unfortunately hospitals do not have the resources to address PTSD. Adding even small amounts to hospital budgets is difficult in our current economic climate. While the military has made some progress in providing adequate treatment for PTSD, little has been done to treat civilian trauma victims. Americans wounded in their own neighborhood are not getting treatment for their trauma; they are not even getting diagnosed.

David Crump works at the Brigham and Women's Hospital in Boston as a Violence Recovery Specialist helping these youngsters and their families deal with their stress, and recover. In Boston, physicians are leaders in seeing guns as a health problem. The Brigham and Women's Hospital is treating urban violence as a disease, and gunshot and knife wounds as symptoms of a larger illness that can be dealt with. David works around the clock to help young people and their families who have been the victims of violence. Like the many physicians who have written articles in medical journals, the hospital sees these wounds as medical problems. Actually David Crump is helping a number of people who have suffered from violence with PTSD, remaining in close contact with them and their families for long periods so that he can notice PTSD, which often does not show up until several months after an injury. David supports them by talking to them about their problems and, especially, by developing caring relationships. But David Crump is the only person dealing with the patients who have been shot or stabbed, and helping their families deal with a disabling wound or a death. He has devoted his whole life to working with young people in the streets because he sees these youngsters not only as desperately needing help, but also as people who deserve a better life. He loves each one of them and treats them as if he were their parent.

David grew up in a small town in Texas with a largely Mexican American and African American population. He spent a lot of time with his grandparents, whom he describes as poor, but "rich in spirit." He feels blessed that his early life helped him to understand the culture of violence and poverty, even though he also lived in middle-class neighborhoods.[3] Like many people who have experienced difficult times, yet also loving family ties, he wants to make the world a better place.

Every day David is a witness to the results of violence that has reached unprecedented heights since the early 1990s, when Dr. John Rich watched as young black men returned repeatedly to Boston City Hospital's emergency room with life-threatening wounds. Many doctors and nurses assumed that the young men were doing something to get shot. Trying to understand how to prevent more violence, Rich began interviewing the young men after they had left the hospital. He found that many of the patients were suffering from PTSD, and that the reasons they had been shot were not what he had expected. His experience of interviewing these people led him to write a book, *Wrong Place, Wrong Time: Violence in the Lives of Young Black Men*.[4]

According to Geoffrey Canada, who has written a ground-breaking book about his personal history with violence, "America has had a long love affair with violence and guns. It's our history, the taming of the West, freedom and liberty, Civil War, World War, what we learn is might makes right. Poor people have never had it and want it."[5] After he graduated from Harvard, he established a community school in Harlem that services youngsters and their families, afternoons, evenings, and weekends. That solution serves the very complex issue of violence and is a rare model. But we need public policies to address the sources of violence, and to help the many endangered communities become stable and healthy.

While Canada has written about Harlem, there are similar issues in every city, including Boston, where too many young people are routinely shot and stabbed. Many years ago a student knocked on a professor's door in a small college. She begged her to help her write her senior thesis because no one at the elite school she was enrolled in (Harvard) would help her or acknowledge her. The professor readily accepted and they discussed the student's thesis, for which she wanted to study which blocks in Dorchester are safe for one group to walk protected by their peers, the line between those blocks that they could not cross without facing physical harm. This was too many years ago to have to acknowledge that Dorchester has not changed. The Bowdoin-Geneva neighborhood, a sixty-eight-block section of Dorchester, has continued to be more dangerous than Boston as a whole for the intervening thirty years.[6]

Eileen McNamara of WBUR has written extensively about gun violence—about the number of people critically maimed, streets littered with shell casings, and bullets landing close to a sleeping baby in an apartment. And she acknowledges how, instead, we focus on the Newtown slaughter in a Connecticut elementary school, or the mayhem in a Colorado movie theater. For a while the media covered Gabrielle Giffords, the congresswoman who was shot in the head and has gone public about guns. But what happens daily in Dorchester and Roslindale barely registers on the consciousness of those who have the good fortune to live outside what is truly a war zone. In her article, McNamara wrote that in a five-month period, nine people were killed and more than fifty maimed by gunfire in Boston.[7]

Schools in this country are dangerous too, because many students carry guns and there are fights and intimidation in classrooms, hallways, and schoolyards. In neighborhoods where youngsters feel powerless, surrounded by hostility and abuse, they often feel like failures in an environment without order or predictability. For them, violence is often a form of twisted self-esteem, a way of asserting personal identity and power.

Guns are a major problem in this country. Even more disturbing is the fact that gun manufacturers are making a lot of money, and have an extremely harmful influence in this country. According to a story on NPR in Boston, Smith & Wesson, the company making assault weapons, is the most profitable business in Massachusetts. Every time there is a widely published massacre, the sales of guns rise dramatically. Worse, gun manufacturers are immune to lawsuits. In 2005, George W. Bush signed the Protection of Lawful Commerce in Arms Act that makes it extremely difficult to sue gun manufacturers for injury. Numerous executives of gun manufacturing companies stated during sworn depositions that it was not important for them to keep track of how often their guns were used in crimes. Unfortunately, in President Obama's administration, the Justice Department has continued to side with gun manufacturers in order to defend the constitutionality of the law. Given his difficult relationship with Congress, the president never succeeded in having another law passed that would make gun manufacturers accountable.

To make matters even more difficult, the power of the National Rifle Association (NRA) is omnipresent in elections around the country. In Colorado, State Senator Angela Giron and John Morse, a former policeman and the president of the state senate, were recalled from office on September 11, 2013, for sponsoring legislation on background checks for private gun sales, which was intended to limit ammunition magazines to fifteen per round. Although they were both popular with strong support in their constituencies, they were unseated by the money that poured in from the NRA, and by conservative groups from as far away as New York and California.[8]

With Washington's inability to impose background checks for gun sales, the states need to solve this problem. Only a few states, including Delaware, Maryland, and New York, have acted to stanch the flow of illegal guns. Nevertheless, illegal weapons from other states land on the streets. In 2006, Michael Bloomberg and Thomas Menino, when they were mayor of New York and Boston respectively, founded Mayors against Illegal Guns that grew to a bipartisan group of one thousand mayors who wanted to do something to help rid their streets of guns.[9] But more and more guns and assault weapons are now available.

Geoffrey Canada has noted that handguns are an important part of young people's experience in the inner cities and that, for them, it is important to know the difference between a Tech 9 and an Uzi. He also noted that when a young person has acquired a gun, he has a strong temptation to use it, "to see what it feels like, sounds like, what damage does it do, how quickly can you fire it, where you can hide it."[10] Like the young man in Boston whose brother was killed, he had obtained a gun to protect himself.

There are no effective policies to prevent violence. The slogan "War on Crime" does not address the issues that create so much "crime." It has created tougher sentencing for young people caught with guns, and brought about the introduction of metal detectors at schools, but these do not address the socio-economic problems, or the bleak and dangerous lives our young people endure. We spend billions of dollars hiring police, and building prisons. By early 1990, the United States had the highest incarceration rate in the world per capita.[11] In 1994, "Three strikes, you're out" laws drove imprisonment rates even higher.

In a number of articles in the *Journal of American Medicine*, experts argue that gun violence should be treated as a public health challenge, just as smoking or car accidents. But here again, Congress removed from the Center for Disease Control's budget, $2.6 million—the amount it had spent on firearm injury the previous year. Further, added to the final appropriation was this stipulation "none of the funds available for injury prevention and control, and the Centers of Disease Control and Prevention may be used to advocate or promote gun control."[12] One physician wrote an article listing ways of preventing so many deaths from guns—ways that have been blocked by legislation, the influence of gun lobbies as well as this country's belief in the importance of possessing guns. Despite this, Dr. Stephen W. Hargarten, emergency medicine chief at the Medical College of Wisconsin who treated victims of the of Sikh temple shootings, in 2012, wrote about creating new social norms including disease patterns, and observing how a problem spreads.[13]

In fact, in Chicago, an epidemiologist, Gary Slutkin, advocated fighting violence as if it were an epidemic, and established a Cure Violence Initiative intended to train people in public health approaches. One group that was trained is Man Up! A cluster of city programs created to help young black and Latino men who are most likely to be the victims of crimes or involved in it. These programs are financially supported by the private philanthropy of former Mayor Bloomberg and the Open Society Foundation and has been very successful in eliminating shootings in a section of Brooklyn.[14]

David Crump sees violence in broader terms. He believes that it includes verbal abuse, egotism, insecurity, overusing a person's authority, and that there are many different kinds of hurtful behavior. He also sees violence in situations many people consider normal: competition in the workplace, people that exercise power and control, as well as those who don't speak to people they know. He keeps a good balance between his keen perception and his heart.

Like Geoffrey Canada, David Crump sees physical violence as a social problem. In a country where wealth and power is a measure of success, he sees the most important part of his life as building relationships in inner city neighborhoods with all the love and competence one person can muster. Also, he works in a country that has continued to deny grief and death—for example, we say "pass away" rather than "die"—even though death is something we will all face. David has attended the funerals of too many young people who died by violent means. He is committed to helping these young people through all their trials and tribulations. He is an amazing person who can accomplish so much that our society wishes to ignore.

David had a long career as a street worker before taking his job at the Brigham and Women's Hospital, and that has prepared him to communicate with the wounded, their families, and the medical staff on their terms. Although he didn't receive a Harvard education, as Geoffrey Canada did, he has developed through his experience a deep understanding of the neighborhoods where fear, insecurity, unpredictability, and guns are the norm. He respects the young people in those neighborhoods, and works with them in many different ways. He seems to be doing ten jobs at once. I would describe him as a spiritual counselor (although he has no connections with the church in his work), an emotional counselor, and a practical counselor. What he has accomplished in his work shows us that one person in a world of power and division can make a great difference. In his work, David Crump reveals the importance of every child who lives in harsh circumstances, and that though their lives are bleak, each one of them is a person with many possibilities that he helps them develop. In a *New York Times* article by an African American writer who was out with his friends, a physician, a filmmaker, an executive vice president, and a writer, revealed how each one was talking about the two worlds they lived in. Each one of them live with searing memories of their childhood worlds of dangerous, crack-ridden inner cities with their own codes, but now thrive in "the other America."[15]

As a street worker David achieved a great deal. He became acquainted with the young people there and directed them to services that could help them, as well as giving them the support they would need to get away from what David calls, "negative activity."[16] Some street workers are assigned to particular neighborhoods, and some work across the city.

He was also involved in Trauma Response, a program that was sponsored by the Department of Social Services, and the Department of Children and Families. In that role he dealt with the death of a young person by going to the crime scene and helping to create a memorial to the youngster. Just like his work at the hospital, he was involved in helping the family deal with the terrible pain of losing a child.

David served as a house manager for an independent living program for young men; some of whom had been in the juvenile justice system, and some who came from homes where they were neglected in a number of ways or whose parents had died. These young people were teenagers, and stayed in that home with David until they were twenty or twenty-one. He worked with them to help them get back into high school or college and prepared them to live independently. He loved these youngsters and felt as if he were a mentor to them.

One of the young men who David was working with was shot and became paralyzed as a result. Because there were no programs for youngsters in his condition, a new program was started for that young person that later included others with similar problems, so David found himself working with two jobs. More importantly, he saw his role as giving these boys the support they needed and further, the emotional care that is such an important part of healing.

Besides these jobs, David started a hip-hop after-school program in three neighborhoods. The first was started in the Bromley Housing Development. Then he implemented a similar program at the Boston Children's Hospital, and then in Harvard Square at the Strand Theater. The goal of that program was teaching young people how to dance and enjoy themselves, and that particular program brought young people from different backgrounds together. Hip-hop is rap you can dance to. Rap began in the 1970s spoke of raw feelings and anger at the plight of African American people or to boast of good times. Today rap and hip-hop are a huge part of pop culture. David knew that young people in poor neighborhoods without the resources to keep them occupied and avoid aggressive behavior needed to have a place to go to after school that would keep them busy, safe, and engaged with each other in a healthy way.

A woman who wished to remain anonymous, recalled her young years in a poor and dangerous neighborhood where she was afraid to walk home from school because of taunts from groups of boys chanting "Fight for your right." She recalls being in fist-fights (this was before the time of guns), and that one of her favorite after-school activities was running between moving cars. Luckily, a neighbor happened to see her, and told her mother. As a result she was made to stay after hours in the Catholic school she attended, sitting at her desk quietly as the nun demanded, with nothing for her to do. Looking back, she considers how lucky she was to have had a safe place. After school, evenings and weekends, too many young people are without resources, bored and often turn to dangerous activities. Unfortunately for the youngsters who enjoyed the hip-hop David provided, the Strand Theater closed at the same time that the other after-school programs ended. Like Geoffrey Canada, David Crump understands that a young person's well-being depends upon the community where he lives. And he also understands the causes of violence. In his own words,

> People have been conditioned to accept this ongoing problem. It all comes down to what your economic level is. We have institutionalized racism. We have these health disparities, economic disparities and it fosters this business. We spend 270 million dollars on the police department, but . . . spend 19 million dollars on the Boston Center for Youth and Families. It's all about the distribution of wealth. There's not enough being done for poor people. These problems were not created overnight. They were created by these inequities, poverty and despair. Racism is a legacy of oppression not just on black or brown people. If you can't pay your bills or have no money, you are oppressed.[17]

What David believes is very compelling. According to NPR, a Boston affiliate, the poverty rate for Boston's metropolitan area has remained unchanged since 2011, and that includes all this country's metropolitan areas. It has stayed at 10.7 percent of the population; in 2007 before the recession, the poverty rate was 9.2. The poverty threshold for a family of four is $23,280 in 2012.[18]

At the Brigham and Women's Hospital emergency room, in its trauma and surgery unit where David works is a program called Violence Intervention and Prevention. He has helped more than a hundred victims of street violence. Of the many patients he has worked with, only a very few have returned to the hospital with violence-related injuries, which is an indicator of great progress. Besides being present for the wounded, David has taught the medical staff about patients who are victims of street violence and how to help them beyond giving them medical care. Because of his extensive network in the inner city neighborhoods, the staff is no longer as nervous with these patients and their visitors. David also helps physicians and the nursing staff to understand why young people are involved with guns, giving them some background information on the patient and helping them see these young people as innocent victims. Because of David's presence and his involvement with the patients and their families, the medical staff now has a greater understanding of them. They have learned that their efforts have gone beyond what takes place at the hospital.

Since staff members only spend as much time as it takes to stitch up a wound or for them to recover from their trauma in the hospital, David becomes an important part of these young people's lives. He meets with the families of the youngsters when they come to visit their child, and spends quality time with the hospitalized. What David has accomplished is to change the perceptions of youngsters who come in with a gunshot or stab wounds. He decriminalizes them and has helped the nurses at

Brigham to be less fearful. It's an important accomplishment to strip away the stereotypes of these young people and give the staff a story which they can relate to.

He not only works at the hospital with the injured and their families, but also goes to their homes and keeps up the close relationships he forges until he feels that they have made progress or have the help they need from other sources. One of the many things that David has accomplished is to create a bond between him and people he met at the hospital. One man who he has become close to was shot twice, just months apart. The second time he was shot fourteen times and was at the hospital for more than a week. David helped that man, who prefers to remain anonymous because he is afraid for his safety, and his family to recover from what occurred and to create safer lives. David still spends a lot of quality time with this person, as he did when he was hospitalized. After he left the hospital, David helped him deal with health insurance and took him to physical therapy appointments. He even helped him find a safer apartment, and a job.[19]

Unlike some physicians, nurses, and administrative workers at the hospitals, David not only identifies with the young people he works with, but is able to communicate with them. The latter is not an easy task, because, in the world those youngsters inhabit, opening up to someone can be dangerous and counterproductive. He is able to have discussions with patients telling them that they are not doing the right things and behaving in ways that could send them to jail or ruin their lives. David has what is now referred to as a very high "emotional intelligence," knowing how to build relationships with people and understand their problems.

One of David's greatest successes has a lot to do with restorative justice, which is about making peace between the victim and the offender, rather than resorting to retribution with the offender jailed. David remembers one patient who refused to talk to him, asked him who the heck he was, and to talk to his mother instead. David developed a relationship with his mother and she shared some information with him. In a few days, David went to the young man's house and also to his school to let him know that he was there. When David became friends with the Dean of Discipline at the school, he learned that both young men who were fighting were suspended. The young man began opening up and finally shared what was happening in his life. He had gotten into a fight with another student at his school, the one who stabbed him. David found someone else to work with that person. He told the victim and his mother that they had to work on this problem because they were also responsible for the aggressive incident, that the perpetrator was human too and had to be met him halfway. He emphasized that since both of them were accountable, the person who was wounded had to see the incident from both sides. David went to court with the young men and the story ended with both of them shaking hands and the court dismissing the case. Further, both young men had friends who wanted to get involved with aggression on the streets and David was able to build trust with them. He told them, "Hey look, these kids are cool now."[20] It made an enormous difference, and was one of his biggest success stories.

Restorative justice is being practiced in schools around the country and its success is being measured in a reduction of the number of fewer children dropping out of school, and winding up in jail. They learn a new way of dealing with their hurt and conflict. Those who founded and practice restorative justice regard the legal system as not giving any opportunities to victims to express their anger, fear, and pain. They view anger as a common stage of suffering while I view anger also as an important part of the grieving process. In general, victims and offenders remain peripheral to the judicial process, which seeks to keep them separate and encourage them to be adversaries. Failure to take victims seriously leaves a legacy of fear, suspicion, and guilt as well as with a growing need for vengeance.[21] Restorative justice also gives space to the needs of the offender. In the neighborhoods where David works, offenders often have a poor sense of self-worth and personal power. An offender may have gotten in trouble with the law because he wanted to assert some control over his own life or the lives of others. As David has shown, those who practice restorative justice see the dividing line in our society as between those with the option to make choices and a sense of power and those without this option or power. Every day poor youngsters see innocent people being arrested, while the guilty go free, so they see little relationship between offense and punishment. Things happen in their lives that are controlled by largely irresistible forces.[22]

David has a way of staying with young people and having frank discussions, which is no mean achievement. When he was trying to talk to a young man who was shot, he wanted him to understand that there was a process that could help him. After the young man lied to him by saying that he was just in the wrong place at the wrong time, he said, "Say man, I know what you went through." David knew that the young man was not telling him what really happened, and responded, "If I am going to help you, you have to be honest with yourself and with me." "But I don't really know you that well," the young man responded. David replied, "Fair enough, but you should look me in the eye and tell me what I already know, which is more than you are telling me."[23] The young man agreed and David thanked him for honoring him with that and told him that now they could do some work together. He put him in touch with another team of people who work on the streets in his neighborhood. Then, the young man asked David to help him to change his ways because he knew that what he was doing was wrong. David was impressed with his bravery and his desire for another way of life. Generally, we don't think of the courage and vision it takes to make changes in our lives, because it is neither obvious nor easy.

In working with patients both during and long after their stay in the hospital David understands the stages a person experiences after he has been shot or stabbed: what caused it; the events leading up to it; then the gunshot or the stabbing; and the reality of life afterward. A young person might still have fragments of bullets inside him, could be walking with a limp or have lost the use of a hand. At the same time there are the emotional scars of what occurred. It is similar to the long and difficult journey through grief.

David is very skilled at working with the families of wounded youngsters who have generally been invisible in emergency wards and hospital waiting rooms. He understands that there are many stages of assistance he needs to give the family. The first stage is one of giving a parent or grandparent information about the child. Once the mother of a young girl who was shot broke down and cried in David's arms. David walked around with her, speaking to her. He asked her if she prayed, and when she said that she did, he sat down with her, took her hands and they prayed together. After that he was able to talk to her about her child, what would happen in the next few hours, that she would be brought into the operating room with intravenous drips in her child's arms. He informed her about where she would be able to get services, and what her life would be like afterward. David helps parents advocate for themselves and to acquire the paperwork from the services that are available, and also to understand that they have a wonderful team at the hospital that will take care of them. He explains what rehabilitation means. After that, he accompanies them to the room to see their child. He understands that when trauma affects people, they are overwhelmed, and nothing seems to make sense to them. There are times when a nurse may seem insensitive in what she tells the parent, so he tells them "If you work with our staff and our team, knowing that they care, we are all going to have the best experience possible."[24] David understands that family members do not want to hear certain things that they are being told. He is their guide through the process, helps them connect to the services available, and most of all, is a source of comfort.

David dealt with a young man who was shot, and so badly injured that he was unconscious for a week. When David walked into the emergency room he found his mother with blood all over her holding her baby. He told her that she needed to change her clothes because she couldn't sit there holding her infant while she was in such a state. He asked her how he could help the boy and his family, and how he could make her to feel more comfortable. Then the mother asked him how she could get her baby into day care. David helped her get a rental car, as there was blood all over the car too, and also helped her continue to go on with her daily life.[25]

When the boy woke up, he saw that his family was still there, and that was a comfort to him. David started an important conversation with him, gaining the boy's trust so that he finally asked David what he could do for him now that he had worked with his family. For David, it is not only the person who was shot or stabbed who needs to be healed, but also his siblings, parents, grandparents, and friends.

He has a deep respect for the patients' families, so he does everything he can to make them feel comfortable and welcome at the hospital. He wants to know if the grandmother who is there is taking her medications, and how her health is, while he keeps her informed and updated about her grandchild. If he is dealing with a homicide, David takes a different approach, and he helps families make decisions. He brings them into a room for families and helps them communicate with each other, share experiences, and even try to help each other. He also understands that everyone grieves in a different way and gives them space for that.[26]

David's other approach with families is to find out what kind of services they need, and then connect them to those services. Perhaps it may be a single mother who is having a difficult time with her son and may not know what her child is involved in or perhaps is encouraging it in her own way. In order to be supportive, David needs to know why a young person is in the hospital. He tries to help those youngsters return to their environment and remain safe. Parents need plans for recovery, and, if they feel that they have no options, David helps them to discover what options they do have, or if they feel they really they have no options, David helps them discover how they are going to remain in their community and keep themselves safe. He often connects them with resources, such as social workers or street workers. Social workers help families do the paperwork that is necessary, if, for example, a child has become disabled as a result of his wounds. Some families need to get out of the city to remain safe, and there are also groups that can help with that. David sees his job not just making sure that his patients and their families are connected to services that can help them, but also following up and ensuring that the connection has been made. Using his knowledge of their neighborhoods, he has contacted people who used to be on the streets, some of them willing to serve as mentors to the youngsters when they leave the hospital.[27]

Once there was a young man at the hospital who had been stabbed, but had been able to make it home as the incident happened near by. His mother brought him to the hospital, so her car was covered in blood. The following day, David went to her home. One of the many things he did for this family was to visit a place that washed cars and persuade them to clean the mother's car for free because she didn't have any money and needed to use her car every day. Although it took a lot of prodding, the car was cleaned and the woman was more than relieved. She was also grateful that David was with her to help with her son's recovery.[28] David developed a good relationship with this young man, and talked to him about the friends he had chosen. Sometimes, he told him, "You have to be smart. You can't go out that late at night and you must keep away from certain parts of your neighborhood."[29] He also connected him to a mental health counselor to help him deal with what happened to him, and to their primary care physician. When David is dealing with a wounded youngster and his family, he cares for them over a long period. He helped the young man get a high school diploma through a GED program, staying with him until he got a job. The young man told David that he stopped seeing the people who weren't living their lives in a sensible way.[30]

David doesn't count the hours that often overwhelm him. He has often worked twelve hours in a row with families whose children had been wounded, after a ten-hour day at court. He does go to court often, and sees himself as a person who connects victims and their families to the services that exist in the community. He wishes that he worked with a team at the hospital instead of being the only person there who deals with the numerous issues facing young people and their families.

He also emphasizes in his work that what really helps people who suffer through such difficult circumstances is compassion and love, and he is generous with both. He sees his work as decriminalizing shootings and stabbings, and regarding them as public health issues, adding "you can't police or arrest away a problem." It's a much more complex undertaking. He wants to transform the culture of fear which these youngsters and their families live in. Also, he wants to change the vocabulary we use. Instead of using the terms "gang violence" or "street violence" that conjures stereotypical images, he would like people to describe these scenes as "rival neighborhoods." Nor does he like the word "gang" because describing a person as belonging to a gang, which the media often do, criminalizes him. Instead he would like us to say, "these are my neighbors, these are human beings" adding, "Talking about someone by using their first name humanizes us. We have to look at what is driving this fear and these problems. We all label people to be afraid of their rights."[31] He admits that he is overworked, that it is very hard to navigate the world he helps, and yet he persists. His courage, vision, and compassion make him more than a hero because of the care and time he has given to so many troubled families.

EIGHT

Jodi Rosenbaum
and
More Than Words

Jodi Rosenbaum's impressive skills and background and business acumen more than prepared her for starting a wonderful social enterprise. Before creating the organization More Than Words (MTW), she had worked in child welfare and juvenile justice, and had a lot of experience working with young people who were removed from their homes because of abuse and neglect and placed in the foster care system. She also worked with young people in juvenile courts on delinquency charges. She was deeply moved by seeing how our young people didn't receive the support, the attention or opportunity they needed, and, consequently, often didn't have good outcomes in their lives. She was also a teacher with Teach for America for three years, a nonprofit organization that recruits people to serve in schools with few resources, and witnessed that the institutions working with children were not helping them. She taught in Houston for two years. Jodi felt that was an even more humbling and challenging experience than starting More Than Words. Her third year teaching in the Teach for America program was spent in Georgia.[1] In child welfare she worked with shelter and advocacy centers for abused children, and with child advocate attorneys who represent young people in the state system.

One day a friend of Jodi's found a pile of abandoned books on the side of the road. She took them home with her, looked them up on the Internet, and discovered that they were worth some money. Jodi and her friend were excited. Jodi saw it as an opportunity to have young people work with books and technology, think critically about how to sell them, appraise them and then raise revenue. It could become a special learning experience that would help them. Jodi had heard about how social enterprise could use business to create a social mission so she started doing a lot of research on the used book industry. After a year, Jodi founded a nonprofit to test her vision.

Jodi quit her job, rented a 150-square-foot office in Waltham, Massachusetts, and began working with a few teenagers who were living in a group home in the foster care system, and taught them how to focus on the Internet. As there are few foster homes for adolescents, they live in group homes providing care and supervision to between eight and twelve young people. In 2004, she began selling books on the Internet with a few youngsters from a group home and who never liked books, worked with books, or had any experience with technology. Nor did they like to be held accountable for showing up on time and acting professionally. However when the books started to sell, they became intrigued and felt empowered because it was they who were selling and shipping the books, and responsible for the money that was coming in.[2] That was the beginning of what has become a model throughout the country.

Jodi will never forget the first book they mailed overseas. A young man, Charles, was packaging it and sending it to South Africa. The title of that book was *Freedom in an Unfree World*. The realization that young man had of his accomplishment—that the book would be in somebody's home in South Africa, that the book was about freedom, and that they were receiving money in exchange—was a powerful moment for him.[3]

The budding organization was housed in a tiny office for just a few months and then moved to a larger office where it sold more books and hired a few more young people to be part of this kind of training and opportunity. In 2005, it became clear to Jodi that this program needed to be a storefront in order for youngsters to engage with customers. She opened a store on Moody Street in Waltham. It was the young people who came up with the name More Than Words for the shop, which also became the name of the organization. They were the ones who painted the walls, put up the shelves, and helped to create some of the organization's policies and expectations. They were the ones who suggested hosting an open mic at the store. It grew quickly and the organization was able to give this opportunity to more young people who were living in group homes, who were at risk of dropping out of school, becoming homeless, or in court. The program was in contact with many group homes, probation officers, and schools who then sent even more people to MTW that accepts young people between the ages of sixteen and twenty-one. Soon the organization became more structured and formal in how it interviewed and accepted youngsters, and also designed the training program.

This was a challenging experience on many levels. On the one hand Jodi and her colleagues were learning how to run the business on a daily basis; on the other, they didn't feel fully equipped to deal with the significant issues their young people faced such as needing housing, and help with figuring out how they could acquire their GED, as well as their health problems and substance abuse. In this early time of their founding, Jodi didn't think that they were ready to support them, although in a few years, they were able to.

Within a year of opening its doors, MTW began to use Constant Contact's online newsletter service, and partnered with that business. Over time, MTW began putting out a monthly digital newsletter that lists its major accomplishments. For example, one newsletter includes a paragraph about the visit of a Congresswoman to the store and the warehouse to meet the young people and the staff. The young people wrote a thank-you letter afterward, which was in itself another important achievement. MTW regularly celebrates the graduates who tell their stories of how they had been in trouble, and of what their experiences at MTW meant to them. One young woman wrote about what she accomplished after she graduated from MTW. She spent a year working and then enrolled in an associate degree program. To quote an important line from the monthly newsletter, "MTW has helped me a lot and I think it's a great program for kids that don't have a direction in their lives or anyone to help support them. I really feel prepared for my future and to be successful."

It celebrates not only its graduates, but also the many visits the young people take while they are at MTW, such as to the Universal Technical Institute, where they learned about automotive school as an option for trade training. These young people are continually participating in discussions about education, and the opportunities available to them, something they would not have known given the childhood they experienced. The newsletter records the generosity of many donors, including local universities and colleges, and countless individuals have sent books to MTW, including one who donated three thousand books. A corporate donor, The Friend Street Bookstore, donated five thousand, and a partner, Cradles to Crayons, gave eight thousand. The newsletters are both a way of keeping the public informed of the organization's continual growth and new projects and of applauding its young people.

Jodi sees this program, in which young people stay from six to twelve months, as a transition department for youth development. It has grown significantly and now has a full-time staff who do not just teach children to sell books, and make lattes at the café in the bookstore, but also help them map out a plan for their lives, starting with getting back in school, or staying in school. Jodi wants them to be accountable for their choices, and set specific goals for their future education, work, and life. The organization helps them research options for housing, and connect them to a number of resources. If young people have court issues, it helps them figure out how to navigate those issues. If there is a case with the Department of Children and Families that is about to be closed and the youngsters need additional services, it helps them with that process. It takes them on visits to colleges, universities, and businesses so they can shape a vision for their future after MTW. It also offers them workshops about how to manage their finances and runs a program about how to make education work for them, how to learn, and how to find their individual skills and intelligence.[4] MTW has created a comprehensive and robust support system to help young people with every aspect of their lives.

The organization in collaboration with the young people has created four positions—trainee, associate, partner, and senior partner—for the youngsters. Working in the store makes the young people feel good about themselves, as well as giving them marketable skills. The staff helps to move young people through these stages and advises them not to get too comfortable as trainees. In so doing MTW makes sure that they are growing and achieving at higher levels. It also ensures that they transition out of MTW, finding work and then moving into higher education. The young people are part of a team, so they learn about leadership by facilitating team meetings, and they give and receive feedback. In addition, they are becoming adept at financial forecasting and the intricacies of a pretty complex online and retail business.

Melissa's story is heart-warming and a wonderful example of how these young people have been moving on to a better life and transforming themselves. A rebellious teenager, she came to MTW after getting into trouble.

> MTW is really amazing with helping young people and reaching out to them. Even when you are not ready to do that, and you don't really care about your goals, MTW will reach out to you and wait until you are ready to do it. That goes against the stereotypes that people put on us. They give every single person a chance even if people don't seem to want it. They reach out because everyone here deserves to live a better life. When I first came here, I had two warrants out and was doing really bad with my life. When I started here, I just realized how much better my life could be, and how many skills I was lacking that I needed. I completely transformed myself within 11 months. It's not just MTWs; it's about wanting to be myself, who I am today. If I hadn't I would still be where I was when I started here.[5]

Melissa is now ready to go to Northeastern University and sees this as a big step for herself, not something she would have seen herself contemplating a couple of years ago. These young people are more than courageous in confronting themselves and their problems.

In mid-2011 MTW opened a bookstore in South Boston where the young people are learning to set up a remote bookstore and an outdoor market, how to give tours, and host events. It's a larger site than the Waltham Bookstore, and has adult staff there too. There are twenty-four spaces for young people at the South Boston store, and twenty-four in Waltham. In addition, there are quiet places in the stores where the youngsters can do their homework. Every year, about 120 young people work in both places. Jodi has found that being capable and active in the stores helps them develop resilience and self-efficacy. The young people receive attention in both stores and learn to be accountable. Many of these youngsters come from environments where they are not missed, where it doesn't matter if they come home or not, or are not held accountable for their failure to accomplish anything. As a result, these youngsters have very low expectations of themselves; if they make a choice they shouldn't have made, the people in their lives are unlikely to respond. But at the stores, the staff is going to have a hard conversation with them if they do not fulfill their duties. At the same time staff celebrate their efforts continually. In fact, both stores always have posters or flyers pinned up that celebrate a particular young person's accomplishments. In Jodi's words, "We are in the mattering business, helping young people radically transform and reclaim their lives, realize at a deep level that they matter."[6] Jodi and her staff understand that the young people have been through years of trauma and that not all of them can move easily through the model and walk out in six to twelve months with a high school diploma or college acceptance. It's not an easy process, and the staff work hard to help the youngsters through it. Jodi believes that they need to have this experience over a sustained period to really make a change. MTW is an opportunity for youngsters to be part of the solution to create new and better lives for themselves.

Evenings, the stores often receive visitors who give presentations on relevant topics. For example, every month the youth partners and senior partners meet for dinner and discuss topics related to running the business. One month, a Harvard Business School professor gave a talk on leadership. Afterward, the young people discussed the different skills they need to be leaders, how to motivate peers, and work with each other.[7] At the Boston store, a panel of experts presented the latest research on youth employment, insight into the state's strategy for preparing youth for career success, and an inside view of two innovative programs aimed at supporting at-risk youth to persist in education and employment. The panel included the Director of Research and Evaluation of Boston Private Industry Council and the Chief Workforce Strategist, College of America. There is always an hour of networking and refreshments, followed by a panel discussion that ends with questions and answers. Another event that addressed the needs of young people was a presentation by Social Venture Partners that spoke on employing youth.[8]

In addition, youngsters from MTW attended the Boston Mayoral Forum and listened to candidates discuss important issues such as education and employment for young people. Afterward, a few of the young people were able to network with some of the candidates, one of whom was invited to visit the store in Boston. MTW has become widely known in Boston and Waltham, and the stores have numerous visitors. They have become an important part of the Boston community, a remarkable achievement for young people who had been marginalized.

The business keeps growing and creating new ways of marketing. In May 2014 they had two mobile events that would begin in May and lasted throughout the summer. One is the Greenway Open Market on the Rose Kennedy Greenway in Boston on Saturdays, where they sell collectible books, records, and handmade objects. The other, SoWa (South of Washington Street) Open Market, is on Harrison Avenue in the South End where they sell antiquarian collectible books, recycled glasses cases, bags, and note cards. And the Boston Store held an evening of music, at which they showed videos and held a contest. It also sponsors playgroups for young children with a story time and toys for children to play with, and puts on events on holidays such as Halloween.[9]

In fact, MTW is not only a business but provides without articulating it, the caring support that too many of these youngsters lack. Camila Batmanghelidjh, a psychiatrist who lives in England and started an organization to help children in need, has written about the significance of the relationship between a child and his or her parent or caregiver, making clear that a child's identity and self-esteem are fundamentally dependent on parental perception and the responses it receives as it grows up.[10] To protect themselves against emotional pain, children develop ways to avoid painful feelings they experience because of lack of care. These include defense mechanisms such as denial and anxieties hidden in behavioral problems.[11] These youngsters internalize a sense of shame, seeing themselves as unworthy and experiencing a significant loss of power. If they have had to survive on their own and meet their own needs, they find it difficult to ask for help and expect others to reject them.[12] Dr. Batmanghelidjh believes that caring for youngsters is about preserving our humanity.

The youngsters at MTW are required to show up on time. MTW has really strict and high expectations of their young people. When they don't meet them, these youngsters know that it means something to be at MTW. If they are late three times in a month, they receive an emergency performance review and are at risk of suspension. If the pattern continues, they can lose their spot. But they always have the opportunity to reapply and earn back their place. Part of the model is making these youngsters realize that their actions have consequences, that they have power and control over the mistakes that they make, and that there is an open door for them to return. What is especially important is that these young people no longer feel lonely or alienated from the world, but are helped to feel that they belong in the community and that they are making a contribution. Also they are constantly interacting with each other in productive ways.

MTW has collated some very impressive statistics that show that, although half of the youngsters who come to work at MTW are court involved, but when the staff does assessments one year and two years later, only about ten percent are still court cases.[13] Sometimes young people who are thriving at MTW meet traces of their former lives when they leave and wind up in prison. Sometimes they need to be at MTW a number of times before they are ready to move on, and many of them return, knowing that they are always welcome. The 80 percent who have changed their lives are engaged in work and in school.[14]

Jodi has created a thriving business to help young people who have been marginalized reclaim their lives. Every year MTW earns about half a million dollars. She is very proud of the fact that the stores are making money and are not just passive organizations asking for help. MTW has twenty-six full-time adult staff in the stores that are open seven days a week, including evenings, and also helps its graduates. It has a manager who trains youngsters for business skills for every operation. There is also a team of development managers who help the young people set their goals and be accountable for working on their plans for the future and dealing with the many issues in their lives. At the Boston store there are three staff members supporting the operations and three youth development positions that support youth with their jobs in the store. There is also a business development department that is responsible for sorting the inventory. The staff in this particular department go out every day on the trucks with the youths to pick up books donated by individuals, libraries, and schools. They also make sure there is sufficient inventory for the numerous events that take place at the stores.

A number of people on the staff have experience working with young people and have backgrounds in social service programs. MTW has recently hired an associate director of social enterprise and a business-oriented entrepreneurial manager to oversee all aspects of MTW's retail, café, and online bookstore. The person in that role works directly with young people, as well as motivating and supervising staff to meet high performance standards on management, cost-effective inventory and distribution, marketing and merchandising, customer service, and profitability. That person is on a flexible schedule and works directly with customers and suppliers.[15] They are expected to help youth understand the role of the shifts, help them figure out who is going to play each role and what responsibility each will have, such as who will be working in the café, how many books MTW is trying to receive, and who is going to find and process the orders. Both the young people and the adults must keep the shifts on track and ensure that they meet the goals that were set. The staff is helping these youngsters in situations where they are having problems with the computers or struggling with the different types of books, or shelving them. They help them design the displays, create new events and in marketing, always making sure that they are held accountable for showing up on time, behaving properly, and acting in a professional way.

At the end of each day, there is an assessment and celebration of what took place during that day. Every youth and adult manager speaks about what went well during the shift, what could have been accomplished in a better way, what they are proud of, and what they didn't do as well as they could. Then, the young people give feedback on what each other had done. They might say, "I really appreciate it that when I was having trouble finding that book, you offered to help me and then we worked together and found that missing order, and I was really excited, so thanks for your help, that was great leadership today."[16] They might also say, "When it was time to clean up, it felt like you didn't pull your weight and it took a lot longer to help carry up the mail to the storefront." Or, "Even though we asked for your help, it took a long time to respond and it felt as if you weren't checking in."[17] Jodi feels that this exchange of feedback is an important skill in this world as it encourages all participants to be professional, respectful, honest, and direct with people.

These young people do not come from the kind of environment in which feedback is given, so it is part of the remarkable training at MTW. Jodi sees this as helping their young people realize who their true selves are, that they don't have to hide or be ashamed about the experiences they have had. At MTW they experience acceptance, support, and inspiration. Having role models who are similar to them who are achieving so much is a way of having them believe "I can do that myself." When they come to MTW they see so many young people who are not unlike themselves who are learning the business, living their lives, and having good outcomes. Then there are all these adults who tell them that they can do so much and are encouraging them. Jodi sees this as an important way of making a change from young people who are not believing in themselves and do not think of themselves as capable to people who see themselves as smart and capable of working and doing things for themselves in this world.[18] This is a deeply healing experience for them. Not only do the young people have past challenges and traumas—the kind of experiences that chip away at their mental well-being—but they also lack the protective skills that can help them rebuild themselves, experience joy and satisfaction, and learn self-advocacy.

MTW is a member of the Opportunity Nation Coalition, a greater Boston Area nonprofit that connects at-risk youth with meaningful employment opportunities that provides them with a structural and accessible ladder to achievement in both their careers and personal lives. The coalition has publicized the alarming statistic that 14.7 percent of America's youth between the ages of sixteen and twenty-four are neither working nor in school and that young people are not engaged in society at an acceptable rate.[19] For a young man named Michael, his concern was to graduate from high school and to get a job. But at fifteen, he was told by MTW that he was too young to apply, although the organization didn't forget him. He was hired shortly after his sixteenth birthday. After a few months of training he soon became an associate. He learned organization, professional customer service, marking strategies, and how to set realistic attainable goals. MTW paid special attention to helping him implement these skills, not just in his job but also in his home life. After months of hard work, he became a senior partner. He described the program as both "strict" and "real." "MTW holds you to a high standard, you have to be as punctual and professional as possible." Still they treat everyone like equals. We were all adults and employees, not just teenagers with bad backgrounds."[20] The summer he graduated from MTW he started attending a foundation year program at Northeastern University, that supports Boston students develop the skills they need to be successful in any college setting. In the process of getting ready to graduate from MTW, youths stop going to their scheduled transition shifts and start attending graduation shifts where they learn how to look for employment and decide what kind of jobs they would like. They learn how to apply for jobs from websites, how write a resume and application cover letter, and how to approach employers.

MTW helps these young people after they graduate and is committed to supporting them for at least two years in their "graduate program." Jodi rightly believes that it isn't reasonable to expect that their lives will be just fine when they leave, but that they need some additional, continual case management, and support. MTW has a growing and developing graduate program that is helping young people transition out of the stores, which can be a hard and stressful time. The staff is ready to help them if they lose a job or if they are ready to apply for trade school or college. Now three full-time staff helps the young people transition out of the core program into other jobs and college by staying in touch with them. These youngsters also stay in touch, coming back regularly to check in and keep their connection by phone, email, or in person. Often they come back to the young people at MTW to inspire them and give them perspective. There is a fixed sense of connection, of community that transcends being at MTW every day. Young people who have transitioned from MTW four or five years ago still reach out when they are going through difficult times or have had a loss in their life. If they lose their jobs or have financial problems, they know that they have support at MTW.

Jay Morgan is a graduate of MTW who keeps in touch with its staff member, Kelly Sullivan. He was living in a men's shelter in North Waltham when one of the people who was working at MTW suggested that he look into MTW. It was a stressful beginning for him. He didn't think that he had the capacity to do anything, and had to learn to deal with discomfort and embarrassment, really pushing himself to talk to people. Working night shifts were difficult for him because he was required to be back in the shelter by 10 p.m. Jay was not only very quiet, but really struggled to make eye contact with people because he was suffering from anxiety. But by the time he left he was the most senior member on MTW's team, one of the strongest trainers, and a really powerful leader and role model whom the other young people looked up to. When Jay was able to redirect a young person who wasn't acting professionally on a shift, he performed admirably. His interpersonal and communication skills grew exponentially during his time at MTW. Kelly thought that it was inspiring to see MTW as a comfortable place for him and gave him the opportunity to grow, as many challenging things happened to him in his previous life. It was difficult for Jay to leave because he felt so comfortable at MTW and he tried to postpone his departure. Kelly calls him at least once a month to check in and see how he is faring. She meets with MTW graduates regularly and if they don't have transportation, she meets them in their community or at a location that is easy for them to get to. Jay's story reveals his many talents as well as his background.[21]

I am currently working at Starbucks during the week and at Panera on Saturdays. These aren't jobs I like and I work fifty to sixty hours a week and am experiencing burnout. A lot of people at Starbucks don't know how to use the machines and grinders to make coffee. I had to work to cover a shift and to tell them that it's not that hard. It is stressful work because it is understaffed. I use my bicycle to get to work and Saturday will take the bus to Panera. I almost doubled what I made at MTW, but it's not a lot. I plan to go to college for commercial art. I have been drawing for comic books, learning story boarding, packaging anything related to images in sequence that's commercial art. It may be painted or in charcoal. I like to do other things like graffiti. There is a graffiti ally in Cambridge close to where I work. I started drawing when I was seven years old. When I was nine, I was in an art class that was into realism. My teacher didn't like my drawings. I went home, used my computer and listed schools that had

comics in their art courses, showed it to her and she gave me
a D. Every other week, I spend a lot of time drawing comics
on paper. I had really bad anxiety issues when I was a child
and didn't talk for two years. Now I talk a lot and am looking
forward to going to college.[22]

Kelly is very proud of him. She describes him as a very humble, but highly intelligent and gifted person. He draws comics for
a small newspaper. He went into the newspaper company, sought
out the editor and was hired to draw comics for them. He wrote
his college application essay about how he responded when he
had the conflict with his teacher about art. Most important, he
got accepted at an art school in Atlanta and began taking classes
there in January 2015. He received a housing stipend because
his father is a veteran. He applied for funding and did receive
some money, even if it was not as much as he was hoping to
get. His many accomplishments reveal the resilience that young
people who have had difficult childhoods develop.[23]

MTW connects to a number of agencies. Jodi and many
people see the Department of Children and Families (DCF) as a
challenged agency. There are two sides to its problems. On the
one hand there are the social workers that often work thirteen
hours a day and are in charge of twenty families—too many for
them to be effective. On the other is the criticism of the agency
because of the death of a five-year-old child whose social worker
did not make the required monthly visits.[24] Former Governor
Duval Patrick has called it a system that performs miracles. Yet
there is also the issue of foster care where children have been
bounced from one home to another and where many have suffered abuse and neglect. According to Children's Rights, which
recently reviewed DCF, some have even been given psychotropic
drugs without a system to monitor the medical records those

in state care.[25] Nevertheless with all its problems, it keeps referring children to MTW, as do schools, probation officers, the Department of Youth Services, and other organizations. Jodi and her staff give many presentations at DCF staff, as they do at other agencies for children in need. MTW has become a place where young people learn self-confidence, gain many abilities, and recover from their past experiences.

MTW is funded in a number of different ways. First there is the revenue earned from its business activities. The organization has decided that its youth needs to generate enough income to cover the cost of their presence, as their stipends are a large part of its budget. The half million dollars they generate is about a quarter of its budget. But MTW has a number of expenses associated with social services, which require a lot of funding. About 41 percent of its budget is covered by grants from foundations, such as the Smith Family Foundation, Mellon Foundation, State Street Bank, the Carl and Ruth Shapiro Family Foundation, Bank of America, Wells Fargo, UPS, Mosaic, United Way, and many more. Individuals fund about 15 to 20 percent of its budget. The state government funds the remaining 20 percent as MTW has a contract with the DCF, the Department of Youth Services, and the Department of Health.[26]

Jodi points out how cost effective they are. The amount of money it costs to put a young person through MTW is miniscule compared to what the government is paying to put youngsters in juvenile detention, or in group homes, or into other interventions to support them. She sees a movement, albeit slowly, that is growing whereby people want to fund projects that are accountable and showing them good results. MTW is constantly advocating the outcomes that the young people are achieving so that it can ensure that all the money our society and government spends goes to making significant differences in the lives of young people. She sees MTW as a small and quiet force trying to shift perceptions of its work as cost-effective, helping young people to develop better aspirations, and dedicated to life changing outcomes.

MTW received an award from the Social Enterprise Alliance (SEA), which describes itself as the "missing middle" sector between the traditional worlds of governments, nonprofits, and business by addressing social concerns. As social needs continue to rise while the government no longer has mandate to solve so many social problems, and the nonprofit sector faces declining funding and increased demands for new solutions, there is a great need for innovation. MTW is a remarkable combination of business and social enterprise. It is saving the state government money by helping young people acquire education and employment, and, as mentioned by the SEA, it is dedicated to achieving social justice. The organization has thirteen chapters in eleven states that provide local networking and collaboration opportunities, and seeks to influence local policy.

The board of directors of MTW meets twice a month and there are committees of the board that meet in between these meetings. The chair, Elizabeth March, is associated with Children's Health Watch, which has a mission that is a good fit for MTW. Its pediatric researchers gather evidence and analysis to inform policy makers and the public of how economic conditions and public policies are reflected in the health and well-being of their youngest patients. It is concerned that the health and learning potential of too many of the youngest children in our country are at risk because of hardships associated with poverty such as insufficient food, unstable housing, and inadequate home heating. It contacts politicians such as the Speaker of the House and the Chair of Ways and Means Committee, on the many issues of family homelessness, and families who are exposed to violence or threatened with violence in and around their homes.

In the summer of 2014, MTW created their first Alumni Advisory Board, which consists of five directors. As part of their first meeting, the board planned and executed a networking dinner that allowed the board to connect with other MTW alumni as well as to discuss their vision for the newly created board. Two networking events took place, one for each site. The alumni engaged in conversations about life after MTW and also talked about possible future events, such as job fairs or fundraising. The board also planned for a future that includes strengthening its network of alumni and advancing MTW's mission.

MTW's annual report of 2014 applauded the outdoor markets such as SoWa, the new sales strategies that the youth organized including several "dollar-day" sales events, increasing their customer base and store revenue while providing them with more opportunities to enhance their skills. MTW also hosted an all-day volunteer event with Goldman Sachs that included an afternoon of "speed-interviewing" and a workshop on financial literacy. Because MTW's Boston store is doing so well, Jodi sees it as codifying MTW and strengthening the organization for long-term sustainability. The report also gives a snapshot of MTW young people: over 45 percent have current or recent court involvement; over 60 percent have recent or current involvement with the DCF; over 50 percent have a diagnosis mental of mental illness; and over 40 percent are in a special or alternative education setting, often for behavioral issues. It includes remarkable stories of young people who have transformed their lives and are applying to colleges after lives of desperate hardships and lack of self-confidence. It is an important lesson on how it is possible to transform one's life and especially, on how one individual such as Jodi and the organization she founded, can make an enormous difference in the world. Although 65 percent of the youth graduate from the program, it's important to remember the other side of that statistic—children who face overwhelming challenges and thus need important emotional support.

Then there are the astonishing statistics of MTW cost effectiveness. It reported a 53 percent increase in earned revenue from the bookstores and 51 percent increase in government funding for 2015. Now that 61 percent of its revenue comes from foundations, corporations, and individuals, MTW has gained wide publicity for its remarkable achievements. Then there is another type of financial gain. The average cost per young person through the program and the two years of follow-up support offset, by earned income is $22,000 while the annual cost to keep one youth in a group home or a locked facility for a year is $70,000.[27]

There are more statistics of its success. The number of youth that MTW has served and employed has increased by 105 percent over the past two years; it grew to 259 youth served in 2015. Jodi contrasts this figures with a disturbing reality in our country: 6.7 million youth between sixteen and twenty-four are out of school and work. The good news is that 81percent of MTW youth have obtained a GED or high school diploma within twenty-four months of graduating. In addition, 34 percent of its young people are in higher education while less than three percent of youth in foster care obtain a college degree. Finally, within two years of graduating, 61 percent of young people have obtained part-time or full time employment, whereas 75 percent of youth in foster care are underemployed or unemployed after they leave state custody.[28]

In July 2014 at the innovation space at Constant Contact's headquarters across Waltham, one of several themed conference rooms meant to reflect the digital marketing firm's various customers was created to replicate the look and feel of the

MTW bookstore. Youth and staff from MTW worked with the Constant Contact team to create a conference room modeled after MTW complete with bookshelves, coffee shop items, and decorated ceiling tiles for the space to mirror the Waltham bookstore. "I wish everyone could have seen the kids' faces at the ribbon cutting," said Jodi. "You just saw it register for them that we matter. We matter so much that this huge company cared enough about us to create this conference room and make it about us. Those external messages and reaffirmations really matter."[29] In fact the partnership between Constant Contact and MTW was acknowledged with the *Boston Business Journal* 2014 Partner of the Year Award. A former executive at Constant Contact is on the MTW board. The company also provides direct financial support, stages book drives and supports employees who donate their own resources with matching programs. One former MTW alumnus now works at the company. The chief human resources officer at Constant Contact was pleased to remark that MTW "perfectly illustrates our philanthropic mission to help organizations grow the next generation of leaders."[30]

The MTW's Annual Report for 2015 celebrates a decade of its work, and that 181 young people were served that year, 78 percent were enrolled in school and 84 percent were passing their classes. As in the previous year, the revenue MTW earned rose 32 percent. This was the second year that graduates had received support from the MTW graduate program's Alumni Advisory Board, which now includes pilot high school and college partnerships, as well as the first year of full-time staffing. In addition, the Youth Development Department launched new networking events at the stores in Boston and Waltham, showcasing twenty different career fields to MTW youth.

In 2016 MTW was one of two hundred social enterprises across thirty-six states that submitted proposals to a federal

Social Innovation Fund, a California based foundation that supports social enterprise and employment opportunities for people facing significant barriers to finding work. It was one of twenty-two that will receive $100,000 annually for five years. Jodi Rosenbaum saw this important grant as a chance to create new innovations that will help MTW grow and serve even more youngsters in Boston.

MTW has received a number of phone calls and emails from nonprofits in other locations that are interested in learning how they could use MTW as an example for creating similar services. Jodi is more than pleased to know that other people and organizations are inspired by MTW. She feels that the organization has a responsibility to use its two stores as models and make them as strong as possible in order to help others create such effective businesses with a social mission. MTW offers an important lesson for all of us. People in this country who are struggling tend to live in the moment, but those who are economically comfortable often think of the future. However, the young people at MTW are part of our future and we need to be cognizant of their situations and give them the support they need. Jodi Rosenbaum has accomplished just that and now has a national reputation.

NINE

Derek Ellerman and the Polaris Project

The Polaris Project is one of top charities that changed the world. In 2014 it received an award for its work in International Peace and Security. Two students at Brown University, Derek Ellerman and Katherine Chon, founded Polaris on February 14, 2002.

Derek was a senior when he founded Polaris (North Star), yet he had been busy for four years running a nonprofit organization on behalf of the victims of police abuse: homosexuals, lesbians, African Americans, and twelve ethnic minorities who were often targeted. He took one course each semester when he started this effort and worked with sixteen volunteers. What inspired him to start this volunteer work was his observation of a young cashier in a store who called the police because she was annoyed that a homeless man was sitting on the steps of the store. When the police arrived, they beat up the homeless man. This is why Derek created the Center for Police and Community and began working with the police, preparing claim forms in Spanish and English for victims of abuse. His major contribution was to train and sensitize members of the police force. Then he started accompanying them when they were on duty and became a strong presence at the city hall in Providence, Rhode Island, where he had conversations with the mayor. His main objective was to create a civilian review board. He researched the best ones around the country. Four years later his proposal passed the Rhode Island state legislature.[1]

When Derek was a senior in college he was stunned by articles about girls and women who were trafficked in the United States and in other countries. One particular article in the *Providence Journal* was about five Korean women who had been trafficked into a massage parlor just outside of Providence, only about ten minutes from where he and Katherine were living. These were people who were hoping to find better jobs, but were locked up and abused instead. They had cigarettes burns on their arms and slept on concrete floors with no bedding. Derek and Katherine were both shocked at the news because what they had been researching trafficking in Thailand, Nepal, and India.[2]

Derek wrote up a business plan for Polaris, for which he and Katherine won second prize in a competition for young social entrepreneurs. Their proposal was the only one for a nonprofit. They packed their belongings in a moving van, drove to Washington, D.C., and set up their organization in a small apartment. Derek's mother helped with early funding. They started bringing in other young people to help them, all of whom worked incredibly long hours for no salary.

These two young people and their staff had no contacts, but basically started their enterprise from scratch. Then they began by connecting with different people who were working on sex trafficking, attending conferences, and meeting with the staff and executive directors of different organizations. A number of different nonprofits were providing services for women and girls who were trafficked, but Derek found that they were waiting for cases to come forward rather than looking for them. One of the early insights of Polaris was to start reaching out to women and girls in the sex industry in the D.C. area, tracing 250 brothels in their first eighteen months through magazine advertisements and Internet sites such as Craigslist.

One of Polaris's first cases focused on two Korean women, who had been trafficked, but were arrested on prostitution charges and about to be deported. Polaris was able to work with the police to get them out of jail. One of them returned home, and the other woman received a T visa, which protects girls and women like her by enabling trafficking survivors to stay in the United States and apply for a green card. Once they started penetrating the different networks, such as the Korean massage parlors, Derek and Katherine acquired an insight into the different ethnicities and how their operations were run. They developed a comprehensive approach through victim outreach and identification. By talking with the women and working on these cases, Polaris developed a sophisticated understanding of how these people are recruited, how they are controlled, and how the money moves.

Soon Derek and Katherine were training police and were called in the middle of the night when the police were raiding a brothel so that Polaris could go and prevent potential traffic victims from being sent to jail. The police had only been taught the paradigm of prostitution, in which the girl or woman who is selling her services is the criminal. The police were not focusing on the johns, but repeating the pattern of arresting the women, but not the pimps. Every night there were children as young as eleven and thirteen who were being pimped out on the street and arrested, but there were no services for them or any kind of child protection.[3]

Recognizing Polaris's knowledge, the police developed respect for its work and knew that its members were available twenty-four hours a day. Polaris built trust with law enforcement over the years, at many levels, and it was reciprocated. The members of Polaris were called as early as 3 a.m. Once the site was secured, they would interview the women to see if they were being trafficked. Polaris had built knowledge of cultural and language differences. Katherine speaks Korean and other staffers spoke Spanish. Then, they would make sure that these girls got the services they needed.

Three times a year Polaris held training sessions for the volunteers. It also developed a leadership program for people who wanted to have careers serving the oppressed. It was a competitive process with people coming from different backgrounds; some were students; some were attorneys in the early years of their careers; some were interested in working on policy. Polaris also provided services, such as housing and attending court when pimps tried to get arrested trafficking victims out on bail. An Internet site, idealist.org, was used to advertise different positions in Polaris. One of the features of Polaris's fellowship program that made it very attractive is that fellows have progressed to careers in larger foundations, and even in the State Department. The fellows worked directly with clients, researched programs and laws that Polaris was lobbying for, and worked on the front line. In the first years the organization had only a few staff and twenty fellows.[4]

Initially, besides their first grant, money was raised from friends and family. The organization then received a grant from the government for its outreach work. It was soon recognized that the work Polaris was engaging in was innovative and important, accessing and identifying victims of a crime that had largely been ignored or invisible. Behind these victims there is a substantial infrastructure that is often hidden.

In its early years Polaris won the support of a few members of Congress who were interested in their program and supported their work. Over time that federal government support has grown, so that the organization now partners with the Department of Health and Human Services, the Department of Justice, and the State Department. Much of the contact with these departments stemmed from Polaris as one of the few groups at the time with a direct and sophisticated knowledge of the criminal trafficking networks. Polaris was uncovering details about the networks that outraged people and gave the organization a good reputation.

Derek found that being in Washington, D.C., was important for Polaris because it is one of the major hubs for trafficking on the east coast, and also the source of the federal government's efforts against trafficking. Early on, Derek and Katherine knew that they needed to work from the top down to build a movement, and that government infrastructure was needed to make a deep impact on this issue. At the same time, they reached out to the victims to earn the credibility to be their advocates.[5]

Polaris started with victim outreach and by 2005, had developed a client service program in Washington, D.C., and in New Jersey. A person coming out of a trafficking situation has a great need for a series of emergency services. Often a survivor has no place to stay, or is still in danger from trafficking networks trying to locate her. Survivors may be foreign nationals, who cannot speak English and have no one to give them support. Polaris's case managers work with them in order to meet their needs. Among its client service staff are social workers. Girls and women coming of out trafficking feel shame as well as fear. One of Polaris's key early members was a trafficking survivor who ended up creating her own organization called Courtney's House.

It is important to understand who the trafficked girls are and how they are perceived, as well as the language of the traffickers. The area where the girls are forced to work is called "the track," her pimp, "her boyfriend," sometimes referred to as "daddy."

The girls who are recruited are called "wives in law." These youngsters, some as young as eleven, many thirteen or fourteen, are usually fatherless, motherless, or have parents who are lost to drugs, or in prison. They may have been sexually abused by an uncle, a cousin, a neighbor, or a teacher, and ran away from their homes.[6] Pimps entice them with the promise of safety and with early kindness. In the early stages, the girls may have felt good because so many of them have never experienced love, a sense of safety, or had good memories. The pimps play upon their desire for family and caring by creating a pseudo family structure of girls, "wives-in-law," headed by a man they call Daddy.[7] Pimps are experts at seeing vulnerability in teenage girls. For example, one might take a girl out for a few meals, and pay her for having her nails done so that she thinks he cares. Then he makes sure that she gets drunk and may take her to a strip club, for example, telling her that he is out of money and could she please do what he asks this one time. Frequently, these girls are beaten into submission, some girls are kidnapped, and forced into a locked room and are gang-raped initially to break their will. The shock and traumatic response a girl leaves her feeling helpless and utterly subdued.[8] The Justice Department has estimated that nearly 450,000 children run away from home each year, and that one-third of teens who end up living on the street will be lured by pimps within forty-eight hours of leaving home.[9]

Ninety percent of trafficked youth have experienced some form of abuse or neglect and the majority are homeless or runaways. Seventy-five percent of the girls were in foster care, and went from placement to placement, often experiencing fresh abuse from a new family.[10] Further, growing up with alcoholic or drug-addicted parents places the girls into codependency patterns that make them feel responsible for taking care of their pimp. Violence in the home trains children to believe that abuse and neglect are normal expressions of love, but such violence can create attachment disorders.[11]

Experts see pimps as using the same tactics as cult leaders, hostage takers, and terrorists—mind-control, brainwashing, and violence—to keep their victims under control.[12] That type of control, which makes traumatized hostages, prisoners of war or domestic violence bond and identify with their abusers, has also been called the Stockholm syndrome. An example of the effects of this syndrome can be found in the situation of a woman who testified in the State Supreme Court in Manhattan to defend her pimp.[13] Unfortunately, the title of the article recording her testimony refers to the young woman as a prostitute. Nevertheless, it reveals how effective pimps are in manipulating women by using kindness followed by violence again and again, jerking a girl back from any attempt at independence. Accompanying the article is a photo of the pregnant woman, which reveals a face that is blank and totally without emotion.[14] She also has the pimp's nickname tattooed on her neck where it can be clearly seen. It's not unusual for the victims to defend their pimps in court. They have not only been physically abused but also brainwashed.

Middle-class girls also become trapped. One of them wrote a book that reveals her innocence.[15] Although Theresa lived in a wealthy town and was a devout Catholic, her childhood did not seem very happy. Her father was away on business trips frequently, and she was put in charge of her younger siblings. Her parents would argue a lot and, since they moved so frequently, she had to continually make new friends. The trouble began when she had a crush on a boy of Arab descent and went to his house at his invitation only to find that it was empty. The kissing turned into rape and photos were taken of her when they were entwined and used as blackmail. Theresa spent two years being followed, called, and raped repeatedly. She was physically abused by a number of men at the same time. She wrote about her shame, embarrassment, pain, and feeling worthless. The men poured alcohol down her throat until she passed out, tied her to a bed by her wrists and ankles, and physically abused her. She thought that nobody would believe her story if she told it, and was convinced that the welfare of her family rested solely on her behavior although she described her parents as "neither affectionate or emotionally attached."[16] What made her vulnerable to exploitation was the lack of support. The teachers in her school never questioned the times they saw her pulled out of class by older Chaldean Arabs. They saw her being slammed against her locker, spied on, harassed, and almost daily watched her leave with them.[17] It took her twenty years to talk about PTSD.

Theresa was fortunate, because one night she managed to run away, barefoot and shivering, and stopped in a small café. A waitress noticed her and asked if she needed help. Eventually the waitress called the police who appeared in minutes and drove her home. He knew exactly what had happened to her. When they arrived at her home, her father was angry, but the policeman asked to speak with her alone because he knew what her situation was. Her father thought that she was just out at night too late and made her stay home for the week, a decision that proved to be a blessing because she was safe at home. The very next weekend he announced that they were moving to Connecticut. Both events saved her.[18]

Years later Theresa became a social worker and human development specialist. She is a sought-after speaker worldwide on the subject of human trafficking. She claims that traffickers come from every ethnic group and class, that the Chaldeans who abused her were evil men, but not representative of their community. Unfortunately, she found at the age of fifteen that evil is not restricted to any group, but is present everywhere.

Trafficked girls live in a culture that objectifies girls and women, sexualizes them, and tries to turn them into commodities. That culture was demonstrated in the behavior of Dominique Strauss-Kahn, the former head of the International Monetary Fund, who might have become the President of France if he hadn't been arrested for assaulting a maid in a New York hotel. He has a shady past of sexual forays. In France, while in court for his pimping activities, he spoke of his liking for "rough sex" and referred to women as "equipment."[19]

Polaris has worked to change the image of trafficked girls as "just prostitutes," willing participants in their own abuse, and prostitution as a victimless crime. Such perceptions are embedded in culture and very difficult to change, but, thanks to Polaris, the United States is beginning to view rape as power, and to understand that it has nothing to do with sex. It has also helped rescue women in the courts, where they were reluctant to speak up, and felt very uncomfortable. Many people wonder why these women don't just walk away from their situations, so it is extremely important that a more complete and clearer account of the lives of these victims is publicized.

Derek has found that sexual addiction among males is a rising problem, and that there is now an epidemic of online pornography. Unfortunately, it starts at a very young age with boys who are eleven or twelve years old. Often parents have no idea what their children are doing because in many cases they are not as skilled as their children in using the Internet. He sees that on the one hand men who use pornography may also use sex victims to make money. Pornography may be a big business, but it's also an industry where small operators are not making much money, which makes them more likely to become involved in the exploitive trafficking of women. Derek has found that research into pornography has documented a desensitization process, and that people who are addicted to pornography over time seek more extreme forms. He sees a strong overlap between pornography, prostitution, and sexual trafficking.[20]

Polaris has shone a light on exactly who the Johns are. People do know that there are pimps, but few realize that Johns are every age, ethnicity, and socioeconomic class. They could be judges, mailmen, truck drivers, janitors, artists, clergy, drug dealers, teachers, and men in well-regarded professions. In fact, a policeman in New York City was discovered working as a pimp by an anonymous phone call that led to an investigation by the FBI.[21] Just calling them Johns minimizes their role as statutory rapists and child abusers. Unfortunately, many of them prefer girls in their teens.

A shocking revelation of the identity of some traffickers came from Kathryn Bolkovac, a policewoman who applied to DynCorp to serve in Bosnia following the three-year war in the Balkans. As part of the Dayton Agreement, the UN Security Council mandated the creation of a mission in Bosnia and Herzegovina to provide an International Police Task Force (IPTF) and a UN Civilian Affairs Office to provide humanitarian relief, refugee aid, and monitor human rights issues, rebuild the economy, and provide civilian police to train and monitor the local police force. As well as working for DynCorp, Kathryn Bolkovac worked for the UN Office of High Commissioner for Human Rights and reported to the UN Special Representative to the Secretary General (SRSG), an American Diplomat.

In one town where she worked, she discovered sexual trafficking of young girls from other countries who were locked up, abused, and whose passports were removed or faked. They worked in restaurants or bars with American names. She also discovered that members of DynCorp, a global leader in military strategy, nation rebuilding, world security, and counterintelligence, were acting as Johns, as were members of the IPTF and an American diplomat.[22] Kathryn sheltered these girls and had them identify the Johns. UN personnel were accused of rape and sexual assault in 2014, with the bulk of the cases involving peacekeepers deployed to some of the most troubled parts of the world. A report released by the UN Secretary General in March 2015 presents the findings of a decade-long effort to stop sexual abuse by UN personnel and soldiers.[23]

The files Kathryn had compiled on their activities disappeared and she was sent back to the United States before her two-year term was over. She left with copies of the files and tried to get the Johns convicted in the United States. Some of them were, but most returned from their tours of duty as if nothing had happened.[24] Other members of DynCorp who had been concerned about the trafficking were also withdrawn while the perpetrators remained.

Nevertheless, Kathryn won a civil law suit against DynCorp for wrongful termination, making a public disclosure. It was a horrific experience, in which she found one of the girls who had been ensnared drowned and floating down the river that changed her life. She has since become an international speaker on human trafficking, ethics, and anticorruption issues. She provides training and instruction at universities, at NGOs, national defense departments, and community organizations, on peacekeeping operations that focuses on human trafficking and violence against women.

Polaris also works on labor trafficking cases. Derek noticed that in Washington, D.C., there were a lot of wealthy diplomats who enjoy diplomatic immunity and brought their servants with them, some of whom may be abused. Polaris helped spearhead a task force for the area and launched a client services program in 2010. A grant from the Department of Justice allows Polaris to coordinate between local, state, and federal agencies to provide more services for victims of trafficking in northern and central New Jersey.

One woman, who escaped from labor trafficking after being held for a year, shared her experiences. She goes by a new name—Maria, because she is still afraid. She had seen an ad in her local newspaper for office work in a hotel in Florida and Arizona. She had received a work visa at the U.S. embassy in the Philippines and arrived in the United States in 2006. When she arrived she found twelve other workers there and was placed with all of them in one apartment. At first she refused to take the hotel housekeeping jobs they offered. They threatened her family with harm if she refused to leave. The others who didn't have work visas were threatened with deportation. Neighbors sensed that something was wrong and someone called the police. The FBI kept the apartment under surveillance, and finally ended the trafficking operation in 2008. After being interviewed by the Department of Justice and the FBI, she and the other women were asked to testify against the traffickers. Even after her captors were in custody she feared retribution.[25]

A former executive director for Partners of the Americas, Maddu Huacuja, had a young man walk into her office. He had been brought to the United States from Chile by a very wealthy couple as an *au pair* for their two toddlers. They promised to pay for his ticket. When he arrived he had no winter clothes and didn't speak English, but the couple left him in charge, and traveled to Japan. He was completely isolated. He cleaned, cooked, and took care of the children from six in the morning until midnight. The couple didn't pay him because they told him that he had to work to pay for his ticket. Every day that he was allowed to have off, he would come into Maddu's office. Little by little, she heard his story. Eventually, he told her that the father started touching him. At that point Maddu decided to take him away. She arrived at 9 p.m. and when the man opened the door she announced, "I am coming to get Alexandro." She just put him in the car and left. She helped him learn English and get a job so that he could earn enough money to return to Chile. She now works in a federal court as a translator and has come up across a number of people who have been in similar situations. They come from poor areas, lack education, and are mistreated. Maddu added, "That's not even the tip of the iceberg."[26]

One type of forced marriage is a "mail order bride." A woman may be brought from another country, married to a U.S. citizen, and then find herself in domestic servitude, and sexually abused as well.[27] Forced marriages are also a human rights issue. There are also cases of children sold and smuggled into the United States to work as maids. For example, a neighbor called an Orange County Child Protective Services social worker to report a case of child abuse. The caller said that a young girl was living in the family's garage, acting as a maid, and not attending school. Along with a police investigator, a social worker came to the house of that family. The father when pressed by the officer admitted that there was a twelve-year-old girl in his household besides his children, whom he described as a distant relative. When the police wanted to talk to her, the father talked to her in Arabic, telling her to deny that she worked for them. When she came down shabbily dressed with red and raw hands, the social worker called a translator on her cell phone and the police officer immediately took her into protective custody. A few hours later he returned with a search warrant, and agents from the FBI and Immigration and Customs enforcement. In the garage, they photographed the girl's stained mattress, a bucket of soapy water, and a broken lamp. The investigator charged the couple that held the child with conspiracy, involuntary servitude, and harboring an alien.[28] As Derek has often noted, it's everyday people who notice such wrongdoing and alert the authorities that lead to rescue and safety in these hidden crimes.

In addition to domestic servitude, labor is trafficked in agricultural work, factories, and restaurants. For example, nine 7-Eleven store owners and managers employed dozens of immigrant workers at their stores and were accused of hiding dozens more illegal immigrants from Pakistan and the Philippines at their stores.[29] Then there are magazine crews— the young people selling magazines from door to door. These impoverished children are moved from city to city in a van and have a quota they have to meet. Often there is a lot of physical and emotional violence involved. If one of them doesn't meet the quota, they just get dumped in a city with no possessions.

There are also begging rings. One of the Polaris's earliest cases was peddling by deaf and mute Mexicans in New York City. Dozens were living in tiny apartments and were forced to sell trinkets on the street. Once back in the apartments all the money was taken from them. Derek found that it took a long time to achieve a breakthrough in their case, but eventually a police officer took their communications seriously. In Washington, D.C., there is a peddling ring that uses children, mutilating them in order to make them more emotionally appealing.[30]

According to Polaris, the roots of labor trafficking are workers who come to the United States on H-28 visas for seasonal nonagricultural jobs, such as construction, harvesting crabmeat, or operating fair and carnival rides. They often fall prey to unlawful recruitment and abuse.

Giant Labor Solutions (GLS) is an international criminal enterprise that recruited hopeful immigrants from impoverished villages around the world. It has transported more than one thousand people to the United States from the Philippines, Kazakhstan, Moldova, Jamaica, Uzbekistan, Poland, and the Dominican Republic, often providing them with fraudulent visas. It also preyed on foreign workers who were already in the United States but whose visas were about to expire. It held workers in virtual captivity, shuttling them to work sites in fourteen states, and often subcontracting their labor to sites that believed GLS was legitimate.[31]

Polaris has worked more behind the scenes with corporations and companies to help them more effectively train their people and establish protocols to strengthen their supply chain protections. It is not one of Polaris's major causes, but it has been noted that another reason that human trafficking is rising is the opportunity offered by the corporate trend toward outsourcing labor. The corporation may not know about it or perhaps hope to stay out of it, because at many levels down, work has been subcontracted to groups who are taking advantage of foreign labor both overseas and recruited in the United States.[32]

Then there is the trafficking of agricultural workers, an area in which there are few protections and regulations. Employers who bring guest workers into the country for just a short time have a tremendous amount of power. Polaris has dealt with such cases in its New Jersey office. There are other organizations reaching out to them directly, meeting with different groups of farm workers, and giving them pamphlets with a hotline number. In some cases, Polaris staff have reached out to farm workers in parts of Northern New Jersey. One owner actually threatened Polaris's staff, telling them that they had to show their legal papers proving that the organization had the right to speak with some of their workers.[33] Groups that partner with Polaris do most of that work.

Polaris has also been working with an organization that raises awareness among truckers. It provides truckers' organizations with training and materials and has received a lot of calls from truck drivers reporting sex traffickers they have come across. Pimps leave a lot of women and children at truck stops. Many truckers are also Johns, but there are also many now who now see that this is a situation of child abuse and who want to help.[34]

Sarah Jakiel, who has skills in international development and worked in Thailand and Eastern Europe, has been with Polaris for several years and was instrumental in starting a national hotline. The hotline is available twenty-four hours and receives thousands of calls every year. Polaris has also publicized its work through a number of signs that show how traffickers victimize a person. They make it clear that the victims are not free to come and go as they wish, are under eighteen, providing commercial sex, work excessively long or unusual hours, and were recruited through false promises concerning the nature of the work. The places where they work or live may have heightened security measures such as opaque or boarded up windows, bars on windows, barbed wire, and security cameras. The signs also suggest that victims avoid eye contact, and are not in control of their identification or passports.[35]

In Washington, D.C., Polaris was contacting community members and conducting awareness campaigns to help people recognize signs of trafficking. It uses billboards, as well as television shows, and documentaries. One area that has recently come to their attention is Chinese buffets, where a customer may just sense that something is wrong, seeing a staff member fearful or unhappy. Derek feels that everyday people are the best eyes and ears for identifying traffic in addition to law in enforcement and organizations like Polaris.

The board of directors has been very helpful with Polaris's multifaceted work. Derek's cofounder Katherine Chon is on the board. She now works for the Department of Health and Human Services in a position that primarily focuses on trafficking. Although the board is heavily involved in ensuring the organization is adequately financed, another of its most important roles is as a partner in Polaris's strategic planning. For example, at the organization's ten-year anniversary, it made the decision to bring its work to the global level. Derek's mother, Mei Mei Ellerman, was once a member of the board, and continues to give lectures on trafficking throughout Massachusetts. Derek became head of Polaris's board of directors in 2010, and his former staff member Bradley Myles, who joined Polaris as a fellow in 2004, became the CEO. Derek describes Bradley as a super-star leader and a hard worker who is knowledgeable about human trafficking.

Bradley Myles was determined to integrate technical assistance with important companies so that the program could reach many troubled parts of the world. It became one of Polaris's most important endeavors and one of its two different programs. There is the BeFree texting, training, and technical assistance for law enforcement and service providers across the country. There is also a policy team that focuses on state and federal policy. It has played a key role over the last seven years helping to pass state laws against trafficking across the country.

Texting is a good way for children or women to contact Polaris because they can delete the text after they have sent them. There have been numerous occasions when staff members received calls from people in bathrooms with the water running and the caller speaking quietly because the pimp is in the other room and would beat her if he knew she was calling. BeFree text shortcode instantly connects victims to services. Polaris now has instant access to victims by developing partnerships with Thorn: Digital Defenders of Children, which allows victims and care providers to connect instantly with the National Human Trafficking Resource Center (NHTRC) hotline operated by Polaris.[36] Since 2007, the hotline has received more than seventy thousand calls from across the country and around the world, connected more than 8,300 victims to assistance, and support and reported more than three thousand cases to law enforcement. From 2012, the calls increased by 55 percent with 31,945 phone calls received in 2013. Since its first year the hotline experienced a 456 percent annual increase in phone calls. The hotline is partially funded by the U.S. Department of Health and Human Services' Anti-Trafficking in Persons Division.[37]

Polaris undertook an important project for global programming in 2013 with funding from the State Department, individual donors and support for data aggregation from the Global Human Trafficking Hotline Network, Palantir Technologies, and Salesforce.com. This project identifies anti-trafficking hotlines around the world and connects with them in order to provide those who are trafficked with opportunities for learning from each other as well as offering training and technical assistance for creating and expanding anti-trafficking hotlines in many countries.[38] Previously Polaris had to navigate between a caller's location on Google maps, and resources available for victims including legal services, shelters, and law enforcement. It meant that a staff member would have to spend ten minutes to find the right person to help her instead of giving her an immediate response.[39]

This important connection occurred after Bradley Myles met with representatives from Palantir Technologies, a data analysis firm whose biggest clients include the CIA, the U.S. military, and major banks. The philanthropic engineer at Palantir helped the two organizations work in tandem. Within a few weeks Palantir created software that gathered Polaris' network of resources into a single dashboard for call specialists to acquire data of the geographical location, age, migration status, language, and shelter requirements that helps to assist a victim's particular situation. This partnership is one of many examples of how big data is being used in the fight against human trafficking. On the one hand the Web is becoming a tool for traffickers seeking to exploit vulnerable populations where sites such as Facebook recruit young people and post their pictures in an advertisement for escort services, only to force them into prostitution. On the other, it also serves as an important source of information that activists and officials can use to prevent such practices.[40]

With the support of a $3 million Global Impact Award from Google, Polaris has joined with Liberty Asia and La Strada, both of which have experience in fighting human trafficking in Southeast Asia and Europe. These two organizations have also received grants from a Google Global Impact Award. This type of collaboration provides much needed help to bypass the new practices of the traffickers. The director of Liberty Asia is working with Polaris to establish a regional hotline for Thailand, Vietnam, Malaysia, Myanmar, Cambodia, Laos, and China. More members are expected to join the Global Trafficking Hotline as it is extended.

Polaris's Global Modern Slavery Directory is a public database of more than 770 organizations and hotlines that identify human trafficking and forced labor. It serves more than 120 countries, helping concerned people, law enforcement officials, and policy makers to identify modern slavery organizations in each country as well as the services that are available. The directory is the result of what Bradley Myles is so concerned about—collaboration between Polaris, the Freedom Fund, and the Walk Free Foundation that can assist concerned services worldwide.[41]

When Polaris first started, only two states had laws against trafficking. Polaris began working with state legislators and local groups in 2003. Washington and Texas were the first to have anti-trafficking laws, followed by Missouri, Florida, Minnesota, and Massachusetts. In 2013 the fiftieth state passed a law against human trafficking. That enables local law enforcement to make arrests and bring charges at the state level. However, there is no national training program as each state has different laws on trafficking, thus the lack of uniformity makes it difficult to deter traffickers. Also, there is a lack of consistency for protecting victims. One state might have services for them while another might have none.[42] Polaris rates states on the laws they have passed to prevent and prosecute human trafficking. Law enforcement officials, in many cases, still mistake trafficking victims for criminals, and Polaris would like more training to help police recognize them as victims.

Many people find it hard to imagine that trafficking for prostitution is happening in their own neighborhoods, even in middle- to upper-class suburbs. For example, in the spring of 2014, an anti-trafficking investigation led to the indictment of people charged with conspiracy to smuggle Asian women into Massachusetts. The victims would be picked up at the South Station Bus Terminal, and taken to apartments and other places in the towns of Stoneham, Wellesley, Newton, Woburn, Peabody, Watertown, and elsewhere.[43] Unlike cities where trafficked girls often are visible on the streets, the problem is more discreet in the suburbs where "trafficked women in the suburbs are offered for sex in ads on Internet sites and often work in brothels advertised as 'massage parlors.'"[44] According to Kate Keisel, director of Polaris's program in New Jersey, they are present in every suburb. A survey Polaris conducted three years ago found about 525 massage businesses operated in New Jersey as fronts for brothels. The businesses were, according to Keisel, "Very discreet operating in extremely affluent suburbs."[45]

Congress passed a bill reauthorizing the Trafficking Victims Protection Act in 2013 as an amendment to the Violence against Women Act. It allocates $130 million to prosecute traffickers and provide recovery assistance to victims, such as housing and legal services. Again, it is as important to practice the law as well as to pass it.

A Trafficking Victims Protection Act was signed in 2000 by President Clinton. It spells out severe penalties for those convicted of human trafficking and provides rehabilitation for victims. However, again, signing a law, and following through are two different things. Cynthia Cordes, an assistant U.S. attorney for the Western District of Missouri, prosecuted more than fifty human trafficking cases in her nine years in that position. Her convictions included pimps who forced preteen girls to walk the "track," a high-ranking foreign official from Taiwan who abused her household staff, a highly organized ring of Chinese traffickers who imported women to work as prostitutes in massage parlors. Also among the cases she prosecuted was the case against Giant Labor Solutions that was shut down after it was raided in May 2009. She rescued 170 people. In 2006 when she brought her first case to court, the district had never filed a trafficking case. When Cynthia Cordes left her position for the private sector in 2013, she had prosecuted more human trafficking cases than any other assistant U.S. attorney in the country, and she never lost in court.[46] She worked closely with the FBI and the police. When she began work in the private sector, Cynthia Cordes helped to develop a training program to educate local law enforcement and community organizations on how to locate victims, provide them with assistance and gather sufficient evidence for prosecution. She played an important role in creating coalitions of federal and state law enforcement agencies, as well as NGOs working on behalf of victims.[47]

In 2014 Polaris partnered with the Wyndham Hotel Group, the world's largest hotel company with 7,590 hotels across seventy-one countries. They developed training for hotel owners, property-level staff, employees, and call centers to educate them about every facet of human trafficking. The chief executive of Wyndham Hotel Group wanted to ensure that the hotel industry is able to make an important contribution to the prevention of human trafficking. The hotel group donated $150,000 and one million Wyndham points in their guest loyalty program that allows people to stay free of charge. Those options support Polaris and its service providers to acquire safe hotel rooms for survivors of human trafficking when they escape a trafficking situation.[48] Too many people are unaware of the fact that many pimps place their girls in attractive hotels that are accessible to middle-class suburban Johns and can attract business travelers. The partnership with Wyndham is an extremely important achievement because the Supreme Court is currently hearing a case to let the police inspect hotel and motel guest registries without warrants. Such surprise inspections are vital to law enforcement because it is one of the most effective tools to deter human trafficking. Although a decision has not yet been made, it reveals how reluctant hotels and motels are to reveal their registries.[49]

In April 2015, the U.S. Attorney's office in Boston finished a five-year joint local and federal investigation into a notorious sex trafficking operation with the sentencing of the final defendant in the case. While advocates for child victims applauded investigations, they insist that it is business as usual in hotels, motels, and inns throughout the region.[50] Since 2007, 1,434 cases of human trafficking in hotels and motels were reported to the NHTRC and Polaris's BeFree. The majority of traffickers are pimps, but a small percentage of labor trafficking takes place in both the hotel industry's work force and the organizations that supply its products. They continue to exploit their victims unchecked because hotel staff, managers, and executives are unaware of what is occurring or how to discover and aid those in need.[51]

The Polaris staff has a Drop-In Center in its locations for local clients. They include four different sources of support to its clients; comprehensive case management, which provides food, clothing, and material assistance; social services, criminal justice, and legal advocacy. Other forms of support include accompanying victims to court and advocating for them. It also provides translation and interpretation services, medical help, support for housing, and partners with convents for transitional housing. The center also provides psychotherapy because its clients experience shame and PTSD that includes nightmares of their past experiences. The fourth area provides workshops that help empower its clients by teaching them English, computer skills, and preparing them for becoming employed.

In 2007, the UN Office on Drugs and Crime found that human traffickers make at least \$32 billion a year.[52] Unlike the illegal arms trade and drug trafficking, human traffickers don't need to pay for the human beings whose services they are selling, and they can be used and trafficked again and again. Because it is so lucrative, it is growing more quickly than the trafficking of arms and drugs.

Polaris sees the greatest challenge in the coming decade to be holding traffickers accountable because they are very adaptable are skilled in evading detection, and move their girls without being noticed. They are very good at sheltering their revenue, often putting their profits in shell names and companies. According to Polaris, the State Department and the International Labor Organization, there are 20.9 million people in slavery across the world, and two million children exploited by the global commercial sex trade every year.[53] The State Department's annual Trafficking in Persons report gives an estimate of the number of men, women, and children who are trafficked worldwide as high as twenty-seven million.[54] Thanks to Polaris, the State Department, Congress, the Secretary of State John Kerry, and President Obama, have spoken out on human trafficking thus helping Polaris to publicize the fate of trafficking victims at the highest level of government. As a result, the Justice Department has defined human trafficking as a major civil rights issue. The Obama administration has encouraged the creation of local and federal task forces around the country to deal with the growing concern.

In 2015, there was disagreement between the political parties on Capitol Hill about an anti-trafficking bill that would provide new financing to help the victims by placing additional fines on people convicted of sex and labor trafficking. The bill passed in the Senate in late April 2015. It encourages the prosecution of Johns who typically escape criminal charges. A second bill gives preference for Department of Justice enforcement grants to states that approved "safe-harbor" laws, ensuring that young people sold for sex are treated as victims instead of being prosecuted. That the bill was approved in the Senate and in the House of Representatives, although with less funding is a sign that, despite disagreements on the inclusion, enormous progress has been made.[55] Bradley Myles and Holly Austin Smith, who was trafficked, spoke about the bill on PBS on March 18, 2015. They emphasized the need for educating the public about prevention as a very important way of stemming the tide of sexual trafficking.

In the past few years, documentaries on sex trafficking have helped to publicize it worldwide. A documentary series on domestic sex trafficking in Boston, and some other cities in the country is the focus of "A Path Appears" aired on PBS. Robert Bilheimer has also made a film on human trafficking that focuses on children. A chilling documentary, *Tricked*, by Jane Welles gives a frightening view of pimps, Johns, the trafficked girls, and the complexity of trying to help them escape. One of the pimps, who were interviewed in the film, laughs and says, "A pussy is a commodity." A policeman in Las Vegas speaks out that everyone could become a victim followed by the story of a university student being invited to a party only to find herself alone with a man who victimized and trafficked her. In the documentary the journalist Nicholas Kristoff tells us that girls and young women who are sexually trafficked are 50 percent more likely to be murdered than the average citizen.

Even the entertainment industry has produced films on the trafficking of children. BBC started a television series about a detective, Kurt Wallander, based on the crime novels of the Swedish novelist Henning Mankell. A film that has sparked wide interest is *Sidetracked*, which reveals that an important member of the government served as a pimp, and that some children were sold by their parents. Another, *The Witness*, focuses on labor trafficking and the terrible treatment of trafficked workers. What makes these so important is that the films take place in Sweden, a country that is highly regarded worldwide for its democratic socialism and the many services it provides for its citizens.

While the statistics may seem overwhelming, Polaris and its partner organizations have not only changed the fate of the victims, but also responded to their needs, helping them heal and reenter society. It's important to remember that Polaris started with a twenty-two-year-old, Derek Ellerman, testifying before Congress, and showing us that it is possible to take on a daunting and complex problem and find a number of different ways to successfully address it. Polaris's work emphasizes how each person who has been saved is important. Enabling girls and young woman to regain their lives and reenter society is a remarkable accomplishment by Polaris that has changed our perceptions of these victims and disrupted the culture of invisibility.

TEN

Yifat Susskind and *MADRE*

Let us globalize compassion.

—Mr. Kailash Satyarthi,
winner of the Nobel Peace Prize 2014

In 1983 an organization called MADRE (mother in Spanish) based in New York City, was formed by Kathy Engel who became its first executive director and was supported by Vivian Stromberg in her plan to help Nicaraguan women who were suffering from the U.S. sponsorship of an undeclared war against the people of Nicaragua. Seven years later Vivian Stromberg left her twenty-three-year teaching career to take over as MADRE's executive director.

Since its founding, MADRE has been committed to women's human rights around the world, partnering with local groups because it understands that women are the backbone of their communities, and that positive change depends upon them. The first program it organized to help the Nicaraguan women was the collection of crayons, books, powdered milk, medical equipment, and art supplies. In 1991, on the first anniversary of the Gulf War when Iraq invaded Kuwait, MADRE organized the delivery of ten tons of milk and medicine to clinics and hospitals in Iraq. Vivian Stromberg, along with a delegation of MADRE members, personally delivered the aid by driving a caravan of trucks across the dessert from Amman, Jordan, to Baghdad.

In 2011 Yifat Susskind became MADRE's executive director after working in every staff position. She was born in Israel and the experience of growing up there inspired her to join MADRE. Yifat always had a sense of the impact of war on families and children. She was brought up with a social justice orientation that eventually led her to question many of the ways that people identified with Israel. After graduating from a university in the United States, that orientation made her decide to return to Jerusalem and work with an Israeli-Palestinian human rights organization.

Yifat has claimed that one has to be a visionary to confront the many problems our world faces, and that, if we internalize the thoughts of policy makers in all fields at all levels, we cannot realize the many avenues for change and improvement. She believes that creating our own perspective on the world enables us to change social reality in new ways. For example, she sees that the jobs and lifestyles of a young adult's parents are no longer available, that those who want to make a good life for themselves and their families will have to be creative and open to constant change. She refers not only to the job market, but also to the way we grow our food, make the energy needed to heat our homes, raise our children, and, especially, resolve international conflicts. Like many others, she is particularly concerned about climate change. Yifat believes that policies in support of the current situation are just benefiting people who share the decision makers' point of view.[1]

When she was a child, Yifat's family would periodically visit relatives along the Syrian border. There were times when the sirens would go off at night, and she would take her father's hand and go down into the bomb shelter where people gathered nervously. One of those nights when her father was trying to get her to go to sleep, she complained that she was too frightened to sleep. He told her to picture a little girl in Syria in bed and also afraid of the noises, and to wish her sweet dreams, adding that it would help her fall asleep and bring peace back. She was very young and remembers a feeling of dissonance and deep confusion that there could be a little girl in Syria experiencing the same fears.[2]

That was how she came to see that some children absorb dehumanizing stereotypes that perpetuate conflict. It was an experience that remains at the center of her political vision. It gave her the idea that she could be part of making peace, and quiet her own fears by reaching out to someone else who is afraid. She learned that offering help is not charity, but self-preservation and that the best way to stop feeling helpless is to help someone. She feels that MADRE is working with the bravest people in the world who survived wars and natural disasters in Syria, Iraq, Kenya, the Sudan, Nicaragua, and other turbulent countries. She has discovered that these women have lived through the worst possible conditions, yet are still filled with hope and continue to work as if their lives depended on it to make a better situation for themselves and their families.[3]

MADRE works with women who were raped or whose daughters were raped during a conflict. Together they strive to work for a world without violence. The organization also partners with mothers who buried every one of their children who died from the famine in Somalia, and yet still dream of a world without hunger, and with women who were never allowed to go to school, and yet want a world where every single child has access to education.

With a staff of eleven MADRE is a small organization. Yet, it has been assisting women around the world by partnering with them on their own terms. Its staff includes women who speak Arabic, Hebrew, and Creole, and women who are able to relate to many different cultures. The organization has been working for thirty years in Nicaragua with the indigenous communities of its North Caribbean Coast Autonomous Region, where it partners with an indigenous community development organization that promotes women's rights, and an indigenous cultural perspective. In their daily work they strive to meet the basic needs of the resource-poor people in these communities, which have lost the forests, lagoons, and waterways that once sustained them because of corporate encroachment, drug trafficking, and climate change. These new threats have emerged since MADRE started its mission there in the 1980s.[4]

Now it works with 115 communities along the Coco River on the Nicaraguan-Honduran border, where the women of these communities face many problems because of geographic isolation, such as access to government services like medical care and the police. Violence against women—domestic violence, rape, and early pregnancy—is a major problem in these communities, and MADRE is working with the women there to build on their own strength in countering it. There is another project the organization has been developing called "Women Water Keepers," which involves cleaning and taking care of water sources to ensure that the water people collect is clean and not likely to cause life-threatening diseases like dysentery, cholera, and typhoid.[5]

Rather than bringing top-down aid from a culture that differs greatly from the one being helped, MADRE programs reflect the needs of the grassroots populations in more than twenty-seven countries. Within each of these countries, they work with numerous groups to further their aims and inspire them. Through its impressive work, this organization is accomplishing two very important goals: making the politically invisible visible, and empowering women who are socially, politically, and economically viewed as powerless.

MADRE has also developed key foundations for social change: access, affinity, and agency. With regard to access, people must be able to recognize the denial of basic resources including clean water as violations of their human rights, and that governments are accountable for upholding these rights. Affinity is the coming together of people to see their own struggle in a broader context and in relation to other people's struggles. For example, Yifat Susskind arranged for women who had been part of successful programs in Bosnia to travel to Syria with a translator in order to share their success and help a sister group. Agency is about women gaining access to arenas of power and being a recognized part of decision making that affects them.[6]

The organization also developed four strategies for meeting immediate needs. Its former director realized that when women are absorbed in the struggle to meet their family's needs for daily survival, they are unable to develop long-term solutions to the crises they face. In 2002, MADRE worked with a sister organization Benumpuhwe in Rwanda, meaning ("from the heart" in Kinyarwanda), to build a water system for a new village of families headed by women made homeless by the genocide in 1994. MADRE installed sixteen water taps, thus reducing waterborne diseases and the time women spent hauling dirty water from great distances every day. These women also took part in MADRE-sponsored health and hygiene workshops to improve the health of their families.

Creating Partnerships for Social Change is the second of MADRE's strategies based in its partnership with community-based women's organizations around the world working for social justice and progressive politics. The women it works with are survivors of war, political repression, genocide, economic and sexual exploitation, and national disasters. With MADRE they work to build health clinics, nutrition programs, establish shelters for women who are subject to domestic violence, community rights organizations, human rights training centers, literacy campaigns, and programs to improve women's political participation. This strategy enables women in communities to strengthen their leadership skills so they can share their important perspectives with other survivors of human rights violations and serve as role models for moving beyond victimization to leadership. Rather than accept the victim-advocate dichotomy, MADRE recognizes that survivors of abuse are often the most powerful advocates for change, thus creating a very important new perspective on the sources of strength. What makes MADRE so compelling is that members of its sister organizations partner with each other in different countries and thus has created an international gathering of women who have overcome marginalization, violence, the traumas of war, and ethnic oppression to help each other heal and make their communities vibrant again.

MADRE's third strategy is advocating for human rights. It has always differed with conventional human rights organizations that see themselves as apolitical. Instead this organization sees the entire process of defining, working toward, and applying human rights as essentially political. When MADRE began working in the international arena, mainstream human rights organizations barely acknowledged the economic issues that MADRE found central for most women around the world, such as rights to food, housing, and health care. Women's rights as human rights were marginalized until the global women's movement won international recognition of broader interpretations of human rights at United Nations conferences in the 1990s.

Seeing their efforts to acquire women's human rights as a work in progress, MADRE worked with indigenous women and advocates of the emergent sexual rights movement in Latin America and Africa to maintain the process of continually expanding the application and definition of human rights.

MADRE cofounded the first and only women's farmers' union in Sudan. The founder and director of its Sudanese sister organization is an agronomist, Fatima Ahmed, who brought together women subsistence farmers to pool their resources and train them. She traveled to MADRE's New York City office in 2013 and 2014, and, on her last visit, she shared the good news with MADRE's staff that the union had grown tremendously and had 5,241 members farming nearly fifty thousand acres across sixty villages. The members are also dealing with the effects of climate change and are being trained in adaptive agricultural techniques, such as water harvesting, which involves plowing deeper rows to hold, water, and planting trees around their farms to prevent erosion and slow down water evaporation.[7]

To further aid this union Yifat Susskind wrote an op-ed in the *Huffington Post* to demand that the international food aid system, rather than continue with the U.S. practice of sending genetically engineered rice from Texas to the Kenyan-Somali border, buy food for Africans from this union, as grains grown and purchased in Africa are easily transported and can be stored for longer periods. The women farmers' union has a strong commitment to organic farming and to persuading its members to never use pesticides partly because pesticides are sold aggressively to communities where there are high rates of illiteracy. Because women farmers are unable to read the directions on pesticide cans, they were having horrible accidents with them that raised the rates of birth defects and cancer among them. These farmers were getting the pesticides on their hands, thus ingesting it directly from their unwashed hands. These women now sign a public pledge with each other not to buy pesticides and are learning about organic methods of pest control. A further goal in helping to change these conditions is to eradicate illiteracy among the women, so the union is part of the women's literacy project.[8] With the money the women earn from farming, they pay for a biweekly program where they can learn to read. In 2013, MADRE gave the union an oil mill to make sesame and peanut oil from their harvests, thus increasing their income so that they feed their families well and also send their children to school.[9]

Given that climate change affects the most vulnerable communities, MADRE sees its work as empowering people at the local level who suffer the impact of national and global policies. The organization felt that it had to become involved in environmental programs in the last eight years because it has increasingly heard from its partner organizations that some of the biggest threats women face are the result of environmental degradation. MADRE is concerned that the international community has overlooked the connection between gender and climate change. While most people realize that it disproportionately affects the poor, many fail to realize that 70 percent of those living in poverty are women. Women are providing subsistence for their households and depend on ecosystem services, free clean water, growing medicinal plants, and a predicable climate for their farming. Deforestation has removed 80 percent of old growth forests in the developing world and threatens the livelihood of local and indigenous people. The many species on which women rely for their nutrition and health care are disappearing. Rural women's work increases dramatically as they are forced to trek longer distances to collect food, water, and firewood. This not only affects the time that women have for political participation and social networking, but also increases exposure to sexual and armed violence as they walk further from their communities to collect much needed resources.[10] At the international level, there has been some progress in debate of this issue, but little action, although some European countries have made important strides.

The United States and China are responsible for the highest carbon emissions, so in 2014, President Obama and China's President Xi Jinping came to an agreement to reduce emissions. In the United States, the president has sought to encourage states to engage in cap and trade schemes, but a number of states are opposing his efforts. He also spoke about climate change at the UN General Assembly in 2014, and has made numerous efforts to create programs in the United States by using his executive powers and has sought to help the developing countries with this problem. India, which is the third largest emitter of carbon, has recently increased its coal mining and has put a global warming pact in doubt.[11] There are numerous organizations around the world and in the United States working to protect the climate. In the fall of 2014, six thousand Climate Reality Leaders brought communities around the world to Brazil to share their views, and discuss ways of mitigating climate change. In the United States there are many organizations rallying people in effective ways, such as Interfaith Power and Light, through which five thousand congregations are encouraging their members to contact their senators. Columbia University is offering a master's degree in Sustainability Management to help educate people. Some groups such as Divest-Invest have encouraged a number of universities and businesses to cut their ties to coal and oil companies by ceasing to invest their endowments in them, and is also working with their shareholders. The important change is that people around the world are feeling the effects of climate change on our planet, demonstrating, and speaking out. China and the United States may have come to an agreement on climate change, but differences between the developing and developed countries emerged at the talks on climate change in Paris, December 2015. However, the conference included a sweeping effort to save the world's forests and created rules to encourage developing countries to preserve their forests.[12] Developing countries have made clear that the more financial help they get, the more they will be able to preserve their forests as they need to encourage economic growth that will bring their large population electricity, transportation, and employment. MADRE, aware of the needs of women in developing countries affected by climate change, seeks to build programs at the local level and seems to be the only organization reaching out to women in this way.

MADRE has created new programs every year. In 2004, it launched a new media program to publicize its work and goals and to disseminate MADRE's perspectives and information about the women with whom it works. Since then its articles have been published in hundreds of newspapers and magazines, having been especially concerned to influence the mainstream media by building relationships with journalists and editors. In 2005, the *New York Times* editorial board requested a briefing with MADRE staff to gain a wider understanding of women's situation in Iraq. The organization continues to build its reputation as a critical resources for journalists in the United States and internationally.[13] Yifat Susskind herself has written extensively on women's human rights and her work has appeared in online and in print publications such as the *New York Times*, *Washington Post*, and *Foreign Policy in Focus* and in her contribution to Laura Flanders' book, *The W Effect: Bush's War on Women*.[14] She has also been featured as a commentator on CNN, National Public Radio, and BBC radio.

Yifat knows that women are not powerless and that they need to be included in local, regional, national, and international politics. She believes that when we think about foreign policy, we don't think about the impact it has on women. Nor do we ordinarily see economic and social policies as affecting women. Yet they are the most vulnerable to policies and the strongest workers on behalf of their county, region or country. For example, many women's groups have left important legacies in this world. Ten years ago, a group of African women were furious that an oil company had fouled their drinking water. Before dawn, a large group of them took a boat to the company's headquarters in their country and demanded that they stop the practices that were causing the problem and they were successful. Then, there is the extraordinary Wangari Maathai who started a woman's movement in Kenya to plant trees. Women were complaining about water and lack of firewood, and in response she organized them and helped them plant trees, at a time when women were supposed to defer to men in decision making, and when the authoritarian President Daniel Arap Moi's government portrayed women as incompetent. Maathai's response was that the most important part of a woman's body was her head. The efforts of this group of women helped an uprising against President Moi that brought him down in 2002 after twenty-four years in power. The Greenbelt Movement, for which Wangari Maathai won the 2004 Nobel Peace Prize, eventually planted thirty-five million trees.[15] In accepting the prize, she emphasized her belief that restoring the environment is peace work, and that her movement had not only planted trees, but had inspired women to take charge of the environment, their government and their future.

A partnership that is close to Yifat's heart is in Gaza. MADRE has worked for years with Palestine medical relief communities that run local community clinics in the West Bank and Gaza. One of them is the Palestinian Medical Relief Society (PMRS), an organization that provides emergency medical aid for women and families caught in the conflict with Israel. MADRE has found that one of the biggest threats to public health in Palestine is the Israeli military occupation, which has undermined health care by exacerbating poverty and malnutrition, as well as by limiting people's access to health service severely by restricting the right of Palestinians to travel, sometimes even from one village to the next.[16] In addition, the Israeli military has launched attacks on hospitals, clinics, and ambulances, which PMRS is helping to equip. MADRE supplies PMRS with medicines, supplies like gauze and bandages, and fuel for ambulances and generators. According to National Public Radio, the war has destroyed half of Gaza's water supply and sanitation infrastructure, and killed more than 2,100 people.[17] According to UNICEF, 90 percent of the water from Gaza's sole aquifer is unsafe for consumption and 90,000 cubic meters of untreated sewage is discharged into the sea daily because the sewage treatment plants are overwhelmed.[18] Potable water flows from Israel to Gaza through two pipelines; a third has been constructed, but not yet commissioned pending broader negotiations.

MADRE has found that this has been a very unpopular issue to take a stand on, and is particularly contentious in the United States because of its close ties with Israel. However, MADRE has always taken the position that the plight of Palestinians is a human rights issue and it is clear in its understanding of the occupation of the West Bank, Gaza, and the Golan Heights as illegal. The Oslo Accords of 1993 and 1995 failed even to meet the basic rights of Palestinians for self-determination. MADRE doesn't have a position on what the outcome should be, but believes that the decisions should rest with the people in that region. The organization also believes that the United States should support those Palestinians and Israelis who share its point of view on human rights, social justice, and democracy. It feels that, regardless of how poor a job the Israeli or Palestinian leadership is doing to move their people closer to peace, there are always people living in those societies who are working for peace and that it is they who should be listened to in determining what they need in terms of international support. [19]

It is also working with a grassroots group of Israeli and Palestinian midwives who are from different sides of the conflict, who feel that they have a connection with each other as women and midwives and have a lot to learn from each other. Midwives for Peace supports their desire for joint professional development workshops every few months. The Safe Birth Project helps Palestinian women in labor to deliver safely, despite Israeli military roadblocks and checkpoints that prevent them or delay their travel to hospitals in the West Bank. It also provides medical kits and sponsors sessions about contraceptives and family planning. Part of their interest in meeting together is that it enables a relationship between people on both sides of the conflict, and gives them an opportunity to learn from their different experiences. [20]

Both groups of midwives are committed to end the occupation, but Yifat has noted many difficult and important issues need to be dealt with to bring it to an end. She sees that Palestinian groups and Israeli groups hold differing views about the continuing violence across the Israeli-Gaza border, but it is clear that, even though Israel has formally ended the occupation, it still continues. Israel controls the borders, the airspace, everything and everyone that moves in and out of the territory. [21] Because of Hamas, Israel regards even the material needed to rebuild bombed homes and institutions as related to the manufacture of weapons. For example, during the winter of 2014 flooding of toxic waste in Gaza caused new illness among its residents and hospitals were bombed. Gaza was not allowed to import spare parts for water treatment facilities, and schools had become places for refugees. The United Nations has noted that it would take more than twenty years to repair the bomb damage. Over the years Israel has refused to allow the occupied territories to pursue their economic development. Yifat feels that people who care about human rights should make it clear that no one should feel that they are in a position to choose between the far right of the Israeli government and Hamas because they don't represent the majority of either society.[22]

Unfortunately, the current situation in Gaza has provoked some unforeseen results in Western Europe, such as waves of anti-Semitism in Germany, Belgium, and France. Chancellor Angela Merkel led a rally against anti-Semitism in Berlin telling Germans, "It is our national and civic duty to fight anti-Semitism."[23] The president of France has also condemned the violence of Palestinian youths when they attacked synagogues and caused French people who are Jewish to move to Israel. The young Palestinians in France are second generation, having been born there, but feel alienated and frustrated by their lack of acceptance. Rioting took place in Sarcelles, a working-class Paris suburb where generations of immigrants are living in government housing, and many peoples coexist largely peacefully.[24] A small, but vocal group of immigrants from the Middle East has become inflamed by the Israeli-Palestinian conflict. When there are no outlets for creating peace and developing relations across borders violence often breaks out.

MADRE is also very concerned about women in refugee camps and works to restore their dignity as well as responding to their needs. Yifat regularly visits refugee camps to which thousands of refugees have fled. When someone asked her how she could work in places that were so depressing, her answer was that she would be more upset if she just stayed at home feeling helpless and watching wars rage from her couch. MADRE is working with different Syrian organizations, some inside Syria and others caring for millions of refugees in Jordan, Turkey, and Lebanon. Some of them were in the Syrian Refugee camp in Kurdistan in Northern Iraq in 2014, where there were very few services for people. What MADRE is doing there is attending to women's most basic needs, such as shelter, food, and clean water for their families.[25]

However, the women from those organizations focus on supplying the aid that women request but are not included in the aid the Red Cross and other humanitarian agencies deliver, such as reproductive health supplies and sanitary napkins. Going without these basic needs affects their dignity and their mobility. Diapers and baby clothes are also needed. MADRE also provides reproductive health services and midwifery care. Many women have come to MADRE for family planning help, as the last thing they want is to get pregnant in the insecure situation of a refugee camp. MADRE provides trauma counseling for the women to boost their capacity as mothers and to take care of other people who have been traumatized. Throughout this war the cell phone fills a vacuum felt by Syrian refugees who are miles away from their homes and loved ones. A reporter who visited Syrian refugees in Jordan discovered that it helps tie shattered lives together, and is as vital to their survival as food, water, and shelter.[26]

A MADRE team was in Iraq a few weeks before their work began with Syrians in 2013, where they had developed a project ten years earlier which had helped cofound the only network of women's shelters in that section of Iraq—a project that has been raided by police several times because it's not legal to run a women's shelter in Iraq. On one occasion the police had returned all the women to their families, the very place these women have fled. It was a tremendous effort to negotiate with the local police to avoid treating the shelter as a brothel, which is what they intended to do. Many young women were running away from forced marriage or had escaped prostitution into which their families had sold them and many were fleeing severe domestic violence. A member of the MADRE team noted that in such a context, a woman would only run away from home if she feared being killed there.[27]

MADRE works with its sister organizations to negotiate with the local police, relying on those organizations for strategy and technical assistance. A few key people in MADRE's partner association speak English and the MADRE team has some Arabic speakers on its staff. Sometimes MADRE's assistance can be very strong because receiving a letter on a letterhead from an international organization in New York City makes it clear to a local police department that they are being watched, and could be reported to the United Nations, and this helps the local organization in its advocacy.[28]

Since the 2003 U.S. invasion of Iraq, more extreme right-wing religious actors have become increasingly empowered. As a result, the tradition of honor killing has skyrocketed in Iraq, even though the American leaders told the United States that the invasion was to protect women and increase their rights. In fact, a civil war between the Sunni and Shi'ite population erupted, as the United States helped a Shi'ite President, Nouri-al-Maliki, into office, who began harassing the Sunni majority and putting their lives at risk. Previously, the United States had put Saddam Hussein into power, an authoritarian who had his own army and the Ba'ath party, but was Sunni, reflecting the majority of the population. Having lost its power, the Ba'athist army became one of the foundations of ISIS (Islamic State in Iraq and Syria) or Daesh, its acronym in Arabic.

Throughout its years of working with Iraqi women, there have been times when it was too dangerous to travel to Iraq or impossible to get visas, and a MADRE team would meet the Iraqi sister organizations in Istanbul or Kurdistan. They also made sure that these women had cell phones, and had access to email and Skype, as well as donating money so that they could have a generator in their office to cope with the sporadic electricity supply in Baghdad.[29]

During the worst of sectarian fighting in 2007 and 2008, MADRE's partner, The Organization of Women's Freedom in Iraq (OWFI) cofounded by Yanar Mohammed who is also its executive director, was one of the only groups in Iraq that rejected the Sunni-Shi'a division. Ten years earlier no one ever talked about what sect they took part in and had friends in both. OWFI held what they called Freedom Space Gatherings at a time when the Shi'a militias were executing anyone who was engaging in cultural expressions that weren't religious, CD vendors on the streets and musicians. People who didn't want to be part of the sectarian war engaged in a traditional form of Arabic poetry performance. Young Sunni and Shi'a men and women came together and performed for each other about their hopes, dreams, and frustrations about their situation. They also did a lot of human rights work, such as peace building between communities and taking a specific stance against sectarian violence. They were constantly under threat, because they spoke out against the killing of gay men in 2012 carried out by militias with government support. In addition, OWFI extended some of the sheltering and counseling work MADRES started for women under threat by including gay men and children who are unable to live at home.[30] Yanar Mohammed operates five shelters in her network and plans to open a sixth safe house for Yazidi women who are escaping sexual enslavement from Daesh. They operate without a fixed address because she has tried and failed to get authorization from the government. In October 2015, she spoke to the members of the UN Security Council telling them that they were partly to blame for the fact that Shariah law and honor killings are rarely punished, reminding them that ten years ago Iraqi women spoke to them about the situation for women.[31]

Yifat has shown that MADRE's work is to find out where there is no form of aid, where the big agencies are not working, what issues are not being addressed, and which people are falling through the cracks, and then to focus their efforts on filling those gaps. MADRE support to its sister organizations is both constant and growing. It helped its partners in Iraq to reopen their Al-Mousawat radio station after it was destroyed by a car bomb in 2013. OWFI had established the station in 2009 to strengthen women's abilities to claim their rights and play a positive role in rebuilding their country. MADRE worked with OWFI to create programming that offered listeners practical information on human rights and aired new perspectives that help transform derogatory and harmful attitudes and actions towards women.[32]

The same year it provided dozens of children born with birth defects access to healthcare in an Iraqi town located near a toxic U.S. military munitions dump. This aid included wheelchairs, canes, prosthetics, and a full medical assessment by a physician. Yanar Mohammed told MADRE that the ISIS advance threatens Iraqi women, in many ways, including summary executions, torture in detention, and the destruction of religious sites. ISIS has treated women harshly, attacking and killing female doctors, lawyers, and other professionals. They also captured five hundred women, taking 150 into the town of Tal Afar, and sending them to Syria to reward ISIS fighters or to be sold as sex slaves.[33] Yet through OWFI, MADRE is sending life-sustaining food packages to families headed by women in Samarra, currently surrounded by ISIS forces where no aid can reach them.

MADRE's work with Syrian women both inside the country and in refugee camps has had positive results. It helps them in an extraordinary way, by using the fruits of its work in Bosnia and Kosovo, it worked with the Women in Black, which began in Israel in 1988 and has become a global network of women committed to peace and justice, and actively opposed to injustice, war, militarism, and other forms of violence. During the war in the Balkans, they supported members of oppressed religions and stood silently in public squares for hours, enduring mockery and threats by passersby.[34] MADRE has worked in that region since the beginning of the 1990s, bringing rape as a weapon of war to the attention of the American public. The organization shipped humanitarian aid during the NATO bombing of Kosovo and has maintained close relationships with partner groups in Bosnia.

When MADRE began working with Syrian women's groups in the context of civil war, Yifat had a ground breaking plan: MADRE's partners from Bosnia could share a wealth of experience with Syrian women. It organized opportunities for them to exchange stories, ideas, and strategies. The exchange occurred on two levels, one being an emotional level because, during a civil war, people have a sense that they have been forgotten and that nobody understands what they have endured. It's a powerful experience for Syrian women to feel the support of women from Bosnia and to know that these women understand what they are facing. For them, the Bosnian women serve as role models for people who have survived in extremely trying situations, and a special and very necessary friendship was created and expressed between the Bosnians and Syrians.[35]

The other level of their exchange is tactical and strategic. The Bosnian women have experience of how women's organizations and civil society groups can have meaningful participation in peace negotiations, and in the transitional justice process.

According to Yifat, one of the Bosnian women told the Syrian women, "Whatever you do, don't allow the constitution to be written in the context of peace accords. If you haven't lived through that historical experience, you are not going to know that it is really important to separate them as well as the time it requires for a society to have a constitutional process really be building democratic sensibility and understanding in the population and to have people involved in that."[36] These women also told their Syrian counterparts that while they don't want foreign intervention in the construction of a constitution, they need international support in peace negotiations.

MADRE was able to work inside Syria because it is a small group working with local partners and can "fly below the radar." International aid groups are unable to enter Syria with food and medicine, but the organization is able to do so even though it is on a small scale.[37] As it did in Haiti, the organization was working with women who are doing what women in crises do, distributing aid because they know the community and which people are the most in need of help, and where they are located, which large aid organizations are not likely to be aware of. Currently Yifat is not sending her staff into Syria because it is so dangerous, but one of the paradoxes of a civil war situation is that often some of the borders are left unguarded. It is possible to walk across the Jordanian-Syrian border any time. The Jordanian army is neither big enough nor concerned enough to control the movement of everyone going back and forth and there is no fence through the swath of dessert across which the border runs.

MADRE trained Syrian women physicians and nurses working inside Syria in Turkey for a few days. Given the fact that so many hospitals have been bombed or taken over by militias that are using them as prisons, such training is extremely important. It collaborates with Circle of Health International to provide trauma counseling for the women and children, and has provided them with medical supplies to bring into Syria. That work started in 2011 when Syria was so closed that MADRE had no contacts there, but they managed to establish contacts in the intervening years.[38]

MADRE also works with Syrian refugees who are not in the large camps in neighboring countries such as Lebanon, which receive a lot of media attention because that is where the United Nations works and where large aid agencies and governments have easy access. Many people wind up outside the parameters of these camps, either because there is not sufficient space for them, or they are afraid to be in large camps. In Jordan, MADRE works with a small organization that has created a clinic and a women's center where most of the refugees are staying, providing recreational and educational activities as incentives for refugee women to bring their children to the center. Members of that organization then engage them in conversations about the importance of registering as a refugee so they can have access to health care and food aid. In 2013 MADRE delivered solar lanterns to that community because women are living in places in with no electricity that are completely dark at night and are afraid of being raped. These refugees may live in places such as behind an abandoned gas station or on the edge of somebody's property.[39]

An impressive contribution to the role of Syrian women was a report produced in 2013 by MADRE and the International Women's Human Rights (IWHR) Clinic, the City University of New York (CUNY), and the Women's International League for Peace and Freedom (WILPF), and Syrian women's organizations. Lisa Davis, Clinical Law Professor in the IWHR Clinic and Human Rights Advocacy Director for MADRE compiled the report. The project is called "Seeking Accountability and Effective Response for Gender-Based Violence against Syrian Women: Women's Inclusion in the Peace Processes." The goal of the project is to strengthen the role of Syrian women in advocating solutions for gender-based violence and future policy changes. The report reveals that when Syrians began peaceful protests against President Bashar Al-Assad, women played an active role in protests and local mobilization, leading and organizing demonstrations. However, as the protests became militarized, women were sidelined and their roles marginalized in political groups that were formed outside of Syria.[40]

Further, three-quarters of Syrian refugees are women and children who fled to escape violence. The women who remained in Syria suffered torture and sexual violence as the war escalated, and the UN Secretary General stated that such violence was part of a widespread and systematic attack by both the government and the opposition. The terrible consequences of such violence are accompanied by social stigma and honor killings. Because these women are often excluded by their families and community they rarely report health problems such as physical injuries, sexually transmitted diseases, and unwanted pregnancies resulting from sexual violence. Women also suffer from domestic violence resulting from the stress of living in unstable conditions.[41]

Also, because most refugees have no way to earn a living, child labor and early marriage are widespread in refugee communities. Young girls are sold as brides and parents also arrange early marriage to protect their daughters from the insecurity of refugee life. Further the UN High Commission for Refugees has reported a large number of refugees as having no officially recognized nationality, both because of lack of birth registration and because people married in religious ceremonies have never completed the process of civil marriage. Syrian parents fleeing the conflict have left behind marriage documentation and, if any of them were able to return, they might find that the civil registration system is no longer functioning.[42]

To deal with these devastating problems, the report makes a series of important recommendations to the UN Security Council and to the United Nation's multilateral donor agencies and donor governments. Among these recommendations are that support be increased for local projects that provide medical, psychological, social, and legal services to survivors of sexual violence, as well as for reproductive health services to counter the threats to women and girls in conflict. Most important is the recommendation to ensure that women are included in the peace process. MADRE has done an important job of publicizing what women face during war, educating the public, and lobbying the United Nations and other international groups to support women.

MADRE's 2013 annual report included a moving testimony from a Syrian woman.

> One of the worst things about being a refugee is feeling invisible. If something horrible happened to me, no one would know about it. I used to think about that and it filled me with a terrible feeling. When I was home, I knew that my family and my neighbors would take care of me if I were sick or if someone tried to hurt me. But I felt so alone now. When we received your help, it changed so much. It told me that someone knows I am here. That someone is worried about me and they want to make sure that I'm OK. Thank you for reminding me that I am not alone.

In October 2015, Yifat Susskind cosponsored a symposium in Istanbul with locally based Syrian and Iraqi women rights activists, including Yanar Mohamed of OWFI to help end the scourge of rape unleashed by the ascent of ISIS. It has used rape to exert control and spread terror, tearing families and communities apart. The participants in the meeting found a great change in the treatment of women and girls after they have been raped, that they are quietly taken back instead of being subjected to honor killing. According to Yifat, it is harder to blame women for being raped when it is so widespread and has unsettled social norms. This group emphasized that the trend is new and tenuous, yet also a rare strategic opening to make that shift permanent.[43] They also spoke about the need for shelters for women and about how the tide is turning; faced with an influx of displaced people, Iraqi NGO shelter providers have successfully negotiated written agreements with local tribal leaders from Karbala and Samarra, permitting them to have safe housing.[44] Women's rights activists are working to obtain similar agreements from other townships and have also turned their attention to Baghdad. Yifat sees that moments of crises are also opportunities these activists to remake their communities.

In addition, MADRE had been working with an International Indigenous Women's Forum (IIWF/FIMI) since it was founded in 2000. The FIMI connects the work of indigenous communities with policy making at the international level, such as climate change negotiations or bilateral trade. It works to ensure that the perspectives of indigenous women are included in human rights discussions by facilitating their participation in regional meetings and UN conferences. It promotes indigenous women's work through advocacy and media initiatives.

Indigenous people are frequently disenfranchised from their local governments, and with no say in policies that may have a negative impact on their communities such as the creation of a gold mine. Distant corporations and governments make these policies. It's important for women to have a voice in these decisions that harm their health, nutrition, and well-being. MADRE is helping them to have a voice in addressing those problems. Women are the ones lying down in front of bulldozers and linking arms to make chains, which are the only actions at their disposal. Such efforts work in places where the community level is coordinated at the national and international level.[45]

MADRE is also working with women in their own communities by providing hundreds of women in impoverished towns with vaccinations, pap smears, eye, ear, and throat exams, and other preventive health tests. At a health fair organized by MADRE and the Women Workers Community it sponsored ten educational sections on sexual and reproductive health. It is also active in communities where human rights violations are common, making sure that the work they do at the local level is connected to the national and international efforts. Without connection to those higher levels of activism, MADRE would be unable to influence broader policies such as government decisions to take possession of their land or an extractive industry moving in their territory. Then there is the issue of climate change, that because governments are not tackling it, community activists need to provide some leadership of policies impacting climate change. MADRE gives them training and access to those empowered to make decisions, accompanying them when they approach those policy makers. It believes that activism in the international community must have relevance and be accountable to people working at the site that is the focus of that activism.

There are success stories of local level activism when it is supported by lobbying at the national level and international intervention. In Tanzania women protested against Chevron, and women won policy changes in Nigeria by protesting against Shell Oil. It's more difficult for local activists in Latin America because corporations conceal their aims with the many shell companies they use, so it is difficult to discover the owners.[46] In 2014, at a huge demonstration on climate change with nearly four hundred protestors in New York City, Patricia Gualinga, a leader from the

Kichwa community of Sarayaku, Ecuador, walked with indigenous leaders in the demonstration, and presented at the People's
Climate Justice Summit that ran parallel to the UN Climate
Summit. She spoke to media reciting her message to "Keep
the Oil in the Ground."[47] The Ecuadorian government publicly
apologized for the human rights violations that occurred in their
rainforest community in 2003, the first time in Latin America
that a government official traveled to an indigenous community
for this purpose.

Thirty indigenous community leaders attended the FIMI
meeting in New York in 2014 and MADRE raised money to pay
for their transportation. It has been working with the people who
attended its programs for a long time in their communities, but
this was the first time they had ever left their community or flown
in an airplane, or had such a cosmopolitan urban experience.
Some of them stayed with a MADRE staff since it would have
been difficult for some of them to stay in a hotel, take an elevator,
or ride the subway.

The meeting was held to ensure that an indigenous women's
perspective was incorporated in the new development policy
framework, the "sustainable development goals," that the United
Nations were preparing to succeed the millennium development goals. These are signed by almost every government in
the world and come with a significant budget to help these
goals be achieved. They have a concrete application rather than
the nonbinding resolutions the United Nations usually makes.
Indigenous women want to be part of that discussion from the
beginning, as mainstream development is often conceived with
a completely different agenda from what these women want and
how they perceive development.

In 2014, people from MADRE's advocacy staff traveled
to Columbia and Guatemala to give a series of workshops

and training sessions for women based on what those women thought they needed to feel that they have justice in the aftermath of conflict. What these women asked for were psychosocial services, and there was much discussion on the ongoing impact of trauma on families and communities. Adult women who are survivors of mass rapes and massacres are aware that, as mothers, their invisible wounds are having a negative impact on their children. MADRE worked with a woman in Colombia that does trauma counseling and somatic exercises with these women to heal the effects of human rights violations and give them easily learned tools to integrate into their daily lives.

An important part of MADRE's strategy is bringing women together from different communities so that they can exchange their stories and their strategies, understanding that it is more important for indigenous women to learn from each other rather from MADRE. A few years ago the organization brought Rose, a Miskita leader and educator from Nicaragua, to work with indigenous organizations in Kenya. Even though they may be worlds apart geographically, they have similar experiences and perceptions because they are indigenous, have a similar relationship to the physical environment that shaped their culture and also experienced exclusion by their national governments. Rose did excellent work in trainings and workshops with groups of Maasai and Samburu women. She speaks English, but had MADRE's Spanish-speaking program director, Natalia, to help her out if she couldn't find the right word or expression at times. In Kenya, English is also a second language.[48] Yifat's concept of yet another kind of partnership has been widely used.

Although MADRE has only a small staff, its members are able to accomplish a great deal because they focus on working in close and constant contact with partner organizations to mobilize their strengths. MADRE makes sure that they have computers and cell phones to keep in touch. This wonderful organization is able to empower women around the world in places that large aid organizations are unable to reach. By working with local organizations, it is able to understand and respond to their needs in unique ways, helping them to grow and reach out as well as to attain their goals. Its philosophy is making connections around the world where women are in need, protecting their human rights and their health and livelihoods, as well as ensuring they have a role at all levels of government. The organization is supported by numerous foundations, and individuals who have enabled MADRE to give millions of dollars in aid to its sister organizations.

Ironically, although MADRE has been working on behalf of poor and disenfranchised women for over thirty years, the United Nations has only recently reported on the disparities between the poor, the middle class, and the wealthy. Although there is increasing education and access to contraception for the middle class and the wealthy, the UN report reminds us that, at a time when the world has prospered, women in the poorest countries, together with poor women in some richer countries, have not seen their lives improve.[49] As the report makes clear, "In conditions of structural poverty, the threats to women's survival are especially acute, due to the lack of access to health services, particularly sexual and reproductive services, and the extreme physical burdens of food production, water supply, and unpaid labor that fall disproportionately on poor women."[50] Making progress in this area is precisely what MADRE has been doing for over thirty years, with its small but dedicated and multinational staff.

ELEVEN

Alan Lightman and the Harpswell Foundation

Dr. Alan Lightman is the first person at the Massachusetts Institute of Technology to hold a joint faculty position in science and the humanities. He is a physicist who has written a number of novels. In 2003, his life changed dramatically when he accompanied his friend, Frederick Lipp a Unitarian minister, to Cambodia. His friend had founded a nonprofit organization in Cambodia to help twelve- and thirteen-year-old girls resume their education. Many had been taken out of school to work in the rice fields. When he saw what his friend's organization was accomplishing, Alan Lightman decided that he too would fulfill his desire to create a humanitarian project.

It was a challenge that required a great deal of effort and hope, because Cambodia is troubled by poverty and its history of genocide and corruption. In 1975, the communist Khmer Rouge came into power and, through executions, starvation, diseases caused by relocation, and forced labor, systemically killed an estimated two million Cambodians—almost a quarter of the country's population. Nearly every educated person was killed and much of the country's infrastructure was destroyed, although some of it has since been rebuilt. The city of Phnom Penh was emptied and whole families were forced into the countryside where they were subject to endless, back-breaking labor, nightly propaganda sessions, and fed so little that many died of starvation, if they were not executed.[1]

In 1979, the Vietnamese army invaded and occupied Cambodia for ten years. During that period, a young Khmer Rouge officer, Hun Sen, was named prime minister and he has proved to be ruthless and corrupt. He has remained in power for three decades and has declared that he intends to stay in office for as long as he lives. Until 1999 the Khmer Rouge senior members remained at large. Pol Pot, its leader, died in 1998 and the arrest the following year of Ta Mok, its last commander, marked the end of the Khmer Rouge movement. A special Cambodian International Tribunal was established in 2006 to try the most senior surviving Khmer Rouge leaders. Comrade Duch, the head of the most notorious of the regime's many torture and death centers, was convicted of crimes against humanity in 2010 and sentenced to life in prison. The trials of two remaining Khmer Rouge leaders are moving ahead but are plagued by procedural delays.[2] But since 1999, for the first time in thirty years, Cambodia has been at peace.[3] Nevertheless, according to Cambodia's Minister of Women's Affairs, who is a physician, many people who survived the genocide suffer from PTSD, which often accounts for outbreaks of anger and domestic violence.[4] Many Cambodian refugees who were resettled in the United States still suffer from PTSD.[5]

According to Loung Ung, twenty-five years after the defeat of the Khmer Rouge, Cambodia was still one of the poorest countries in the world with an average annual income of

U.S. $254 and over a third of its population living below the poverty line. Because the Khmer Rouge targeted professionals in all fields—doctors, lawyers, architects, professors, and other talented people—the country was unable to pass on its skills and knowledge to the next generation.[6]

Hun Sen's Cambodian People's Party (CPP) dominates the economy, as well as a political system characterized by widespread corruption. CPP is responsible for the destruction of Cambodia's forests where people lived and worked and which contained sought-after hardwood trees that had been a source of wealth throughout its history. After the fall of the Khmer Rouge, the trees were harvested and sold abroad. The World Bank required the government to hire Global Witness as the country's first forest monitor. It mapped a broad network of illegal logging, cataloged bribe payments, and named Hun Sen's cronies and family members as complicit. After presenting its report, Global Witness was forced to leave the country and the razing of most of the forests continued. In addition, government officials seized and sold off Cambodia's land for development, displacing thousands of Cambodian citizens who were dumped miles away.[7] The United Nations and many NGOs, such as USAID, remained in Cambodia, contributing half of the nation's budget. Every U.S. Ambassador there, together with the World Bank, demanded an end to corruption.[8] The government did pass laws to respond to the criticism, but failed to enforce them.

Dr. Lightman decided to improve the lives of Cambodia's people whom he found to be in a very fraught situation. After that first trip, he spent a great deal of his time fundraising and was able to build a school in a small village. He placed advertisements in local newspapers to find people in construction and oversaw their work. When the school was completed, he registered it with the government, making it a Cambodian public school and taking on an obligation to teach the government's curriculum. The government also supplied a teacher, but, since teachers are very poorly paid, it was difficult to find teachers willing to move out to the countryside, far from any city. Consequently, Dr. Lightman supplemented the government salary.

Most villages now have schools, although 60 percent of the country's women older than about thirty-five to forty are illiterate. Dr. Lightman's decision to supplement the salaries of the teachers in the school he established is very important, because students in other village schools are required to pay bribes in order to attend classes.[9] Because of the teachers' demands for bribes and the widespread poverty, between 15 and 20 percent of children never attend primary school. Those who are able to go to school find themselves in classes with up to eighty students. Fewer than 13 percent of young people are able to continue their education and attend high school.[10] A 2009 report by the World Bank on education and competitiveness warned, "Cambodia cannot grow until it reforms its education system."[11]

After the school was completed, Dr. Lightman proceeded with two more projects in that village—building a mosque, as the village was Muslim, and helping to build a drip irrigation system for farming. He also developed a sewing business. Since there is no electricity in the village, he donated pedal powered sewing machines. The salary of the women in this business is twice that paid in the garment factories. They are even able to make a profit, half of which they give to the village elders. Since the mid-1990s, Cambodia has built garment factories that employ women, selling almost 75 percent of their products to the United States. Although the garment industry accounts for a large proportion of the nation's GNP, women receive low wages, living six to a small dingy room they rent near the factories. They work six days a week and have miserable lives, but that work is necessary for their families as they are earning more than their parents.[12]

Dr. Lightman's foundation has a staff member in that village, Tum Yousos, who is a director of Cham (Muslim) programs and administers the school Dr. Lightman built, as well as a high school scholarship program in the village of Tramung Chrum. He also helps administer grants from the U.S. Embassy to promote human rights and training for democracy.

The success of Dr. Lightman's project of building a school in a small village made it easier for him to convince people to donate money for building a women's dormitory and to establish the Harpswell Foundation, dedicated to helping women achieve a truly unique and outstanding education. To start a foundation in such a setting requires foresight and courage. Alan Lightman felt that educating women was the best way to rebuild a country mired in poverty and led by an authoritarian government. What sparked this effort was meeting Veasna Chea on his second trip to Cambodia. She was a young woman who told him the story of her college attendance in 1990. Male students were living in Buddhist temples while they were studying at the university, but there was no housing for female students, which prevented young women from the countryside, where 80 percent of the population lives, from receiving college education. But Vaesna Chea and other female students did not accept being denied an education and lived underneath the university building for four years, in what was nothing more than a crawl space between the bottom of the building and the mud. Seeing at firsthand such a crucial need, Dr. Lightman returned to the United States with the goal of raising money to build housing for female students.[13] Historically and culturally, women are supposed to defer to men in Cambodia and are in great need of empowerment. World Bank studies have shown that educating and empowering women is the most effective way of helping developing countries.

The first dormitory for women was built in 2006 at Phsar Daeum Thkov, Phnom Penh. It provided free room and board for thirty-six women. Since demand for this dormitory was heavy, the foundation was able to be very selective and accommodate the brightest and most ambitious women in the country. Dr. Lightman also decided to create an in-house academic program that the students could attend during the evenings and weekends while not at their universities. The program offers English classes, leadership and history seminars, discussion of national and international news to sharpen critical thinking skills and classes on debating, analytical writing, and on Southeast Asian geography. Genocide studies classes are also available, in which the genocide committed by the Khmer Rouge is put into an international context of instances of genocide. The students have access to computers connected to the Internet. Because of the skills they acquire during the dormitory's academic program, they are at the top of their classes in three out of the five major universities in Phnom Penh.[14]

A second dormitory was built in the Teuk Thla area of Phnom Penh in 2009. The new facility houses forty-eight students, which brings the number of women students in the program to eighty-four. There were forty-five graduates from the classes of 2010 to 2013. Now the foundation is enabling twenty students to graduate every year, accepting twenty new students who have completed high school. The women in the two facilities come from poor families in rural villages without electricity or running water. Without the foundation's help, these young women would only be able to work in the rice fields and in the garment industry.[15]

Each dormitory has eight leadership residents each year, who stay for three months or so. They are generally women from the West with international travel experience who are sensitive to other cultures and interested in the empowerment of women. They live in the facilities as volunteers to teach the students, as well as to help them. Mira Weisenthal, a volunteer from the United States, is responsible for selecting these volunteers and the foundation advertises the opportunity on its website and through the idealist. org website. Mira interviews the women who want to be involved on Skype and decides if they are qualified to be leadership residents. The foundation pays for their room and board and gives them a small stipend, but does not pay their airfare to Cambodia, although Dr. Lightman often helps them raise funds for their round-trip tickets. Not all of the leadership residents come from the United States, as the foundation prefers to have mentors from all over the world. Volunteers have come from Britain, Austria, Australia, New Zealand, and the Philippines. The fifty leadership residents who have worked at the dormitories in the past eight years serve as useful contacts for new residents.[16]

As well as leadership residents, the dormitories have a very impressive administrative staff. The senior manager, Varony Ing, is the manager for the dormitory and leadership center at Teuk Thia and supervises both facilities. She has a BS in electrical engineering from the Institute of Technology in Cambodia and a master's degree in public administration from the University of North Texas. In addition, she has many years of experience in working with international organizations to improve the quality of life in Cambodia and is especially committed to the empowerment of women. Every year, she has meetings with each student to monitor their economic progress, as well as keeping the dormitory buildings and facilities in good shape and ensuring that all the bills are paid. She sends Alan Lightman a weekly facilities report and puts together a monthly financial report.[17]

Varony Ing's assistant manger, Sophal Som is responsible for the dormitory and leadership center in Boeng Tabaek. She earned a BA degree in archaeology from the Royal University of Fine Arts. She was the vocational skills supervisor at Hagar International, an organization that rescues women and children from violence abuse and sexual trafficking and helps them become strong members of their communities. At Hagar, she worked in everything from financial reporting to teaching vocational skills to counseling families in desperate situations. At the dormitory, Sophal Som is directly involved with paying the bills, helping to prepare weekly financial reports, and running any errands that need to be done in order to keep the dormitory running smoothly. Although supervised by Varony Ing, she is the person who has direct contact with the maintenance personnel.[18]

Kim Henry is the Director of English Instruction at the facilities. She received a Certificate of Teaching English as a Foreign Language from the Worldwide Teachers Development Institute in Boston. Before coming to Cambodia, she taught English in Nepal, Ecuador, Vietnam, and Thailand for several years. She also teaches English and supervises all the volunteer English teachers in both dormitories. She is in charge of teaching materials and designs tests for the fourth-year students that helps her to decide which of them have a good enough command of English to come to the United States. Kim Henry has lived in Cambodia for many years.[19]

A house-mother is also on the staff in the larger facility. Malis is in her fifties and lives in the dormitory to provide maternal care to all of the students, who miss their families and value the presence of someone who can respond to their emotional needs around the clock.

Both dormitories have twenty-four-hour security and are surrounded by high walls of barbed wire, which is reassuring for the parents of the young women. The main danger experienced by these young women in the dormitories is theft. Most parents who live in the countryside are very nervous about their daughters moving to the city because sex trafficking is a large problem in Cambodia. It is, unfortunately, a very common occurrence for people from the city to go to villages and tell parents that they have a job for their daughter, which turns out to be in prostitution rings. The parents need to be sure that the Harpswell Foundation is legitimate and that their daughters will be safe in their care. Dr. Lightman has discovered that it is almost impossible to stop sex trafficking in Cambodia, because it represents a large part of its GNP, alongside the garment industry and tourism. He is aware that the government and the police are involved in trafficking. To allay the concerns of the students' parents, the foundation sponsors an event for them at the facilities every two years.[20]

Given the nature of the political system in Cambodia, the students and the staff at the dormitories do not talk about politics outside of the facilities. The government is informed about the dormitory and the leadership sessions, but not about the details of the curriculum. Several government ministers have visited the facility, and the foundation is on good terms with the Cambodian government.

Dr. Lightman stays in Cambodia for between two and four weeks twice a year. In the United States, he spends four hours a day on foundation work, fund raising, keeping the programs running, corresponding with the leadership residents and the managers, and working with the students who are studying abroad. He also keeps the Harpswell Alumnae Association connected. Two other trustees on Harpswell's board play important roles. Rangita de Silva de Alwis is an international lawyer and head of a local women's leadership initiative in Washington, D.C., and has many contacts around the world with people interested in encouraging women. In the future, Dr. Lightman will be looking for more members of the foundation that will eventually be able to extend the role and the life of the organization.[21]

For the past five years, the Harpswell Foundation has brought four graduates to the United States each year for postgraduate study. They do not obtain master's degrees but take part in a one-year certificate program in which students can take any course that they want to at an American university. Most of the universities they attend do not have postgraduate programs so they have created them especially for the Harpswell Foundation. Students are able to attend Northeastern University in Boston, Bard College in New York, Bowdoin College in Maine, Agnes Scott College in Atlanta, and Rhodes College in Memphis Tennessee. Thanks to arrangements made by Dr. Lightman with these institutions, the Harpswell Foundation students are granted free tuition while the foundation provides them room and board, the airfare to the United States, a laptop for each one of them, and money to cover their personal expenses.[22]

Maggie Doyle is the coordinator of the Harpswell-U.S. Fellowships for the four students traveling to the United States, and supervises the selection process that begins with the international English language test system (IELTS). Students interested in study abroad need to write an essay about why they want to come to the United States and how it would benefit them, and submit a list of their extracurricular activities and their academic record. The senior manager, Varony Ing, and Dr. Lightman make the final decisions. One factor that must be taken into consideration is their level of maturity and their adaptability to American culture.

Alan Lightman has found that it is quite a challenge for these students to live in the United States for a year. They miss their families and their country and need to adjust to very different kinds of food. They also have trouble with the open display of sexuality in the United States, as it is rare in Cambodia for a couple to kiss each other before they get married. One of these young women was sharing a room in a dormitory with an

American student who brought her boyfriend in for the night, which she found profoundly shocking and offensive.[23] Here again, Alan Lightman helps the students with these problems, finding another room for them if need be. He believes that, even though the United States can be a strange new world for them, the year that they spend abroad expands their horizons by exposing them to more of the ways in which the world can work. This is truly a different and important way of learning for these young women, as they need to adapt and, in a sense, reinvent their ways of thinking and seeing.

Some of the students have wanted to continue studying after their year in the United States in order to complete a master's degree, so they are now in master's programs at the University of Massachusetts in Lowell, at the University of California, the American University in Washington, D.C., the University of Hong Kong and in the Philippines. Alan Lightman wants these young women to become the leaders of their countries, heads of banks and businesses, ministers, heads of law firms and hospitals—in short, to become leaders in whatever field they have chosen. Although Alan Lightman did not read the World Bank's report about the role of education in changing a country, his foundation is doing just that. He is pleased that his graduates are project managers at NGOs, journalists at some of the major newspapers in Cambodia, working in law firms, and teaching in high schools and universities. Two of them are working in the Cambodian Ministry of Women's Affairs. Dr. Lightman believes that the Harpswell graduates can realize their potential to become leaders of Cambodia.[24]

Villages are also being changed by the experiences of Harpswell students. They share what they have learned when they visit their families and neighbors. They have been involved in a charity event to help disadvantaged children. Dr. Lightman always tells them that with privilege comes responsibility to help people who are not as well off as they are.

Chandy Eng finished her year at Bowdoin College and was applying for admission to a master's degree program. She has shared her story so that people can gain some understanding of what Cambodian students are thinking and what their goals are.

> I believe that there is nothing that a girl cannot do. In my family, my father is the breadwinner. He supports our family by working as a porter in Sihanouk Ville Autonomous Port. My mother is a housewife. I know that to facilitate my studies and the studies of my younger sisters and brother, my parents work very hard. My father has spent his life on the sea working on ships but I have never heard him complain about having to work hard to support his family because he always believes that he has a good wife and he has four good children.
>
> My mother is a normal Cambodian woman. After marrying, she has been a housewife, staying at home and doing most of the housework. She does not want her daughters to become housewives like her. She is a great mother.
>
> High school was a very challenging period in my life. I clearly understood that my family would not be able to financially support me to study higher education, so the only way for me to compete for a scholarship was by having exceptional grades in the final year of high school. A tear is dropping in my heart all the time when I think about this. I thought: I have to be stronger and stronger to show everyone how much I am trying so they will not be disappointed. After high school, I realized that I was passionate about studying law and managed to win a scholarship to study at the oldest and best law school in Cambodia, The Royal University of Law (RULE). Moreover, it is the priority class for scholarship abroad.
>
> Leaving home to find more education is not an easy thing for Cambodian women. However, I knew I had to leave and

seek more education far away from home. I was ready for the challenge and I had a strong desire to study in a foreign country. As Nelson Mandela, Nobel Peace Prize winner in 1993 said, "Education is the most powerful weapon which you can use to change the world." In Phnom Penh, luckily I was selected to be one of the students residing in the Harpswell Dormitory, which provides leadership training and free accommodation, supported by Dr. Alan Lightman, whom I call Dad and other donors. I got this chance due to my good results in high school. Opportunities like this one are so important for Cambodian women, who have great potential but lack the money to have the chance to continue their studies. Harpswell provides me the chance to empower myself to be the leader, live in a community with many women from different provinces. The love, care and understanding are found in Harpswell.

Many people ask me about the thing that inspires me to study hard and never be hopeless. I always laugh and silently think about how much I miss my parents and siblings, who always encourage, give hope, believe and kindly help me. I promise myself never to let them down. I want to be a leader in a high position in Cambodia and show the potential of what women like me can do. I am convinced that a belief in your dreams and ambition will lead you to success. My parents always tell me: "Daughter life is difficult and being a girl is even more difficult, but you have to try hard because there is nothing that a girl cannot do if you really want it. You must walk to find your way; you cannot sit and wait for your chance." Those words stay deep in my heart and give me the energy to continue fighting obstacles.

To succeed there are many difficulties that I need to face and solve. Being the oldest daughter in a Cambodian family, I need to do much housework and act as a role model for my younger brother and sisters. The most difficult thing is to show other people that I am a fearless woman. "The future is not predicted, but planned," the founder of Toyota once said. It is my strong belief that having a dream is how we help ourselves direct the way we live our lives. My long-term dream is to be a high-ranking leader in Cambodia and I am striving to achieve it.

I want all women in Cambodia to be able to access their rights and have the opportunity to change their lives. Seizing opportunities is so important to make change and help Cambodian women to have brighter futures. Men have more opportunities than women in Cambodia and some men do not share those opportunities with women. I do not understand this, but I think one reason is that they are afraid. Some men think that if women have rights they will become better than them. I really want to tell them that women work hard and can help to develop this country with you. We do not want to compete with you. We can work together. Now I am the one who has a chance and I need to share it with other girls. I believe Cambodian women are brave and have great abilities but they are diamonds that are not yet made up. Women from all over the world have this right to opportunity, no matter whether they live in Europe, Africa, Asia or elsewhere. We all deserve a better world.[25]

There have been important improvements in Cambodia as slow change takes place. An example of such improvement is a pilot project for farmers to use better tools on small plots of ground, which has gained the government support. The nation is growing more prosperous. Now that the country has enjoyed more than a decade of stability, tourism, an important part of the economy, continues to grow and draws over a million visitors to Cambodia each year. The number of urban Cambodian college graduates is growing, with over forty thousand people entering college every year and a growing number studying abroad.[26] As a result, educated Cambodians have become more skeptical of the leadership and more critical than they have generally been. Gaffar Peang-Meth, a Cambodian with a doctorate from a U.S. university and a professor of political science at the University of Guam now feels that Cambodia will be able to move on from the domination of Hun Sen, as he had noticed that "not only are some students and recent graduates dissatisfied, but I also know some people in the current regime, in the military, as well as the bureaucracy who are unhappy."[27]

Even though the presence of the United Nations left an enduring structure in Cambodia, with a system of government divided into executive, parliamentary, and judicial branches, the current system is still supported by vested interests. Hun Sen is still unwilling to allow dissent, but it has been growing. In December 2013, tens of thousands of anti-government demonstrators marched through Phnom Penh in one of the biggest acts of defiance of Hun Sen's three-decade rule. The peaceful procession stretched for several miles, bringing together protesters with a varied list of grievances—garment workers, farmers whose land had been taken, supporters and leaders of the opposition Cambodia National Rescue Party (CNRP) led by Sam Rainsy and Kem Sokha.[28] It marked the beginning of months of protest, when rallies of sixty thousand people became common, as unions demanded that the minimum monthly wage rise from $80 to $160. They called for Hun Sen's resignation, believing that he had rigged the July 2013 election. The footage shot by protesters and journalists went viral on social media and images of the violence against garment workers were seen even in the villages.[29] In addition to the protesters who were killed and wounded, many were detained and others went into hiding after government thugs smashed through the park in the heart of the capital where protesters had established a base.

The CNRP leaders were summoned to appear in court, but went into hiding instead. One politician elected as a lawmaker in July 2013 has boycotted Parliament, along with the rest of the opposition that claims "They are in a safe place." The CNRP is seeking alternative ways to continue its campaign against the government.[30] Sam Rainsy plans to organize anti-government forces into many small groups and spread them out across the countryside where they would be harder to detect and suppress. Hun Sen's popularity is already declining and his new repression will sap it further. Even though the July 2013 elections were rigged and fraudulent, he lost a humiliating number of seats, while the CNRP won fifty-five of the 125 parliamentary seats. By April 2014, both sides were under pressure to come to terms. In addition, while Hun Sen usually shrugs off criticism from his Western detractors, China, his main source of international political and economic support, has also censured him. In return for ending its boycott, the opposition has won important concessions, such as the reform of the National Election Committee so that its members are chosen by all parliamentary parties and not just appointed by the government, which would give more hope of fairer elections in the future.[31]

Further, although the government may be authoritarian, it does not control the whole country. There are two independent, foreign-owned newspapers that are popular and one independent radio station run by Mam Sonando, who is a thorn in Hun Sen's side. Sonando was arrested three times over reports on his radio program that offended the government. His third arrest two years ago on charges of insurrection led to a long prison sentence, but the ruling was overturned after considerable pressure from Western governments. His radio talk shows regularly discuss topics ignored by most of Cambodia's news media, including the illegal seizure of land, the destruction of the country's forests, and corruption.[32] Generators power the radio station because Mam Sonando is afraid that if he is connected to the national grid, the government might cut off his broadcasts. Cambodia is ranked 144 of 180 countries in the World Press Freedom Index.[33] However, outlawing all dissent seems unimaginable. Though the television stations and Cambodian language newspapers are almost entirely controlled by Hun Sen, the Internet is uncensored and the two foreign-owned newspapers, *The Cambodian Daily* and *The Phnom Penh Post* regularly run reports that are critical of the government. Mam Sonando believes that the public is more politically aware these days and will not accept the government's attempt to block independent voices for much longer. Despite Hun Sen's recent clampdown after the demonstrations, his popularity has declined and he is vulnerable to change.

Alan Lightman sees his university graduates as having an impact on this vulnerability. The students not only find important work, but they also share their experiences in different communities, which helps to reduce the isolation of villagers. For example, one graduate Sivghech Chheng, who studied in the United States and found an excellent job when she returned, volunteers as a project trainer at an NGO called Kampuchea Action for Primary Education. She has arranged and organized multiple educational projects to share with other female university students in the province. She has taught them some of the important skills that she learned at the Harpswell Foundation as well as at her university, such as public speaking, communication, self-confidence, and English.[34]

In addition, over the last five years, the Harpswell Foundation has formed partnerships with other organizations around the world that are devoted to the empowerment of women. Alan Lightman has also connected the students and graduates to the Cambodian Women Entrepreneurs Association, a group of women in Cambodia who have started businesses, and also with the Global Women's Leadership Initiative (GWLI), founded in 2011 by Hillary Clinton with the mission of increasing the role of women in government and parliamentary positions. In partnership with GWLI, the foundation has established a two-week summer institute that includes classes on the skills women need to enter public service. One of the two weeks is to be held at Harpswell and the other at a Cambodian university.[35] The Harpswell Foundation hopes that its students will feel that their efforts to become leaders will not only benefit Cambodia, but will have benefit throughout the world.

TWELVE

Vidya Sri
and
Gangashakti

We live in a multicultural society, although the media do not reflect that sufficiently. Vidya Sri was brought up in New York City, enjoying her life, until she was severely traumatized and lonely when her parents decided to send her back to India for a forced marriage. Her pain was invisible to her family and to the man she was obliged to marry. The invisibility of her misery made it worse. She began to question herself, and the world she lived in, thus her story is also the universal saga of gender violence. She was deeply unhappy in her marriage, but led another life as a highly successful executive. After her divorce in 2010, she started Gangashakti, an organization to help women in forced marriages of all cultures and ethnicities in this country. Gangashakti partners with organizations around the world. Despite her difficult family situation, she succeeded in defining her interests, achieving a personal identity, and pursuing a goal beyond being a wife, mother, and dutiful daughter.

Vidya Sri lived in India with her grandmother until she was two years old. She then moved to join her parents in Queens, New York City, where she grew up. There was no tradition of forced marriages on either side of her family, although marriages on both sides had been arranged as was customary. Her parents, however, had met each other, fallen in love, and faced with great opposition on both sides of the family, had eloped. Vidya grew up as a typical American child, going to New York City public schools, riding public transportation, and loving to eat bagels and pizza.[1]

She became interested in boys when she was sixteen years old, and had her first real boyfriend when she was eighteen. She remembers him as a wonderful Irish-Catholic young man, with blue eyes and blond hair, and the sweetest disposition. He had strong values and a caring family, and she will never forget him. They dated for quite a long time before her father found out about him. For her father it meant only one thing—that she was going to marry this young man, and bear his children. Vidya tried to tell her father that it was just her first boyfriend, and that he came from a wonderful family.[2]

What Vidya had not foreseen was her parents' reaction. They constantly abused her, verbally and physically, telling her, "You have brought shame on us, you've disgraced and embarrassed us."[3] Vidya was shocked. It was a moment that changed her life and her future. Her father told her that she needed to return to India, that she wasn't fit to live the way she was living, and needed to learn how to be an Indian. To her, India was a remote place, and she thought of herself not as Indian, but more as an Indian American. For several months, Vidya tried to argue with them, but to no avail.

Her parents had a difficult marriage and were incompatible from the beginning. Her mother came from a progressive family that had converted to Christianity, and the women were educated and went to college. Her father's family was orthodox, conservative Hindi. His sisters were required to end their schooling at the equivalent of fifth grade, as it was the norm in his youth for people to perceive girls who were educated as likely to create problems for the family, a perception her father shared. Vidya's reaction to her misery and her unwillingness to go back to India was to drink too much alcohol. She even tried to commit suicide because she was terrified of what lay ahead for her.[4]

Imagine a young woman being thrust into a different country across the world where the climate, customs, language, and attitude towards women are totally different from those of her childhood. Her mother and brother moved to India with her and her father returned to Long Island, but visited often to supervise her. Upon arriving in Madras she was criticized for the way she spoke English, the way she dressed, and the fact that she used eye contact with people. Madras, one of the hottest and most humid places on earth, was a shock to her body as well as to her emotions.

As soon as they landed, her parents tried to find a college for her, but there were few spaces and the courses were already in session. Vidya's maternal grandmother had political contacts, and found a college where she knew the principal and where Vidya was immediately admitted. First, it was a woman's college, and second, although the courses were given in English, she had great difficulty understanding the way it was spoken. Vidya had never been in an environment with only women. She felt that it was a terrible punishment, and reinforced the way she was regarded as a shameful and bad person.[5]

Vidya had physical problems for the whole time she was there. She was constantly dehydrated, because during the day it was 120 degrees in the shade and very humid. She didn't drink water as she should have because there were only two latrines for several hundred women, and they were not clean. In addition, she had an upset stomach for four and a half years; even today she has great difficulty with her digestive system.[6]

Unexpectedly, Vidya found herself as an outcast where she was studying. The other young women would make fun of her, saying, "You must have done something really bad to get sent back here. Did you get pregnant, or did you sell drugs?"[7] Vidya was a very obedient child and she was shocked by the allegations. Even the professors mistreated her. First they told her that it was not correct to raise your hand and ask a question. At the end of the second day, one of the professors took her outside and told her, "It's not proper for a young woman of your age to be asking questions or raise your hand. You must have picked up this bad habit when you were in America."[8] The fact that Vidya was a gifted student made it all the more difficult. She began drinking alcohol every day, and once again tried to commit suicide a number of times.

To make matters worse, her father kept telling her that if she wanted to return to the United States she would have to get married, and she continued replying that she was only eighteen years old and didn't know what she would do after she finished college. Six months after her arrival, her parents brought a young man and his family to their home. They told her to go into another room and have a conversation with this man. Vidya was ready to marry anyone just to be able to return to her home, but the young man told his family that she wasn't the right woman for him.[9] After that Vidya kept telling her parents that she wanted to finish school, and then go back home to find work. This was the subject of their continual arguments, in which her father made it clear that there was no way she would return without a husband.

After she finished college, Vidya wanted to continue her studies in graduate school, but her father would not allow her that path. Instead she worked in his office. Given her unhappiness she became severely alcoholic. Alcohol is readily available in India, so she would start drinking in the morning, but nobody in her family realized what was happening.[10] Then one day, Vidya's family brought a man to meet her who was well educated and lived in the United States. When they met, they talked for a few minutes, and one week later they got married. This is not uncommon, even in arranged marriages. Vidya didn't tell the man that she was being forced into this marriage. She wept before and during the marriage. This man, who was a complete stranger, thought that he was entering an arranged marriage and that everything was fine.

When they returned to the United States, Vidya was very unhappy in her situation. She told her parents and her grandmother that the marriage was not going to work, that she didn't feel any intimacy, and that they weren't compatible. They dismissed her objections, telling her that her husband was so well educated and from a good family. They also told her that she should be grateful, because it was the best thing that ever happened to them.[11] These conversations were frequently repeated. Besides, her father believed in astrology and thought that their astrological charts showed the two were destined for each other. Vidya was terribly unhappy, stressed, and had difficulty pursuing her daily life.

Within a few months of their return to the United States, Vidya's father-in-law moved in with them. She begged her husband not to let him stay because they were complete strangers. He simply replied that his father had a right to live with them. Her husband was ten years older than Vidya, yet was always obedient to his father, a very traditional man who wanted to be listened to, and obeyed. In short, he was domineering.[12] In fact her father-in-law was home all day and she had no privacy. This was far from the life that a bright student and an "Indian American" girl had hoped for.

Vidya didn't know how to cope with her misery, so she began drinking once again until it became constant and she decided to attend Alcoholics Anonymous. She told her husband about her drinking problem, and that she had been depressed for years but he didn't take her problems seriously. It's possible that her husband lived in denial for many years. Vidya was married for eighteen years, during which she looked for support from her parents, her grandfather, her aunt, and uncle telling them she didn't want to stay in an unhappy marriage. What she didn't realize at the time was that she couldn't change strongly held cultural views of women and marriage. Her parents and extended family believed that a girl was meant to marry and have children, thus maintaining the integrity of the family. After many years she realized that her family didn't see the nature of her abuse, addiction, and violence. She was told that if she had children, everything would change.

After six years, Vidya found a job both to pay for her higher education, and, because she wanted a divorce, to support herself. She went to night classes and earned an MBA, finding a job in a bank. She moved through the ranks to become the manager of the bank, and then a regional manager of sixteen branches with over a billion in assets.[13] Meanwhile she had two children, a girl and a boy. Her husband moved first to Spain and then to California for his work. To say the least, she was extremely unhappy to leave her job. But she felt that, as always, she was the problem in her marriage and that she needed to be supportive to make the family work.

When they finally returned to their home in New Jersey, she became even more successful in her work. She became a vice president in a bank, managing over a billion dollars in assets with 160 people reporting to her. She loved working in teams and was well regarded and complemented for her leadership. But at the end of the day, she would come home to a different identity where she didn't matter and felt invisible. For years she wanted to leave with her family's help, but now she had her own options, as the money she earned gave her strength and set her free. She realized that she could buy a house, support her children, and feel secure.

She then started reading about forced marriage, and that opened a door for her. Before that she didn't have the words for what she had experienced, believing that she had failed her family. All of a sudden, she realized that she was not to blame for her situation. She told her husband that she wanted a divorce, and for the first time that hers was a forced marriage, not an arranged marriage. The first years after her divorce were tense because she endured hostility from her father, brother, and husband. With time, the tension eased and her work became a major neutralizing factor. Vidya became very close to her mother. Her parents had divorced many years earlier, but she had only heard her father's side of the story.

After she left her marriage, Vidya founded Gangashakti (Ganga, for the Ganges River, which signifies the life-empowering planetary energy of Mother Earth, and Shakti, meaning the power within) because she was sure that there were thousands of women like her. She had made enquiries of self-help groups and South Asian women's organizations, only to hear that they were sure that there weren't any forced marriages, so she knew that she had to start an organization. The idea was empowering and helped her chart her own path. A woman who had been criticized all of her life suddenly felt useful and filled with hope.

Forced marriage is something that very few people know about or understand. It is clearly a matter of human rights and social justice, but its victims hide in the shadows and their plight has been socially invisible. According to Article 16 in the Universal Declaration of Human Rights, "Marriage shall be entered into only with free and full consent of the intending spouses."[14] During rebel conflicts, such as in Sierra Leone, or in Nigeria, where over two hundred young girls were kidnapped, the public was awakened to what social media portrayed as a widespread and systematic attack on the civilian population. However, there has been no mention that hundreds of girls were subjected into forced marriage.

The stress of forced marriage was evident in Vidya Sri's married life and in the years preceding it. She was under physical duress before the marriage and, thereafter, she experienced psychological, financial, sexual, and emotional pressure. In short, forced marriage is a form of violence against women. Women often are unable to leave such marriages because of their continued surveillance by the extended families on both sides of the couple. In particular, culturally shaped views of gender roles dominate the experience of some immigrant families, as well as a desire to stem the influence of Western culture over their daughters, or to end their relationship with men they regard as unsuitable partners for their daughters. Some immigrant families wish to adhere to traditional cultural practices and thus maintain links with the communities from which they migrated. The *New York Times* gives an account of Amina Ajmal, an American citizen who was held captive for three years by her relatives in Pakistan and forced to marry a man there under the threat of death.[15] She escaped to an American embassy that sent her to a secret hideout in the United States. Her case went to court because Amina's father, a Brooklyn taxi driver, murdered members of the family of the person who helped her escape.

Forced marriages are not a phenomenon that occurs only within ethnic communities. In the words of Gangashakti: "Forced marriage impacts a wide variety of communities in the

United States. It crosses religious, cultural, and social-economic lines. No religion advocates forced marriage."[16] Western critics of forced marriage view it as an integral part of the cultures that enable it, while considering date rape and domestic violence as individual acts of violence.[17] But forced marriage occurs in Africa, China, British aristocratic circles, Ireland, and in many different ethnic communities in the United States. According to Dr. Shamita Das Dasgupta, historically forced marriage was practiced in Western societies among the upper classes and religious groups such as fundamentalist Mormons. From the late nineteenth century to the mid-twentieth century, state prosecutors in the United States often charged men with rape to force them to marry their sexual partners.[18] Forced marriages still exist in the Fundamentalist Church of Jesus Christ of Latter-Day Saints and the Tony Alamo Spiritual Ministry.[19] The UN Secretary General's Report on Violence Against Women states that gender violence "is manifested in a continuum of multiple, interrelated and sometimes recurring forms. It can include physical, sexual, and psychological-emotional violence and economic abuse and exploitation, experienced in a range of settings from private to public, and today's world, transcending national boundaries."[20]

Gangashakti is a small group, but it partners with many different groups that help women. It has a staff of three: a bookkeeper and accountant, a person who manages the outreach, and a case manager. A board of three provides strategic direction. Vidya works at the Carr Center for Human Rights Policy at the Harvard Kennedy Center as a fellow in the Initiative on Violence Against Women, while hard at work with her organization. Although her organization has accomplished a great deal, Vidya feels that forced marriage is a poorly understood situation in the United States. Fundraising is a problem for her organization because a lot of money is already spent in the United States and abroad promoting different aspects of forced marriage. She has identified a network of people who are spending millions in support of anti-Islamist movements around the world, but incidents of forced marriage or honor killings are very rarely brought to the attention of the general public.[21] Forced marriage is practiced in Hindi, Jewish, Catholic, and other Christian communities, but those that are intent on ostracizing Muslim communities do so with a political intent, which is a problem she deals with on a daily basis in her work. One has only to think of the right-wing leader, Marine Le Pen in France, to realize that people do not understand Islam.

Gangashakti performs a number of needed supports: managing individual cases; assisting survivors; transporting survivors across state lines; helping the women acquire new identities; and changing their social security numbers. It has had successes in advocating for survivors. Vidya works with a number of different services that interact with survivors, including those of physicians, social workers, and shelters for women who have experienced violence, as well as managers who work at domestic violence centers. The organization is very effective in advocating for a survivor every step of the way, staying in constant touch with her, and managing the services that she needs. Because of the many death threats the organization has received from families of survivors, Gangashakti no longer advertises its services on its website or anywhere else.

The organization also works with women who have endured domestic violence. It has received inquires from African American, Latin American, and Jewish women. It even helped a young Irish American woman who was in a forced marriage. Although she was pregnant, her husband brutalized her, and she lost the baby. He told her that he never wanted to marry her anyway and the woman told Vidya that she couldn't understand why her family had put her through her ordeal. She was without support because her parents blamed her for leaving the marriage, and they ostracized her.[22]

Vidya believes that forced marriages are the result of extreme interpretations of scriptures and social norms. In today's world, extreme interpretations of religion are more ideological than spiritual. Forced marriages take place on the fringes of society. She has found that there are thousands of cases in the United States, but that there is no infrastructure to provide support or services for women forced into marriages. The view she wants to make public is that forced marriage is not a mainstream practice, as arranged marriage, a safe well-intentioned practice that requires the consent of both parties. Arranged marriage doesn't involve physical abuse, trafficking, immigration fraud, or forcing people to cross borders. Unfortunately, there is a lack of understanding of the distinction between these two practices.

Gangashakti collaborates with two important organizations that serve women from South Asia. Manavi is dedicated to empowering women who trace their cultural heritage to South Asia, India, Pakistan, Nepal, Sri Lanka, and Bangladesh, making them aware of their rights in America. It is based in New Jersey, in an unmarked storefront, and has more than 300 clients. The organization received public attention when it conducted a candlelight vigil at Duke Island Park in Bridgewater to honor forty-three-year-old Janaki Dantulurui, a Bridgewater woman beaten to death by her husband, who has been indicted in her murder. Violence against women in the family has been normalized and hidden in South Asian societies, and Manavi aims to make it public.[23] The organization has more than fifty trained volunteers who staff a hotline twenty-four hours a day, seven days a week. It's difficult for abused women to come forward and make a telephone call, because they are often dependent on their husbands, especially economically, which makes them reluctant to seek help or leave an abusive situation, much less admit that they are victims. The biggest problem is shame because they believe that they may be bringing shame to their families. Confidentiality is at the center of the trust between clients and Manavi's staffers and volunteers. As that trust develops, counselors begin to explain the nature of abuse, and the options available to them. The women who come forward also learn that not all abuse is physical, but that emotional abuse can also be debilitating and leave permanent scars. Husbands are abusive when they exert power and control over their wives. Mothers-in-law can be the abusers, when they criticize their daughters-in-law for not fulfilling their duties to their husbands.[24]

Manavi was founded in 1985, the first South Asian Organization in the United States dedicated to raising awareness of women's rights and to advocate for change in South Asian communities so that all forms of abuse come to an end.[25] The core of that empowerment is education. Counselors explain how a victim can apply to the courts for a temporary restraining order, and the legal processes that follow. It offers semimonthly free legal clinics. Confidential advice is available on divorce, alimony, and child support with lawyers present to discuss immigration issues. The organization maintains a network of lawyers trained in the issues faced by South Asian women.[26] Manavi has offices in Washington, D.C., Baltimore, and Texas.

Vidya gave a presentation at a national South Asian Women's Conference that was hosted by Manavi, and that brought together all the South Asian women's organizations which work on domestic violence in the United States. As a result of her presentation, Gangashakti has built many different partnerships. It also partners with the Tahirih Justice Center, which protects immigrant women and girls who seek justice in the United States for gender-based violence, and that also coordinates the National Network to End Forced Marriage.[27] It provides pro bono legal services on immigration, family law, and social case management services to assure that its clients become self-sufficient. Since it was created in 1997, it has assisted over fourteen thousand women and girls fleeing abuse. In its survey on forced marriage in immigrant communities, it found an increasing number of women and girls as young as thirteen who by force, fraud, or coercion were compelled to marry men from their families' countries or region of origin.[28] Women that are U.S. citizens like Vidya might then be forced to sponsor a fiancé or spouse to enable them to come to the United States.

Gangashakti also partners with a network of domestic violence shelters and women's organizations in a number of states. Their locations are kept confidential because there have been instances in which young women have tried escaping, and their families tracked every domestic violence shelter in the country, and even threatened their staff. Vidya has found that threats are not always made by the groom, but, very often, by the parents or the extended family. In societies such as South Asian and African, girls are brought up to obey their parents and to carry the responsibility of their families' honor and respectability. As Jasvinder Sanghera points out in her book *Shame*, daughters are closely monitored while sons are given respect and freedom.[29] For a daughter, her whole world is caught up in her family, and thus even if she rebels and runs away, as did Jasvinder, she will miss and long for even those family members who treated her cruelly.

Vidya works to raise awareness of the plight of women in forced marriages throughout the country and around the world. She wants to lift the curtain on hidden abuse that is widespread but all too often invisible. Two distinct communities composed of women ages sixteen to forty-five years old are reaching out to Gangashakti. One community comprises a larger number of women looking for support to stay in a forced marriage where there has been no rape or brutality, and which they have no desire to leave. What they are looking for is a community to support them to stay in that marriage. The other smaller group is made up of women who are experiencing physical and psychological violence, including rape, and are looking for support to leave forced marriage. Vidya has found that some of them are so confused and upset that they need to know that they have some recourse. In these cases, it is usually a matter of time before they reach out.[30]

In order to reach these women, Vidya has been giving talks and workshops around the country that help women who need her support. If there is no one in the audience who needs her support, some people in the audience know women who do need it. She has received substantial information from her presentations at universities, including students and student organizations. There hasn't been an instance when somebody has not reported known cases of forced marriage. In fact, Vidya has found that students seem to know more cases than domestic violence workers, case managers and professionals, reinforcing that this is an issue that is underreported.[31]

Gangashakti has developed a questionnaire to broaden its information on forced marriage. The respondents were students primarily of South Asian origin. There were 521 confirmed or suspected cases of forced marriage, and 61 percent of known cases of forced marriage that were reported by students.[32] Vidya has found that typically fewer survivors attend her talks than friends or relatives of survivors. An important trait of forced marriage is control by their husbands and families on both sides. The group is very diverse, with many coming from affluent families with good educations, as well as women who live in poverty.[33] These results are reminiscent of the fact that in the U.S. domestic violence has nothing to do with economic status.

Vidya and her co-author Darakshan Raja, a researcher who evaluates criminal justice interventions with a focus on evaluating responses to crime victimization, have studied comprehensively how forced marriages violate women's human rights. They interviewed 524 people—students, domestic violence professionals, and refugee service providers. However, this group only represents a small number of cases that occur throughout the United States. The results of the survey found that 55 percent of women in forced marriage experienced emotional violence, 54 percent domestic violence, 50 percent depression, 35 percent financial and economic abuse, and 15 percent had attempted suicide.[34] Although the survey was conducted in just a few countries and with a small number of respondents, its results are representative of the many thousands, possibly even millions, who suffer abuse.

Forced marriage is very embarrassing for most people who suffer a great deal of shame for being in such a situation, as well as the pain of being brutalized. Vidya has been frequently asked why she just didn't refuse to simply obey her family. Survivors are burdened with their inability to say no, and have a deep need to be obedient, and to seek the love and validation of their families. In the case of *Shame*'s author, Jasvinder Sanghera, she was shown a photo of the man she had been promised to when she was only fourteen years old. When she wanted to get in touch with her mother after she ran away because she missed her, her mother screamed that she had disgraced the family and no longer belonged to the family she loved. Her mother's main concern was that her daughter must reflect the family's good name, and grow up to be a respectful and subservient daughter-in-law who could cook well. Jasvinder's mother married when she was fifteen and her older sister married at sixteen, again to a man she never met. She visited her married sisters, and saw how unhappy they were, while her mother told them to serve their husbands and stop complaining. One of her sisters committed suicide.

Jasvinder lives in England, and after she had created a new life for herself as a single woman, she founded Karma Nirvana, an organization similar to Gangashakti. Karma Nirvana operates a refugee center for women and girls who were running away from forced marriage, where the food is South Asian, and where they receive emotional support in an Asian atmosphere. Jasvinder found that the suicide rate in England among Asian women is three times the rate in the general population.[35] As among such families in the United States, secrecy is a cornerstone of family life, required by the insistence that family honor be maintained. In the United States, the studies that Gangashakti initiated found that the students it surveyed were the only group who knew about women who had committed suicide, constituting 2 percent of the responses to the survey. None of the professionals who worked with domestic violence cases or refugees reported knowing about suicides or attempted suicides.[36]

This harsh treatment of young women stems from a perceived need to control their chastity, which is equated with purity, a desirable quality for a potential bride.[37] Often what triggers a family's outrage is the discovery that a daughter has a boyfriend and that she doesn't want to get married. Members of the extended family as well as the parents tell them repeatedly, "You can't have a boyfriend. We are going to tell you who to marry," just like in Vidya's case.

Forced marriage is also used to address issues of homosexuality, because families believe that marriage will be a cure. There are also many cases of women being forced into marriage with men who have disabilities. Gangashakti has had a case in Texas where a young woman who was nineteen years old was forced to marry a man from another country who was severely disabled. She was brought there to become his caretaker without knowing anything about him, and he turned out also to be violent. Vidya found that both men and women suffer from violence in the process of forcing homosexual men to marry.[38]

Gangashakti has had numerous cases involving identity theft, and immigration fraud. Young people are being brought to the United States from other countries that might only be sixteen years old with a passport giving their age as eighteen or nineteen years old. The organization has dealt with a particularly difficult case of immigration fraud, in which a young woman who was a U.S. citizen, had a gun held to her head by her father who said "I will shoot you if you don't sign the sponsorship papers."[39] Gangashakti removed the file on this young woman because the family had access to the immigration file online and regularly checked its status. The removal was not only to protect the young woman, but also to remove it from processing so the person would not be brought to the United States. Furthermore, her family had created false documents for the prospective groom, claiming that he had a college education and faking a school certificate. In reality, the man had stopped his education at fifth grade.[40] Criminal acts related to immigration are frequently committed in the context of forced marriages.

Vidya noted that there is a lack of national data to present an accurate picture of the prevalence, need, challenges, and responses available for victims of forced marriage. The only national statistics are from a survey conducted by the Tahirih Justice Center of over five hundred agencies across the United States.[41] The findings from that study revealed that these agencies received approximately three thousand known and suspected cases of forced marriage, and that 67 percent of respondents reported cases of forced marriage that weren't being identified. Finally, the survey found that most agencies were not equipped to handle forced marriage cases.[42]

Vidya and her co-author also referred to a study by the Sauti Yetu Center for African women and families on early and forced marriage within the African immigrant communities in New York City. The findings were similar to those in South Asian communities—pressure from their families, friends, and extended families in New York, and around the United States. Also, these young women wanted to keep their relationships with their families, communities, and their culture, as an important part of a woman's identity lies in her culture, especially if it differs greatly from the dominant culture in the United States.[43]

Compared to England, the United States is far behind, not only in awareness but also in developing remedies for victims of forced marriage and a coordinated response to its practice. For example, Karma Nirvana helps women fleeing forced marriages. An important part of Jasvinder's work is listening to her clients because it makes them feel valued, probably for the first time. That involves ending secrecy because, if women remain silent or can't find the words to describe their situations, it is not possible to give them the help they need. What is remarkable is how closely the organization works with the police. Jasvinder has addressed police forces to explain the issues surrounding forced marriage and honor-based violence. Consequently, Karma Nirvana is supported by the head of the Metropolitan Police Violent Crime Directorate. Jasvinder installed a panic alarm button in her shelter for her clients who are at risk of physical harm. If she presses the button, a group of police will be at the shelter in minutes. The Home Office and Commonwealth Office established a Forced Marriage Unit for the rescue and protection of British girls forced into marriage in the United Kingdom and abroad. Furthermore, a Forced Marriage (Civil Protection) Act was passed in 2007 to give British courts the power to pass protection orders or injunctions preventing or preempting forced marriages from occurring.[44]

Vidya travels a great deal, to give workshops and attend conferences where she gives presentations and also for cases in several states that require one-on-one case management. She has traveled to the United Kingdom, which she views as being thirty years ahead of the United States, where she has met with the Forced Marriage Unit, and the head of a unit that is run by the Home Secretary's office. She has spent considerable time in the United Kingdom to gain a clear understanding of their processes and practices. She found that they have a number of civil protections and also a unit that can go into a foreign country and actually remove a victim who is being imprisoned or brutalized. Further, and most significantly, the United Kingdom has criminalized forced marriage, which Vidya is opposed to because she believes it will push all forced marriages and their extended families underground. European countries have signed the Istanbul Convention on Violence against Women, which requires its signatories to criminalize forced marriage. Vidya believes that this too will alienate many communities.

As if her work with forced marriage was not enough, Vidya leads a global research project with fifteen interns from around the world who are looking into specific acts of violence against women. The project is examining differing conventions of violence against women, such as the Convention to Eliminate All Forms of Discrimination against Women (CEDA), and their legal and implementation gaps. She sees this as a very long-term undertaking. She works with Rashida Manjoo, UN Special Rapporteur on Violence against Women. Rashida Manjoo and Vidya have a global working group made up of survivors, practitioners, and human rights attorneys. Vidya networks with a wide range of organizations specifically addressing violence against women, including grassroots, regional, and national organizations, as well men's organizations such as the Right Woman Coalition, and Men Engage, to address the issue of violence with both the survivors and the perpetrators.[45]

Vidya has launched collaborations with human rights clinics and law schools, such as at Yale University. The purpose is to find the gaps in CEDA, which is the only convention that attempts to address violence against women. Yale is helping her look into CEDA's long list of limitations. The University of Chicago and the Santa Clara Law School are helping her to look at a convention in Latin America and its effects on domestic legislation in certain countries. Vidya feels that it is important to engage a wide variety of students and research centers in order to get a diversity of perspectives.

There is also an activist component in Vidya's work. She partners with Lisa Shannon, a grassroots activist who has worked on violence against women in the Congo. Her executive director has worked in El Salvador. Vidya is concerned about the gap between international organizations and what happens locally, and feels that she is an example of someone who has fallen through that gap. When she fell through the cracks, no one saw the violence she experienced or did anything to help her, and she did not have the vocabulary or the skills to help herself. Gangashakti has given her a unique platform and autonomy because she refuses funding from political entities, which makes her feel all the more independent. Her own life has taught her that without grassroots efforts, an international law cannot be effective within a single country where there are so many different ethnic groups and practices. For example, when writing about legislation on the sexual assault of women, Amartya Sen describes India as a collection of distinct countries with diverse records, experiences, and problems.[46]

There are different kinds of intelligence—intellectual, on the one hand, and emotional, on the other. It is emotional intelligence that is needed to understand how to manage relationships. Vidya was a highly gifted student and successful bank manager. Nevertheless, she experienced loneliness and suffering, and it is that experience that inspired her to create an organization to help bring women with similar experiences out of the shadows and to provide services that respond to their particular communities.

THIRTEEN

Eric L. Adams:
Racism
and
Criminal Justice

In the fifty years since Martin Luther King, much has changed. There is a thriving black middle class and professionals in many fields. We have the first black president who has made important changes, such as making health care available to the disenfranchised, and Loretta Lynch is the second black attorney general to head of the Department of Justice. Yet, the institutionalized racism that affects voting rights, neighborhoods, jobs, poverty rates, racial profiling, education, and incarceration persists and needs to be addressed. There are two stories occurring in a nation that has remained divided, and a number of outstanding people who are working to bridge that divide.

One person who has spent his life trying to bridge that divide is Eric L. Adams, President of the Brooklyn Borough—the first black American to hold that office—and former state senator. Adams experienced horrific racism as a child. When he was fifteen years old, living in South Jamaica, Queens, he and his brother were arrested on a criminal trespass charge for unlawfully entering and remaining in the home of an acquaintance. The police took the brothers to the 103rd precinct, where an unarmed Sean Bell was later shot and killed by the police. They took the two boys down to the basement where they assaulted them, kicking them repeatedly in the groin, before they were taken to spend the night in the Spofford juvenile detention center. For a week after the boys were released there was blood in their urine. The brothers never talked about it or shared it with their parents until Eric Adams became an adult. They were confused, because they had regarded the police as a symbol of authority.[1]

As Eric Adams grew up he worked hard to put aside that shame and affront. Yet new incidents similar to his compelled him to relive those memories: Randolph Evans, Patrick Dorismond, Abner Louima were killed, and Amadou Diallo was severely wounded with a broomstick. Too many other young men reminded him of his own dark secret and what it did to them. Reverend Herbert Doherty and leaders in the community wanted Eric Adams and other young black men to go into law enforcement in order to fight from within. When Mr. Adams joined the New York City police department he felt that he was so recklessly overt about police infractions and racism that the people he worked with thought he was a man possessed. "I just had a reckless disregard for the career to just fight for dealing with the issue of racism in the police department in our lives. Much of what I was saying and what I was demonized for saying is materializing in today's times."[2]

Yet Eric Adams spent twenty-two years in the police department, becoming a police captain, as well as attending college and graduate school. When he first joined the police he saw officers touching the lockers of their fallen brothers and beginning their shifts on the defensive, thinking about protecting themselves rather than the communities they served. One of his white fellow officers told him that if he saw a white individual with a gun, he took extra care for himself and that person. When he saw a black person with a gun, he took care only of himself.[3]

In 1995 Mr. Adams was one of a group of concerned African Americans who founded 100 Blacks in Law Enforcement Who Care. In its first year, $10,000 was collected from the membership and distributed to needy individuals and organizations throughout the city of New York. The organization grew quickly and understands that social problems are at the core of too many criminal actions and unfair responses. It states its mission in religious terms, because black churches across the country include caring for their congregations' problems and are an important base for grass roots activity. Its other missions include advocating for justice for people who have not traditionally had a voice in our society, challenging racism and sexism, as well as economically empowering black people by pooling its resources. It has a regular spot every Tuesday evening in the call-in show Community Cop, on the Manhattan Neighborhood TV Network, and runs survival workshops and a website that people can refer to if they are involved in an incident with the police. Eric Adams and 100 Blacks in Law Enforcement Who Care understand that social and economic policies are needed to address racial disparities in the crime rates in some urban areas and that police need guidance to prevent them from making biased and unethical choices.[4]

Thanks to Eric Adams, our country is just beginning to have a conversation about institutionalized racism, which white people have hitherto ignored. Racial profiling defines so many areas of people's lives, especially in police stops when racial minorities are questioned, handcuffed, and searched at dramatically higher rates than whites. Black people regard these stops as unfair and distrust the police, as such profiling makes innocent people look like criminals, feel like second-class citizens, whose privacy has been invaded and their dignity undermined. These unjust stops are not the result of a discriminatory police officer but a countrywide practice with a structure of incentive-driven training and policy that make it more likely that officers will base their decisions on stereotyping that reinforces racial disparities. For example, a well-known black baseball player was sitting in his car going through his papers in a parking lot outside of a bank in an affluent, mainly white, and town was arrested for a theft he was not aware of. Fortunately, his fame protected him.

Investigatory stops focus on young black men in poverty-stricken areas. They involve probing questioning and invasive searches. Those investigated, seemingly for no reason, feel that these stops are unfair. They view how they are treated as a measure of their standing in the community, and these stops confirm that they are not considered full and equal members of society. These practices harm people, most of whom are innocent. Yet, the police are awarded and celebrated for making these arrests. It is easier to make arrests in the disorderly setting of poor, urban neighborhoods where residents spend more of their time and conduct their transactions outdoors, where they are most vulnerable to surveillance. An important feature of police work is a strong commitment to fighting crime, with a focus on poor neighborhoods and there is a collective belief that authority must be exercised firmly to head off threats of violence.[5] Because the federal war on drugs targeted low-level drug dealers and users and was deeply biased and based on the belief that minorities are the primary users and traffickers of illegal drugs, police and highway patrol officers became the enforcers of drug laws. The Drug Enforcement Agency taught ordinary frontline officers how to carry out investigatory stops and make arrests, guided by profiles of drug couriers that highlight ethnicity and race.[6] Following a Supreme Court Decision ruling that stops are legitimate if based on any objective violation of the law, no matter how minor, officers may use minor violations as a pretext for questioning about more serious criminal acts. Thus the difference between a legal and an illegal stop is not a matter of what an officer said and did, but of how he or she describes it.[7] The usefulness of such stops is greatly exaggerated, as their costs are substantial and barely recognized. Such stops violate the norm of fair treatment. While black drivers commonly report being subjected to intrusive investigatory stops, the few white drivers who are stopped describe them to be brief and based on plausible reasons. In fact, black people are 270 percent more likely than whites to be subjected to such stops.[8] In addition police act more intrusively toward black people than whites, as they tend to handcuff black drivers, giving them sobriety tests and ultimately arresting them.

Eric Adams believes that it is necessary "to peel back the onion," and examine the many layers of black peoples' lives. One in particular layer to be examined is that millions of young black men in poor communities are targeted for prison, which is an important part of racial oppression. How many people notice that the growing number of prisoners come from poor and segregated black communities around the country? Black people are 13 percent of our population, but 37 percent of our imprisoned population as President Obama pointed out in 2015. Racial differences are reinforced by class differences. Incarcerations of young black males means that they are out of school, work and family life, only to return with felony convictions, which result in lower wages and gaps in employment. In many states, people with felony convictions are denied the right to vote, access to many government jobs, public housing and other benefits.[9] Even worse, the tough-on-crime policy affects family, friendship, and community relations. The police disrupt these relationships, not only by cultivating informants, but pitting family members, friends, and neighbors against each other. Police departments across the country have installed computers in police cars so that officers can access social security records, court records, hospital admission records, and electricity and gas payment records. A police officer can visit a suspect's home or the street corner where he is likely to be, threaten his family and friends if they refuse to cooperate, and even has the ability to track people's cell phones.[10]

Fear of capture and imprisonment is more than hard on young men with arrest warrants or on probation or parole and have restrictions placed on them such as going out at night, driving, drinking alcohol, seeing their friends or visiting certain areas of their community. Given their intense policing, encounters with police are very likely while they are under such restrictions and could result in the violation of the terms of their release and a quick return to prison. Consequently, these young men may be prevented from visiting their girlfriend at the hospital after the birth of their baby, attending a funeral, or carrying on a normal social life. It also means that these young people fear using the courts, or calling the police if they need help. They are thus vulnerable to threats of violence by people who know they won't retaliate by pressing charges. Sometimes they too may use violence or defend themselves. Members of their community or neighborhood members experience frequent acts of violence in the streets, such as people getting kicked or beaten, but view the authorities as useless for protection, despite their constant presence.[11]

Of the many stops and frisks one of the most memorable is the story of Sandra Bland, a black woman pulled in Texas by the police because she failed to signal that she was changing lanes. She was arrested and later committed suicide in prison three days after her arrest in July 2015. She told her jailers that she suffered from depression, but they failed to keep watch on her or provide her with the help she needed.

Sandra Bland's story highlights another issue; although Texas state law forbids "ticket quotas," state troopers are evaluated in part according to their numbers. The institutional practice of tying a police officer's career advancement by the money he garners from stops undermines fair and just results. A Department of Justice Report of March 2015 found that in Ferguson, Missouri, black people bore the brunt of a policing and law enforcement system designed to generate revenue. After that scathing report on its police and municipal court practices, the manager, judge, and police chief resigned. One of Ferguson's two newly elected black council members said that the practices that fell under heavy scrutiny were being corrected. The Governor of Missouri signed a bill that limited revenue from traffic to 12.5 percent general operating revenue rather than a much higher rate, but that was the only law that was passed after the turmoil following the death in 2014 of an unarmed teenager Michael Brown.[12] Other bills that would have made Missouri's use of force compliant with a 1985 Supreme Court decision, made body cameras mandatory, and required special prosecutors to investigate officer shootings, were not passed.[13]

Yet one year after the shooting of the young man, a commission appointed by the governor of Missouri came out with a long report calling for sweeping changes across the St. Louis region on policing, the courts, education, housing, and more. The top priorities include increasing the minimum wage and consolidating the sixty police forces and eighty-one municipal courts that cover St. Louis and the suburbs. It reveals what black people have known for decades: black drivers are 75 percent more likely to be pulled over for traffic stops in Missouri and 14.3 percent of black elementary school students were suspended at least once during a recent school period compared with 1.8 percent of whites.[14] The most important recommendations are those relating to policing, such as assigning the state attorney general as a special prosecutor in all cases of police force resulting in death, requiring the statewide use of forces database, following up use of force complaints, and the revision by police departments of their policies and training to authorize only the minimum use of force required. But as already noted, only one law was passed by the Republican-controlled state legislature after the Ferguson incident, so there is little expectation that any of the commission's recommendations will be implemented.

But the report has spawned an engagement with grassroots organizations that are launching campaigns to work toward the commission's recommendations for racial equity, justice for all, economic mobility, and more. Reverend Starsky Wilson is very active in working toward change and plans to create an organization that will support different actors and groups in the community that are seeking change and to work with elected officials to achieve bipartisan support to pass bills. In the black community churches are very involved in social issues and justice, and their outreach is an important part of change. Wilson hosted Black Lives Matter to join the community in its efforts.

Another of Eric Adams's layers of the lives of black people relates to the story of the many black journalists who converged on Ferguson to write about Michael Brown and the protest movement. In the year since Michael Brown's death, the national conversation about police brutality has expanded, in part because members of the National Association of Black Journalists have become part-time police and criminal justice reporters. It is as if they are on the front lines, the same way as reporters covering overseas wars, but the events they cover are the stories of their friends and families. For example, *New York Times* columnist Charles Blow wrote about how his son, a student at Yale, had a gun pulled on him by the campus police who thought he didn't belong in the college library.[15] The people who are the focus of these stories bring up every aspect of their painful encounters with police, turning news-reporting into a very emotional job and leading to burnout or thoughts about resigning, when in fact, more black reporters are needed. The treatment of Wesley Lowery, a reporter for the *Washington Post*, who covered the 2014 demonstrations in Ferguson is a relevant example. He was detained while reporting and charged in St. Louis County with trespassing and interfering with a police officer and ordered to appear in court. Reporter Ryan Reilly of the *Huffington Post*, arrested at the same time, will face the same charges. In both cases, the reporters will have the wholehearted support of their newspapers.[16]

Police Departments take a "broken windows" approach that allows them to enforce laws intended to control ordinary street disorder, such as loitering, drinking, but, of course, it was that approach that resulted in the widely reported case of Eric Gardner who was selling cigarettes on the streets of New York and died in a police chokehold. In addition, the war on drugs of the Reagan administration and the first Bush administration fostered the arrest of a large number of ordinary drug users and low-level dealers, which was guided by a false premise of black people as the main users and sellers of dangerous drugs.

Eric Adams points out that the police departments responded in an aggressive fashion because they were able to do so under the cloak of editorial boards and newspaper headlines. For example, how many people realize that the news reports of rising drug addiction in Massachusetts never included the wealthy white town of North Andover? Eric Adams has claimed that it's possible to create laws that criminalize any kind of behavior—that groups can be studied and the things that they do identified and determined as criminal offenses. In the world of crack and cocaine, police arrest those who use the drugs as well as those who sell them. Eric Adams found that in one cocaine racket, the district attorney was uncovering a major drug delivery service, but not one of the buyers of the drug was arrested, many of them were professionals such as doctors and lawyers.[17] He has raised his voice to ask why the lists of buyers were not turned over to the relevant professional organizations, so that if the district prosecutors are not interested in charging these people, they should at least seek the censure of professional oversight bodies.

On a website called Thee Rant, founded by a former NYPD officer Ed Polstein in 1999, members of police departments post ugly racist comments that, according to Eric Adams, help us "realize the depth of the psychologically damaged people who have a gun and a shield and take away two of the most precious items we hold dear in America that is life and liberty."[18] Racists post comments defining black people as "apes," and a retired police officer wrote, among other racist comments, that a Middle Eastern cab driver berated by an officer was "a 'third worlder' who should have 'his head split open.'"[19] Garner's death prompted substantial support for the officer and a number of ugly comments on Thee Rant.

Given the widespread coverage of police brutality against black people and other minorities, there have been disclosures of racist text messages around the country. For example, two high-ranking officers in the Miami Beach Police Department sent around 230 emails containing racist and sexist jokes from 2010 to 2012. A former police captain was fired and a major retired before the investigation was made public.[20] There were similar incidents in Edison, New Jersey, Baton Rouge, Louisiana,

Castleberry, Florida, Clastine, Oregon, and in Georgia. In San Francisco, a city known for its liberal politics, inflammatory text messages that circulated among fourteen police officers became public as part of the corruption trial of two officers. Black people have complained for years about harassment and the excessive use of force by police. And while black people comprise 5 percent of San Francisco's population, they account for half of its arrests and prisoners, and more that 60 percent of the children in juvenile detention.[21] Fortunately, a task force of prosecutors was already scrutinizing three thousand cases that included 1,600 convictions related to arrests made by these fourteen officers to determine if any biases led to any unlawful arrests or wrongful prosecution. The panel is also examining whether racial biases exist in the police department. Seven of the officers who had exchanged racist text messages were fired.[22] The chief attorney in the public defender's office said that, over the years he had listened to many clients claim that officers lied in their police reports or gave false testimony to a judge. This investigation by a panel of judges represents a dramatic change, as such practices have occurred for decades. The news and television station CBS San Francisco has this case on airtime, which is a welcome change in the coverage of racist behavior by members of the police force.

Consequently the secrecy that protects police files is now being challenged, and there is a national push to obtain law enforcement information that has been unavailable outside its ranks for too long. Journalists and civil liberties advocates have long clamored for the release of data about questionable police actions, but it has been the crisis of confidence in law enforcement following the death of Eric Garner and the fatal shooting of Michael Brown that has propelled the issue onto legislative and political agendas across the country. In addition, the many demonstrations after these deaths that were widely publicized at both the national and the community level, have brought the behavior of some police officers to public attention. In addition, cell phone cameras capture their behavior in these events. Before he resigned in April 2015, Attorney General Eric Holder invoked the issue of transparency as a key element of restoring trust between the police and the people they serve. Law enforcement leaders across the country are increasingly confronting demands for police information and transparency in the criminal justice system.

New York City gives the police more protection from scrutiny than most states; section 50-a of the New York Civil Rights Law of 1976 protects officers' personnel records from being released to the public, or from being cited in court without judicial approval.[23] In some states such as California and New Jersey, courts ruled that, unless an officer's safety is threatened, police departments must name officers involved in shootings. Although the police commissioner William J. Bratton has identified officer Pantaleo following Mr. Garner's death, which has helped defuse tensions, the names of other officers involved were not disclosed. Secrecy still prevails in most misconduct cases, including those investigated by New York City's complaint board.[24]

Then there is the issue of harsh arrests, what Eric Adams has called "the culture of police brutality." In a mistaken sting operation for credit card fraud, a well-known biracial tennis player James Blake, who left Harvard University to pursue his career, was flung to the sidewalk in New York City, demanded to turn over and shut his mouth, and then was handcuffed. Police Commissioner Bratton and the mayor of New York City spoke out against what occurred and apologized to Mr. Blake. Mr. Blake told the reporter, "This happens too often and most of the time it's not to someone like me."[25] Commissioner Bratton did not learn of what happened until members of his public affairs staff told him about the news reports of the episode. In other words, this would have been another case that never came to light if the victim had not had such a high profile. Mr. Blake's meeting with both Mayor de Blasio and Mr. Bratton was successful in the sense that he and his lawyers clearly stated that he wasn't after money from a lawsuit, but rather wanted significant changes in police behavior. It was an important beginning.

Before this incident two police officers sitting in their patrol care were murdered by a black man who had traveled to New York with the aim of killing policemen to avenge the deaths of Eric Garner and Michael Brown. After killing them, he later killed himself, but it was an incident that publicly divided the city. Former mayor Rudy Giuliani was one of the many who linked the national protest movement, a civil rights movement against racial injustice, to the killing. He claimed, "We've had four months of propaganda starting with the president that every one should hate the police."[26] The president of the Patrolmen's Benevolent Association criticized Mayor de Blasio by saying, "The Mayor's hands are literally dripping with our blood because of his words, actions and policies and we have for the first time . . . become 'a wartime police department.'"[27] Thousands of officers, many from across the country, attended the funeral of one of the policemen. When Mayor de Blasio took his place at the pulpit to deliver his eulogy, he bowed his head, grief stricken and deferential, while the policemen all turned their backs on the mayor. Some of the officers claimed that what offended them most was the mayor's recounting his conversations about the police that he and his wife had with their son Dante who is black, "Don't move suddenly, don't reach for your cell phone."[28] The population of New York City is 33 percent white and 51 percent of the NYPD is white, whereas 26 percent of the population and 16 percent of the NYPD are black. Many black police officers have recounted that they had been harassed or racially profiled by police when they have been off duty. While this incident has revealed the divide in our country, Mr. Bratton has spoke about the continual distortion through which police and black Americans see each other and how we needed to vanquish this unfortunate distortion.[29]

Eric Adams claims that it still difficult for black people to get into NYPD and that there is a need to break down those barriers to ensure that all groups are allowed in. He added that we should live in touch with our culture and honor our diversity. Corye Douglas, a twenty-eight-year-old black college student who is also a sergeant in the National Guard, is an example of how difficult it is for a highly qualified black person to enter the NYPD. He passed the police officer exam in 2011 before he started undergoing background checks in 2013, after which the process stopped and he endured silence for eighteen months. White men who apply to join the police force are more likely to have friends and neighbors on the force, and often know someone who can navigate the bureaucracy. The percentage of white candidates who pass the exam and are hired is higher than the percentage of black people who pass the test. NYPD surveyed eleven thousand applicants who were trying to join the force in 2013. The candidates said that they had received inadequate information on how the hiring process worked and cited a lack of support from the employees who process applications and a lack of communication from the department as reasons for dropped out during hiring.[30] At a time of increased tensions between the police and minority communities eliminating such hurdles is critical.

Eric Adams has also shed light on the "no-snitch" culture. Members of the police force believe that they have to speak with one voice and cover up for the costly errors of their members. He knows that "there is a real culture of us against them in the police department right now. With that culture comes the feeling that there should be a blue wall of silence rule to cover up the wrong doing of your colleagues."[31] Mr. Adams believes that the police should police themselves and make sure that those who are not worthy of their jobs should not be part of the department.

The racism of incarceration is linked to the police and the criminal justice system in our country. According to Eric Adams, "We should stop using prison as an answer to the problems we are facing and need to move away from a prison industrial nation to a nation of creating and identifying what causes people to do particularly drug related crimes, identifying paths to sobriety, and making people productive citizens."[32] No country in the world imprisons as many people as the United States does, and none hold its prisoners for such a long time. The United States has more than 5 percent of the world's population but about 25 percent of the world's prisoners. Furthermore, African Americans and Hispanics are imprisoned at six times the rate of whites. A third of young black men will be incarcerated at some point in their lives. Most of the inmates are men, but at 113 per 100,000, the incarceration rate of black women is higher than the overall incarceration rate in France of Germany.[33] Reforms by Eric Holder may explain the small recent fall in federal prison numbers. However, even if there is a perceived desire for reform, the expanded prison system has built itself into the fabric of society and the economy. Judges, district attorneys, state and federal politicians, police forces, prison guard unions, federal agencies, and private firms that build and run prisons have not only contributed to the rise of mass incarceration but have benefited from it. In rural areas, prisons are now the biggest employers.[34] The "Three Strikes" sentencing provisions that require a prison sentence for anyone committing a third offence, even if it is minor like stealing a bicycle, has resulted in the incarceration of too many people who present no threat to society.

People are held in terrible conditions in the bigger prisons. Amnesty International found thousands of prisoners confined to windowless cells for twenty-three to twenty-four hours a day, without any education or sensory stimulation. Most prisons in Texas where the summer heat can rise to 140 degrees and have no air conditioning. In many women's prisons, inmates are routinely raped, and those who complain are punished with solitary confinement or threats of violence. When prisoners are released they get a bus ticket and $100 while those out on parole receive $50.[35] Such lack of help promotes recidivism. In many states former felons cannot receive food stamps, or get into public housing. In a number of trades, having a conviction excludes a person from employment.

The issue of gun control is extremely important given the number of guns in the United States. Eric Adams can see no reason for the proliferation of assault rifles in our country, or for the use of high-capacity magazines that are able to carry too many bullets. "It is imperative that our law is applicable to the present times and to be sure that we are not allowing the over proliferation of hand guns."[36] While a state senator, Eric Adams was co-chair of New York's State Legislators against Illegal Guns. He also introduced a proposal to allow cameras on guns and police vehicles.[37] Yet in the heated presidential nomination campaign in 2015, although candidates have spoken out against violence, none of them have offered policies to address gun violence given the NRA's powerful role in politics and society. Leading Republican presidential candidates are overwhelmingly opposed to any efforts to restrict access to guns. And, after Dylann Roof killed nine people at the Emanuel African Methodist Episcopal Church in Charleston, South Carolina, Hillary Clinton made sure to acknowledge that "gun ownership is part of the fabric of many American communities."[38] She has, however, called for universal background checks, and for stronger efforts to block people who are on the terrorist watch list, who suffer from mental illness, or have records of domestic abuse from obtaining firearms. (It is perhaps significant that the background check on Dylann Roof was not completed.)

Although the FBI counts over four hundred justifiable homicides by police every year, this only includes those shot while committing crimes, and, as reporting such shootings is voluntary, the real number is higher. Attorney General Loretta Lynch has started a program in the fall of 2015 to create more openness on police homicides. She has also been an important presence in Baltimore after Freddy Gray died from a spinal injury in a police van. The program has a long way to go given the no-snitch culture of many police stations in poverty-stricken and segregated neighborhoods, but her openness about her plan has created hopes for change.

In contrast to the United States, in the year 2013, police in England and Wales fired weapons three times and killed no one. American police work in a country with three hundred million guns and a murder rate six times that of Germany.[39] One in three families across the United States own guns. Even President Obama, whom Eric Adams refers to with much pride, has spoken about the failure to control the sale of assault weapons. After Dylann Roof's crime, President Obama said that we have to confront the fact that this type of mass violence doesn't happen in other developed countries. Unfortunately, after mass shootings such as the one in Newtown, and at the community college in Oklahoma, the purchase of guns and of publicly traded shares in gun companies, such as Smith & Wesson, surged.

Despite what Eric Adams has referred to as police brutality, he believes that there is a new kind of police officer throughout the country who is striving to hold their profession to a higher standard. For example, Durham, North Carolina, and an increasing number of cities are using the stop and search data collected by their departments to galvanize supporters and pressure departments to change policies. In Austin, Texas, written consent is now required for searches without probable cause, after an independent police monitor reported that whites stopped by police were searched one in every twenty-eight stops while blacks were searched in one of eight stops. Following a similar initiative in Kalamazoo, Michigan, traffic stops declined 42 percent.[40] More than fifty police departments across the country have begun participating in studies that use traffic stop data as a powerful tool in analyzing police behavior.

Although the findings may have demoralized police officers, the black community has offered to help. In North Carolina, the organization and prominence of a community group, The Durham Congregations, Associations and Neighborhoods was very important in bridging the divide. In addition, a lecturer at the University of North Carolina who trains defenders has written a new manual for defense lawyers, prosecutors and judges with a chapter that shows how stop and search tactics can be used by the defense to raise challenges where race may have played a role.[41]

Police have a close relationship with prosecutors, which helps lead to the fact that our criminal justice system is also a source of oppression against black people. Local prosecutors, with close relationships to the police and sheriff's officers, choose the witnesses and ask the questions. Victims or their lawyers can submit questions from a public gallery, but they have no power to question witnesses themselves. The failure of grand juries in Ferguson and Staten Island to indict white police officers that killed black men has created outrage across the country. In most of the cases, the grand jury is a brief pro-forma event in which the prosecutor presses the criminal charges, putting forth only the most damning evidence against the accused. Eric Adams has proposed that special grand juries should be convened for a police-related event, and independent agencies should gather evidence before they convene when a death has occurred during a police encounter.[42]

Then there is the fact that that in most states there are few black prosecutors. About 95 percent of the elected state and local prosecutors across the country are white and 79 percent white men. Yet white men are 31 percent of the population.[43] While the numbers of black people in mayoral positions, police forces, and state senates are increasing, there is a need for black prosecutors. This paucity of prosecutors is in part responsible for black people's lack of trust in the judicial system. In addition, many innocent people are subject to a demand from their prosecutors and from the lawyers advising them to consider plea bargains. Fortunately, the Innocence Project is working in many states to release innocent people from jail, but they are not able to help the many thousands who need them.

The criminal process ensures that impoverished black men who cannot afford lawyers will have almost no access to pro bono legal aid. A two-year study at the Vera Institute of Justice found a pattern of racial disparity at many stages of the criminal process. When they involve plea bargains, which is how the majority of criminal cases get resolved, Manhattan prosecutors consider a defendant's prior arrest record in making a decision. Since black people are more likely to come from heavily policed neighborhoods, where arrests for minor offences are part of life, the study found that if prosecutors based plea bargains on a person's previous prison sentences, instead of their prior arrests, much of the racial disparities would disappear.[44] The same process takes place in New Orleans that has one of the highest incarceration rates in the state of Louisiana and in the United States. There, the lack of public defenders creates serious problems. A public defender spends five minutes on each of many defendants; judges spend about ten minutes on each case and set bail at $5,000 and even $10,000. The defendants are poor, black, and often innocent. Given their poverty, they end up behind bars.[45]

There is also a great racial gap in selecting jurors. One has only to remember that in the Trayvon Martin case in Sanford, Florida, all the jurors were white. Eric Adams wore a hood similar to the young man who was killed, when his killer, George Zimmerman was acquitted. In many states, prosecutors use preemptory challenges three times as often to eliminate black potential jurors as others.[46] The acquittal rate of black people depends upon the number of black jurors. The presence of more black prosecutors in our courts would ensure that jury selection is less biased.

Yet, under President Obama the Justice Department made important changes by filing documents in cases where people were too poor to be adequately represented in municipal court cases. Under federal law the attorney general can argue on behalf of the government's interest in any court in the country, as has happened in previous administrations. Government lawyers do not argue the facts of a case, but give clear support to plaintiffs and put the federal government on the record in cases that are at the forefront of civil rights law where legal aid is implicated. Rather than the time-consuming effort of lawsuits, the practice of filing statements of interest in local court cases helps to promote civil rights.[47]

An important response to police behavior toward minorities comes in the numerous and frequent op-ed essays and bold graphs by Charles M. Blow in the *New York Times*. They have the striking effect of showing the white readership of that newspaper the profoundly different attitudes of different races towards the police. Other responses are the work of the National Association of the Advancement of Colored People (NAACP) and the Southern Poverty Law Center (SPLC). For over forty years SPLC has done invaluable work monitoring hate groups across the country and giving legal support to their victims. It contradicts views that Dylann Roof's killing is just that of an angry, isolated young man. SPLC works hard to bridge the gap between races and promote justice. Roots Action, the Color of Change, and the movement Black Lives Matter are all signs of changing times. Recently the Color of Change donated five hundred books to Texas schools to emphasize the omission of slavery, Jim Crow, and the Ku Klux Klan from children's textbooks.

Then there are people like Ta-Nehisi Coates, recent MacArthur Award winner, and frequent contributor to the popular *Atlantic Monthly Magazine*, on issues of black lives and the problems of racism, and Mychal Denzil Smith contributor to the *Nation*. The widely read *Time* magazine has also recently published an article with many grim color photos of a policeman chasing an unarmed Walter Scott in North Charleston, South Carolina, in April 2015 and then shooting him eight times in the back as he was running away. The article emphasizes the importance of the damning video that captured the killing and lists the names of black people, with their photos, killed by the police. Online investigative journals like *Pro Publica, Daily Kos, Take Part Daily,* and *Black Community Kos* focus on the oppression of black people and attempt to bridge the racial divide in their wide audiences. *Daily Kos* was founded by Shaun King who was outraged by the injustice he witnessed and gave up his job to create and focus on the online magazine.

Eric Adams has frequently spoken out about the need for technology to create transparency of police behavior. If it were not for the video, the police officer's story would have been believed and the country would never know about Walter Scott. Thanks to the video, Officer Michael T. Slager was fired after the shooting and a few months later he was indicted by a grand jury on a murder charge.[48] Also Walter Scott's family received a large settlement. A video shows the 2014 police shooting of twelve-year-old Tamir Rice in Cleveland, Ohio; it also shows how his fourteen-year-old sister rushed to help him, only to be grabbed by police officers, handcuffed, and thrust into a police van while Tamir bled to death. Such widespread use of videos and their easy distribution hold up a mirror to white people, making them conscious of the unfair treatment of black people whose problems they are not aware of, and helping some of them to reassess their attitudes.

Images captured by car dash cameras in squad cars, which previously have been kept from public viewing by the police department, are increasingly made available. For example, in 2014, the public pressured the police to reveal the actions of officer Jason Van Dyke in Chicago. A year after the death of Laquan McDonald, a video of his killing showed the officer shooting the seventeen-year-old sixteen times for no apparent reason other than the story given by the police. As a result of releasing the video, Van Dyke was charged with first-degree murder. Peaceful marches of outraged people of all ages and races, especially members of Black Lives Matter, were held. Groups of people demonstrated on Black Friday 2015, not only in Chicago, but also in Seattle, Minneapolis, and New York, linking their protests over police conduct and the treatment of black people to a day when the nation's focus is on shopping.[49] Five days after the release of the video, under great pressure from the public, Chicago mayor Rahm Emanuel announced he would expand a program for body cameras that started in one police district in January

2015.[50] In fact, many people are asking for his resignation for not releasing the video. In Chicago, the nation's third-largest city, police officers shot and killed seventy people, most of them black, in a five-year span ending in 2014. The Chicago police department has been known for issuing little or no punishment on its own, even after a 2007 overhaul of its discipline system. Under that system, the vast majority of complaints still do not result in discipline. The police superintendent and the police board have the last word in settling the most egregious cases.[51]

As a result, on December 7, 2015, Attorney General Loretta Lynch announced that the Justice Department would investigate whether the Chicago Police Department has systematically violated the civil rights of citizens when it uses deadly force and how it held those officers who used excessive force accountable.[52] She added that the Justice Department would look at the constitutional practice of the use of force, then issue her findings publically, create an accountability system such as a monitor for police behavior in Chicago and work collaboratively with the police department. Attorney General Lynch has emphasized that building trust between the police and the communities they serve is one of her highest priorities.[53]

Eric Adams has been active on such issues throughout his working life. As someone in political office he knows that the time to tell the truth is when there is public awareness. He wrote an op-ed about police brutality in 2014, and in 2015 he wrote a long article for the *New York Times* about the way policing used to be and the horrific practices in which the community was treated when an officer was assaulted. He stated that this was an inextricable part of the policing culture in the United States.[54] Stories that would have never come out are now widely published by newspapers and magazines. For example, the *Guardian* published a story about how the Chicago Police Department, supported by Mayor Rahm Emanuel, kept the secret of people in a facility, Homan Square, where they were brutally interrogated without access to lawyers or their families. Not surprisingly, 82 percent of the detainees were black, and many of them charged with minor infractions such as driving without a seat belt.[55]

Eric Adams concluded, "Rarely has a profession with so much unchecked power been checked in an emphatic fashion by ordinary citizens, not the government."[56] Throughout his working life, Eric Adams has insisted that the police adopt body cameras and release footage in all situations, except when public safety is at risk. Relying on his own experiences as a policeman, he has also been concerned about improving the training of police especially what takes place in precinct lockers and on street patrols. He concluded, "The era of darkness is over."[57] He has defined his work as the President of the Brooklyn borough as furthering digital education, hosting workshops in a variety of areas for young people, providing affordable transportation, helping to create newspapers for ethnic communities and more. He is constantly in touch with the events that occur and with individuals in need of assistance and even joined a protest march. If there were more people like Eric Adams who define their work as improving the lives of individuals in need, our country would honor our common humanity.

An important step toward transparency was taken by the ACLU in California when it released a free smartphone app that allows people to send to ACLU cell phone videos of police encounters automatically. The ACLU will preserve the footage even if the police seize the phone and delete the video or destroy the phone. The app, Mobile Justice CA, works for both iPhone and Android users. It has a record button in the middle of the screen, that when pressed, transmits information about the locale of the incident and the people involved can be transmitted to the

ACLU. ACLU may then share that video with news media, community organizers, or the general public to call attention to police abuse. ACLU affiliates in other states have developed other versions of the app with similar capacities.[58] These apps put into the hands of ordinary citizens the means to introduce transparency into police use of unwarranted force in many situations.

Boston is unusual because there is ongoing communication between the police commissioner with community leaders, local officials, and local clergy. Michael Curry, the president of the Boston NAACP, praised the sharing of information and the response to questions by the police about the video footage of incidents. There are continuing conversations about police transparency, police body cameras, and independent investigations of police-involved shootings. Michael Curry continues to call for increased diversity in the Boston Police Department and has praised the action of a black police officer interacting with a crowd questioning why officers fired. The deputy director of the Lawyers Committee for Civil Rights, a nonprofit organization that handles discrimination cases and issues related to police misconduct, also meets with the Boston police. He expressed hope that the conversations around police transparency will continue, given the history of our country and the lack of trust between the community and the police.[59]

Now that President Obama is nearing the end of his second term, he is able to speak out on racial issues. He not only speaks out, but also takes important actions such as speaking at the pulpit of the African Methodist Church in a eulogy for the nine people who were murdered by Dylann Roof. For the first time in American history, an American president has walked into a federal prison to see for himself a small piece of what mass incarceration has wrought. He also freed forty-six prisoners. These actions ended a week in which the president spoke powerfully about the failings of a criminal justice system that has damaged an entire generation of Americans, disproportionately black men, at a huge cost to themselves, their families and their communities, as well as to the taxpayers and society. He then gave a speech to the NAACP about how the exploding prison population does not include people who commit violent crimes, but instead nonviolent low-level drug offenders caught up in harsh mandatory sentencing that is unrelated to the seriousness of their offence or public safety. He also spoke about the lack of support and resources that would keep them from recidivism and about the overuse of solitary confinement. Many of these inmates subjected to these intolerable conditions are being punished for minor infractions or are mentally ill. He also stressed the need for preventive efforts, such as early childhood education in lower income minority communities, as well as removing the barriers to employment, housing, and voting for former prisoners. Now that there is a national conversation of our policing and criminal justice system, there is hope and some signs for bipartisan legislation that would receive the support for such programs.

One very great and poorly addressed need is for the rehabilitation of prisoners. Some money that could have been spent in prosecutions is instead spent on prevention. At a gym in a poor neighborhood in Harlem teenagers are taught basketball by professional coaches under the watchful eye of police officers and staff. Similar sessions take place every weekend at ten different places across Manhattan. Firefighters helping eliminate the wildfires in California are low-level offenders in prison. One of them commented in an interview by the BBC on September 24, 2015, that he felt as if he were in a family while battling the fire and that he was proud of his work. As a country with such a large prison population, a number of whom have committed minor crimes or are even innocent, we should think about rehabilitation and its implications of not only a lower cost to taxpayers, but also the reintegration of people who will contribute to society.

A further issue is that of anger, an emotion that has many different connotations, but most importantly anger at injustice that empowers people to make important changes. It is not something new. Twenty years ago, Dolly Burwell a black woman, stood up against the dumping of toxic wastes in her neighborhood to become a member of the local government, and The Mothers of East Los Angeles, Hispanic women, who came together to fight against similar issues as well as the operations of drug dealers in their neighborhoods.[60] Both of them ended unjust policies. Eric Adams grew up with anger at what happened to him and he went on to make dramatic changes in New York.

In a scathing op-ed piece Charles M. Blow wrote about the pervasiveness of racism, the need for structural changes in our society, and the need to dismantle oppression from the top down.[61] Two months later, Senator Elizabeth Warren traveled throughout the country to support Senate candidates and build a progressive agenda for the Democratic Party. She gave a very important speech on racial justice as part of the Edward M. Kennedy Institute for the U.S. Senate's Getting to the Point Series. She also focused on the top-down and criticized the trickle-down theory. She emphasized the need to protect black people from violence and that economic justice is not sufficient to ensure racial justice. While supporting the police officers that serve their community with respect, she focused on what she described as a racist criminal justice system and emphasized that police are not "occupying armies." She also referred to Dylann Roof as a terrorist and reminded us that white supremacists with weapons walk the streets.[62]

NAACP president, Cornell William Brooks, has said that he feels that we are moving backward on race. Yet, racism is multifaceted and appears at many levels in our country, and we are moving forward as well with people like President Obama and Eric L. Adams, in ways we need to celebrate and follow. Mr. Adams's goal is to use his experience with policing and as a state senator and in his role of Borough President of the larger New York to make important changes in our perceptions and behavior. That part of the city is multicultural and he is handling differences with tact and concern. He also works with young people in the Brooklyn Borough to promote their education and their self-esteem. As Mr. Adams reminds us, it takes knowledge and skill to move us in the right direction. He is having the tough conversations and meeting the challenges to accomplish just that.

Notes

INTRODUCTION

1. Jonathan Moore, "In a Polarized Age What Does We the People Really Mean?" WBUR. 3/17/14.
2. Vaclav Havel, *Living in Truth* (London: Faber and Faber, 1989), 89.
3. Ibid., 103.

CHAPTER 1

1. Translated text of a scroll found at the Dead Sea and estimated to be an Essene document, supplied by David Milarch.
2. Interview with David Milarch, March 2012.
3. Melissa Fay Green, "The Ancient Tree Archive." *Readers Digest* (April 2014): 1.
4. Ibid., 2.
5. Ibid., 3.
6. Diana Beresford-Kroeger, *The Global Forest: 40 Ways Trees Can Save Us* (New York: Penguin, 2010), 49.
7. Green, "The Ancient Tree Archive," 6.

8. Juliet Eilperin and Stephen Mufson, "Activists Arrested at White House Protesting Keystone Pipeline," *Washington Post*, February 13, 2013.

Jim Robbins, *The Man Who Planted Trees: Lost Groves, Champion Trees, and an Urgent Plan to Save the Planet* (New York: Spiegel & Grau, 2012), 77.

9. Interview with David Milarch, March 2012.

10. Jim Gillis, "Rush for Clues in Melting Ice," *International Herald Tribune*, July 1, 2012.

11. Raymond A. Moody Jr., *The Light Beyond: New Explorations by the Author of Life After Life* (New York: Bantam Books, 1989), 2.

12. Ibid., 48.

13. Juliet Eilperin and Stephen Mufson, "Activists Arrested at White House Protesting Keystone Pipeline," *Washington Post*, February 13, 2013.

14. John H. Richardson, "When the End of Civilization Is Your Day Job," *Esquire* (August 2015).

15. "A Clearing in the Trees." *The Economist*. August 23, 2014.

16. Ben Caldecott, Guy Lomax, and Mark Workman, *Stranded Carbon Assets and Negative Emissions Technologies: Working Paper* (Oxford: Smith School of Enterprise and the Environment, 2015), www.smithschool.ox.ac.uk/research-programmes/stranded-assets/ Stranded%20Carbon%20Assets%20and%20NETs%20-%2006. 02.15.pdf.

17. Interview with David Milarch, November 2013.

18. Green, "The Ancient Tree Archive," 8.

19. Ibid., 9.

20. Interview with David Milarch, November 2013.

21. Green, "The Ancient Tree Archive," 10.

22. Interview with David Milarch, November 2013.

23. Ibid.

24. Jennifer Greenjeans, email to David Milarch, August 13, 2014, with subject "Everyday Sustainable Living."

25. Interview with David Milarch, November 2013.

26. Hank Becker, "Phytoremediation: Using Plants to Clean Up Soils," *Agricultural Research Magazine* 48, no. 6 (June 2000).

27. Interview with David Milarch, December 2013.

28. Bob Frost, "Muir's Sequoia Is Dying," *East Bay Express*, April 23, 2014.

29. Darragh Murphy, "Jurassic Bark: Ancient Irish Trees Brought Back to Life," *Irish Times*, October 28, 2014.

30. Green, "The Ancient Tree Archive," 9–10.

31. Quoted in Robbins, *The Man Who Planted Trees*.

32. John Flesher, "Group Kicks off Planting of Ancient Tree Clones," posted on Tumblr blog, April 23, 2013.

33. Jim Robbins, "Building an Ark for the Anthropocene," *New York Times*, September 27, 2014.

34. Justin Gillis, "Panel Says Global Warming Risks Sudden Deep Changes," *New York Times*, December 4, 2013.

35. John Vidal, "UK's Ancient Forests Could Spread Again Thanks to Plan to Clone 'Super Trees,'" *The Observer*, June 30, 2013.

36. Permaculture was defined by Bill Mollison in 1978 as a philosophy of working with rather than against nature and looking at plants and animals in all their functions rather than treating them as single product systems (Jennifer Greenjeans, email to David Milarch, op cit.).

37. Daniela F. Cusack et al., "An Interdisciplinary Assessment of Climate Engineering Strategies," *Frontiers in Ecology and the Environment* 12, no. 5 (June 2014): 280–87.

38. Archangel Ancient Tree Archive, "Partnership Announced to Reverse Deforestation and Global Warming," *Newsletter*, February 17, 2014.

39. Jonathan Lear, *Radical Hope: Ethics in the Face of Cultural Devastation* (Cambridge, MA: Harvard University Press, 2006), 129–30.

40. "Pre-Columbian Civilizations," http://www.britannica.com/EBchecked/topic/474227/pre-Columbian-civilizations/69366/Late-Classic-Maya-Meso-America-600-900, and Matt Walker, "Sacred Plants of the Maya Forest," *BBC Earth News*, June 5, 2009, at http://news.bbc.co.uk/earth/hi/earth_news/newsid_8083000/8083812.stm.

41. Thomas Pakenham, *Remarkable Trees of the World* (New York: W.W. Norton, 2003), 14–16.

42. Ibid., 26.

43. Diana Beresford-Kroeger, *Arboretum America: A Philosophy of the Forests* (Ann Arbor: University of Michigan Press, 2009), 2.

44. Justin Gillis, "Restored Forests Are Making Inroads against Climate Change," *New York Times*, December 24, 2014.

45. Laurie Goodstein, "In the Footsteps of Popes, Francis Seeking Worldly Change," *New York Times*, June 18, 2015.

CHAPTER 2

1. Tim Arango, "Concern and Support for Iraqi Christians Forced by Militants to Flee Mosul," *New York Times*, July 20, 2014.

2. Vera Laska, *Women in the Resistance and in the Holocaust* (Westport, CT: Greenwood Press, 1983).

3. Misha Glenny, *The Fall of Yugoslavia: The Third Balkan War* (New York: Penguin, 1992), 162–69.

4. Radmila Manojlović Zarković (ed.), *Sjećam Se: I Remember* (San Francisco: Aunt Lute Books, 1997).

5. Adam Seligman, *The Problem of Trust* (Princeton, NJ: Princeton University Press, 1997).

6. Interview with Adam B. Seligman, April 2014.

7. Interview with Rahel Wasserfall, April 2014.

8. "France's National Front: On the March," *The Economist*, March 29, 2014.

9. Dan Bilefsky, "European Candidates See Opportunity on Extreme Edge," *New York Times*, May 11, 2014.

10. "Europe's Roma Bashers," *New York Times*, April 30, 2014.

11. Alice Goffman, *On the Run: Fugitive Life in an American City* (Chicago: University of Chicago Press, 2014).

12. Eliza Griswold, *The Tenth Parallel: Dispatches from the Fault Line Between Christianity and Islam* (New York: Farrar, Straus & Giroux, 2010).

13. Ibid.

14. Ibid., 9.

15. Uwem Akpan, *Say You're One of Them* (New York: Back Bay Books, 2008).

16. Ibid., 263.

17. Jason Straziuso, "U.N. Expresses 'Horror' at South Sudan Massacre," *USA Today*, April 24, 2014.

18. Courtesy of CEDAR (http://www.cedarnetwork.org/2014/02/19/can-accept-different-south-sudan-can-peace-noel-santo/).

19. Paul Rusesabagina, *An Ordinary Man* (New York: Penguin Books, 2006).

20. Courtesy of CEDAR (http://www.cedarnetwork.org/programs/ongoing-initiatives/the-equator-peace-academy/whose-community-memory-conflict-and-tradition/).

21. Ruseabagina, *An Ordinary Man.*

22. Sudarsan Raghavan, "Rwandans Mark 20th Anniversary of Genocide amid Reminders That Justice Has Yet to Be Done," *Washington Post*, April 7, 2014.

23. Courtesy of CEDAR (http://www.cedarnetwork.org/).

CHAPTER 3

1. Interview with Dr. James O'Connell, February and March 2012.

2. Bobby Watts, "3 Jobs and No Apartment?" *New York Times*, September 23, 2013.

3. U.S. Census Bureau, *American Community Survey Report*, September 2012.

4. Ibid.

5. Jeremy C. Fox, "Boston's Homeless Population Increases as Federal Housing Assistance Cuts Loom," *Boston Globe*, March 4, 2013.

6. US Conference of Mayors, *Hunger and Homelessness Survey*, December 2012.

7. Fox, "Boston's Homeless Population Increases."

8. WBUR, October 16, 2013.

9. Alejandro Ramirez, "Homelessness in Boston, 1 Year after Losing the Long Island Shelter," WBUR, August 11, 2015.

10. Ibid.

11. E. Fuller Torrey, *Out of the Shadows: Confronting America's Mental Illness Crisis* (New York: Wiley, 1997), chaps. 1, 3, and app.

12. Ramirez, "Homelessness in Boston."

13. Interview with Dr. James O'Connell.

14. Russell Spooner, *Seeking Signs of Sanity: A Veteran's Account of his Role in World War II* (New York: iUniverse, 2005), 142.

15. Interview with Dr. James O'Connell.

16. Ibid.

17. Ibid.

18. Philippe Brouqui et al., "Chronic Bartonella Quintana Bactremia in Homeless Patients," New England Journal of Medicine 340 (1999): 184–89.

19. Ibid.

20. Ibid.

21. Interview with Dr. James O'Connell.

22. Ibid.

23. Ibid.

24. David Nakamura, "Obama on Telemundo, Rules out Freezing Deportations of Most Illegal Immigrants," *Washington Post*, September 17, 2013.

25. Interview with Dr. O'Connell.

26. Ibid.

27. Bill Mitchell, "Risks of Living on Street in Bitter Cold: When Not to Walk on By," WBUR, January 31, 2014.

28. Ibid.

29. Ibid.

30. Ibid.

31. Martha Bebinger, "Why Some Bostonians Refuse Shelter in the Dead of Winter, and How They Survive," WBUR, February 19, 2014.

32. Interview with Dr. O'Connell.

33. Gabrielle Emanuel. "McInnis House Provides End-of-Life Care for the Undocumented and Homeless." WBUR, June 28, 2014.

34. Interview with Dr. Jim O'Connell.

CHAPTER 4

1. Charles M. Blow, "A Town without Pity," *New York Times*, August 10, 2013.
2. Ibid.
3. Barbara Ehrenreich, *Nickel and Dimed: On (Not) Getting by in America* (New York: Picador, Henry Holt, 2001).
4. "Houston Area Kossacks and Hunger in America," *Daily Kos*, January 16, 2014.
5. Kathleen.Care2 Action Alerts, December 2, 2013.
6. The Sequester refers to a law passed by Congress in 2011 to reduce a $4 million deficit. The cuts disproportionately affected the poor, such as the reduction of funding for the food stamp program (SNAP).
7. Annie Lowrey, "As Automatic Budget Cuts Go into Effect, Poor May Be Hit Particularly Hard," *New York Times*, March 4, 2013.
8. WBUR. December 16, 2013.
9. "The Sequester and the Homeless," *New York Times*, March 23, 2014.
10. "Tales from the Streets," *The Economist*, December 7, 2013.
11. Steve LeBlanc, "A Tough Quest to End Family Homelessness in Mass.," WBUR, January 1, 2014.
12. Ibid.
13. Maine State Housing Authority, "Homeless Department Memorandum," July 15, 2013.
14. Interview with Sister Lucille MacDonald, February and March, 2013.
15. Helen Marie Burns and Sheila Carney, *Praying with Catherine McAuley* (Winona, MN: St. Mary's Press, 1996).
16. Mary Joanna Regan and Isabelle Keiss, *Tender Courage: A Reflection on the Life and Spirit of Catherine McAuley, First Sister of Mercy* (Chicago: Franciscan Herald Press, 1988), 25–26.
17. Ibid., 27–33.
18. Interview with Sister Lucille MacDonald.
19. Ibid.
20. Ibid.

21. "Maine Shrimp Season Is Called Off," *New York Times*, December 4, 2013.

22. Eduardo Porter, "In the War on Poverty, a Dogged Adversary," *New York Times*, December 18, 2013.

23. Interview with Sister Lucille.

24. Ibid.

25. Interview with Renée LaCasse, January 2012.

CHAPTER 5

1. NPR, January 19, 2015.

2. Hiroko Tabuchi, "Rushing to Cater to America's Rich," *New York Times*, February 9, 2015.

3. Motoko Rich, "Number of Poor Students in Public Schools Rises," *New York Times*, January 17, 2015.

4. Small Business Majority, March 6, 2014.

5. NewsNation with Tamron Hall, February 7, 2014.

6. Charles M. Blow, "How Expensive It Is to Be Poor?" *New York Times*, January 19, 2015.

7. David Leonhardt, "Looking Abroad for Solutions to the Great Wage Slowdown," *New York Times*, January 15, 2015.

8. Interview with Sam Polk, June 2014 and August 2015.

9. Linda Tirado, *Hand to Mouth: Living in Bootstrap America* (New York: G.P. Putnam's Sons, 2014), xv.

10. Blow, "How Expensive It Is to Be Poor?"

11. Interview with Sam Polk.

12. Melinda J. Watman, "Obesity: A Disease by Any Other Name," WBUR, April 5, 2014.

13. Julia Lurie, "Black and Hispanic Kids Have a 50 Percent Chance of Developing Diabetes," *Mother Jones*, August 3, 2014.

14. Ibid.

15. Jon Le Bon, "How the Feds Help McDonald's Sell Junk Food," *Mother Jones*, June 23, 2014.

16. Gary Ruskin, "The Calorie Control Council," posted January 17, 2015, on US Right to Know website.

17. Interview with Sam Polk.
18. Ibid.
19. Ibid.
20. Ibid.
21. Ibid.
22. Ibid.
23. Mary MacVean, "South L.A. Women Changed Their Lives, and It Started with Food," *Los Angeles Times*, August 28, 2014.
24. Interview with Sam Polk.
25. Ibid.
26. Ibid.
27. Ibid.
28. MacVean, "South L.A. Women Changed Their Lives."
29. Ibid.
30. Sam Polk, "Friends with Weight-Loss Benefits," *Los Angeles Times*, January 29, 2015.
31. Courtesy of Angela Carrasco.

CHAPTER 6

1. Interview with Wendy Young, December 2013; January 2014.
2. Ibid.
3. Ibid.
4. Ibid.
5. Sonia Nazario, "Children of Cartels," *International New York Times*, June 13, 2014.
6. Francis Robles, "Wave of Minors on Their Own Rush to Cross the Southwest Border," *New York Times*, June 4, 2014.
7. Sonia Nazario, op cit.
8. Frances Robles, "Fleeing Gangs, Children Head to U.S. Border," *New York Times*, July 10, 2014.
9. David Boeri, "Brutal Gang Violence Reigns in El Salvador," WBUR, December 16, 2014.
10. Ibid.
11. BBC Television, August 26, 2013.

12. Elisabeth Malkin, "Guatemala Court Rules Against Official," *New York Times*, February 7, 2014.

13. Minority Rights Group International, *State of the World's Minorities, 2008*. http://minorityrights.org/publications/state-of-the-worlds-minorities-2008-march-2008.

14. Ibid.

15. Jennifer Medina, "Most Migrant Children Entering U.S. Are Now with Relatives, Data Show," *New York Times*, July 26, 2014.

16. Manny Fernandez, "Towns Fight to Avoid Taking in Migrant Minors," *New York Times*, July 16, 2014.

17. Simon Rios, "800 Young Immigrants Have Arrived in Massachusetts since January," WBUR, July 25, 2014.

18. Michael D. Shear, "Obama Approves Plan to Let Children Apply for Refugee Status in Central America," *New York Times*, October 1, 2014.

19. Wendy Young and Megan McKenna, "The Measure of a Society: The Treatment of Unaccompanied Refugee and Immigrant Children in the United States," *Harvard Law Review* 45 (2010), 248.

20. Jim Dwyer, "A 12-Year-Old's Trek of Despair Ends in Noose at the Border," *New York Times*, April 20, 2014.

21. Nick Cumming-Bruce, "Syria and Iraq Called Urgent by New U.N. Rights Chief," *New York Times*, September 9, 2014.

22. Ibid.

23. Paul Ingram, "Rights Groups: Border Patrol Abusing Minors Held in Custody," *Tucson Sentinel*, June 11, 2014.

24. John Burnett, "U.S. Border Patrol's Response to Violence in Question," NPR, May 15, 2014.

25. Interview with Wendy Young.

26. Ibid.

27. Young and McKenna, "The Measure of a Society," 250.

28. Ibid.

29. Interview with Wendy Young.

30. Young and McKenna, "The Measure of a Society," 250.

31. Interview with Wendy Young.

32. Ibid.

33. Ibid.
34. Ibid.
35. Ibid.
36. Courtesy of Wendy Young.
37. Courtesy of Wendy Young, KIND website: https://support-kind.org/stories/jeannettes-struggle-to-find-a-pro-bono-attorney/.
38. Ibid.
39. Courtesy of Wendy Young.
40. Sonia Nazario, "Child Migrants Alone in Court," *New York Times*, April 11, 2013.
41. KIND Pro Bono Attorney of the Month, June 2015. Courtesy of Wendy Young, https://supportkind.org/stories/alex-hess/.
42. Interview with Wendy Young.
43. Julia Preston, "Advocate for Immigrants Up the Ante in a Capitol Sit-In That Brings Arrests," *New York Times*, August 2, 2013.
44. Julia Preston, "Immigrants Fitting in to U.S. Reports Says," *New York Times*, September 25, 2015.
45. Ibid.
46. Ted Widmer, "The Immigration Dividend," *New York Times*, October 6, 2015.
47. Interview with Wendy Young.
48. Ibid.
49. Ibid.
50. Ibid.
51. Ibid.
52. Ibid.
53. Minority Rights Group International, op. cit.
54. Interview with Wendy Young.
55. Kids in Need of Defense, *Annual Report 2014*, https://support-kind.org/resources/2014-annual-report/.
56. Ibid.
57. Ibid.
58. Ibid.
59. Ibid.
60. Ibid.

CHAPTER 7

1. Jenna Russell, Meghan Irons, Akilah Johnson, Maria Cramer, and Andrew Ryan, "68 Blocks: Life, Death, Hope," *Boston Globe*, December 16–20, 2012.

2. Lois Beckett, "The PTSD Crisis That's Being Ignored: Americans Wounded in Their Own Neighborhoods," *Pro Publica*, February 3, 2014.

3. Interview with David Crump, February 2014.

4. John A. Rich, *Wrong Place, Wrong Time: Trauma and Violence in the Lives of Young Men* (Baltimore, MD: Johns Hopkins University Press, 2009).

5. Geoffrey Canada, *Fist, Stick, Knife, Gun: A Personal History of Violence in America* (Boston: Beacon Press, 2010), x.

6. Russell et al., "68 Blocks: Life, Death, Hope."

7. Eileen McNamara, "There's the Violence That Makes the Headlines, Then There's the Rest of It," WBUR, May 3, 2013.

8. "Colorado Lawmakers Ousted in Recall Vote Over Gun Law," *New York Times*, September 11, 2013.

9. "The Iron Pipeline Thrives," *New York Times*, September 8, 2013.

10. Canada, *Fist, Stick, Knife, Gun*, 99.

11. https://www.washingtonpost.com/news/fact-checker/wp/2015/07/07/yes-u-s-locks-people-up-at-a-higher-rate-than-any-other-country/.

12. Arthur L. Kellermann and Frederick P. Rivara, "Silencing the Science on Gun Research," *Journal of American Medicine* 309, no. 6 (2013): 549–50.

13. Marilynn Marchione, "Doctors Target Gun Violence as a Social Disease," *USA Today*, August 12, 2012.

14. Jim Dwyer, "No Shootings or Killings for 363 Days, but the Fight Is Far from Over," *New York Times*, July 19, 2013.

15. Ta-Nehisi Coates, "Beyond the Code of the Streets," *New York Times*, May 4, 2013.

16. Interview with David Crump.

17. Ibid.

18. Benjamin Swasey, "Boston Metro Area's Income; Poverty Rate Unchanged in 2012," WBUR, September 9, 2013.
19. Interview with David Crump.
20. Ibid.
21. Howard Zehr, *Changing Lenses: A New Focus for Crime and Justice*, 3rd ed. (Scottsdale, PA: Herald Press, 2005), 31.
22. Ibid., 52–55.
23. Interview with David Crump.
24. Ibid.
25. Ibid.
26. Ibid.
27. Ibid.
28. Ibid.
29. Ibid.
30. Ibid.
31. Ibid.

CHAPTER 8

1. Interview with Jodi Rosenbaum, March 2013, May 2014.
2. Ibid.
3. Ibid.
4. Ibid.
5. Interview with Melissa, December 2014. (To protect her privacy I omitted her last name.)
6. Interview with Jodi Rosenbaum.
7. Ibid.
8. Ibid.
9. Ibid.
10. Camila Batmanghelidjh, *Shattered Lives: Children Who Live with Courage and Dignity* (London: Jessica Kingley Publishers, 2006).
11. Ibid., 29.
12. Ibid., 67.
13. Interview with Jodi Rosenbaum.

14. Ibid.

15. Ibid.

16. Ibid.

17. Ibid.

18. Ibid.

19. Ibid.

20. Bryan Schoen, "More Than Words: A Great Member of the Opportunity Nation Coalition," August 6, 2012, https://opportunitynation.org/latest-news/words-great-member-opportunity-nation-coalition/.

21. Interview with Kelly Sullivan, December 2014.

22. Ibid.

23. Ibid.

24. Michael Norton, "National Organization to Review Mass. Child Protection Agency," WBUR, January 9, 2014.

25. "Massachusetts Fails to Ensure the Safe Administration of Psychotropic Medications to Children in Foster Care," October 3, 2012, http://www.childrensrights.org/press-release/massachusetts-fails-to-ensure-the-safe-administration-of-psychotropic-medications-to-children-in-foster-care/.

26. Schoen, "More Than Words," *Year End Report*, 2014.

27. Ibid.

28. Ibid.

29. Keith Regan, "Partners of the Year: Connection between More Than Words and Constant Contact Easy to See," *Boston Business Journal*, September 12, 2014, http://www.bizjournals.com/boston/print-edition/2014/09/12/partners-of-the-year-connection-between-more-than.html.

30. Ibid.

CHAPTER 9

1. Interview with Mei Mei Ellerman, November 2012.

2. Ibid.

3. Interview with Derek Ellerman, March 2013.

4. Ibid.
5. Ibid.
6. Rachel Lloyd, *Girls Like Us* (New York: HarperPerennial, 2012), 25.
7. Ibid., 45–58.
8. Ibid., 74.
9. Erica Ritz, "FBI Rescues 105 Children from Horrific Sex Trafficking Operations in 76 U.S. Cities," WBUR, July 29, 2013.
10. Lloyd, *Girls Like Us*, 41.
11. Ibid., 43.
12. Ibid., 133.
13. Russ Buettner, "Prostitutes Testify in Defense of Pimps at Sex Trafficking Trial," *New York Times*, May 29, 2013.
14. Ibid.
15. Theresa L. Flores, *The Slave across the Street* (Garden City, ID: Ampelon Publishing, 2010).
16. Ibid., 117.
17. Ibid., 119.
18. Ibid., 113–14.
19. Dan Bilifsky, "In Strauss-Kahn Trial, France Discards Its Privacy Taboos," *International New York Times*, February 19, 2015.
20. Interview with Derek Ellerman.
21. Rick Rojas and Al Baker, "Authorities Say a Fired Officer Operated a Prostitution Ring at Motels." *New York Times*, February 3, 2016.
22. Kathryn Bolkovac, with Cari Lynn, *The Whistleblower: Sex Trafficking, Military Contractors, and One Woman's Fight for Justice* (New York: Palgrave Macmillan, 2011).
23. Somini Sengupta, "United Nations Workers Accused of Sexual Abuse," *New York Times*, March 16, 2015.
24. Bolkovac, *The Whistleblower*.
25. Linda Ocasio, "Sex and Labor Trafficking in the U.S.: A Q&A on the 21st Century Slave Trade," *The Star Ledger*, March 14, 2013.
26. Interview with Maddu Huacuja, February 2014.
27. Interview with Derek Ellerman.
28. Mary A. Fischer, "The Slave in the Garage," *Reader's Digest*, May 2008.

29. Nita Bhalla, "'Modern-Day Slavery': State Dept. Says Millions of Human Trafficking Victims Go Unidentified," September 16, 2013.

30. Ibid.

31 Art Jahnke, "Deliverance," *Bostonia*, Winter–Spring 2015.

32. Ibid.

33. Interview with Derek Ellerman.

34. Ibid.

35. The Polaris Project.

36. Yamiche Alandor, "Texting Increases Human Trafficking Victims' Access to Help," *USA Today*, March 28, 2013.

37. Ibid.

38. "Polaris Project Launches Global Human Trafficking Hotline Network," Polaris, April 9, 2013, https://www.polarisproject.org/news/press-releases/polaris-project-launches-global-human-trafficking-hotline-network.

39. Ibid.

40. Tierney Sneed, "How Big Data Battles Human Trafficking," *U.S. News and World Report*, January 14, 2015.

41. "Worldwide Directory of Modern Slavery Organizations Launches," Polaris, October 9, 2014, http://live-polaris.gotpantheon.com/news/press-releases/worldwide-directory-modern-slavery-organizations-launches.

42. Ocasio, "Sex and Labor Trafficking in the U.S."

43. Phillip Martin, "Human Trafficking: The Crisis in Boston," WGBH, February 21, 2015.

44. Carolyn Davis, "Human Trafficking: Suburbs' Dirty Little Secret," *Inquirer*, August 6, 2013.

45. Ibid.

46. Jahnke, "Deliverance."

47. Ibid.

48. "Wyndham Hotel Group Partners with Polaris. . . ," Polaris, November 17, 2014, https://www.polarisproject.org/news/press-releases/wyndham-hotel-group-partners-polaris-help-prevent-human-trafficking.

49. Adam Liptak, "Supreme Court May Be Open to Hotel Registry Checks," *New York Times*, March 3, 2015.

50. Phillip Martin, "Sexual and Human Trafficking," WBUR, March 2, 2015.

51. "Human Trafficking and the Hotel Industry," Polaris, March 15, https://www.polarisproject.org/resources/human-trafficking-and-hotel-industry.

52. Ibid.

53. Ocasio, "Sex and Labor Trafficking in the U.S."

54. www.state.gov/j/tip/rls/tiprpt/2014/226649.htm.

55. "Steps against Juvenile Sex Trafficking," *New York Times*, March 5, 2015.

CHAPTER 10

1. Yifat Susskind, "Fighting the Poverty of Imagination: Building a Future That Has Never Existed," TEDx Talk, Saint Peter's University, March 21, 2013, https://www.youtube.com/watch?v=XOg_Dq6EJfg.

2. Ibid.

3. Ibid.

4. Interview with Yifat Susskind, May 2013.

5. MADRE unpublished documents provided by Yifat Susskind.

6. Ibid.

7. Interview with Yifat Susskind.

8. Ibid.

9. Ibid.

10. "Chad: No Protection from Rape and Violence for Displaced Women and Girls in Eastern Chad," *Amnesty International*, July 26, 2007, https://www.amnesty.org/en/documents/afr20/008/2007/en.

11. Gardiner Harris, "Coal Rush in India Could Tip Balance on Climate Change," *New York Times*, November 18, 2014.

12. Justin Gillis, "Climate Talks Also Focus on Saving World Forests," *New York Times*, December 11, 2015.

13. Interview with Yifat Susskind.

14. Laura Flanders (ed.), *The W Effect: Bush's War on Women* (New York: Feminist Press, 2004).

15. Wangari Maathai, *The Greenbelt Movement: Sharing the Approach and the Experience* (New York: Lantern Books, 2004).

16. Interview with Yifat Suskind.

17. NPR, March 25, 2014.

18. Catherine Weibel and Sajy Emulghanni, "A Fresh Solution to Gaza's Water Crisis," UNICEF, January 14, 2014, http://www.unicef.org/mena/media_8765.html.

19. Interview with Yifat Susskind.

20. Ibid.

21. Ibid.

22. Ibid.

23. Jim Yardley, "Europe's Anti-Semitism Comes out of Shadows," *New York Times*, September 24, 2014.

24. Ibid.

25. Interview with Yifat Suskind.

26. Dana Janbek, "For Syrian Refugees in Jordan, the Cellphone Is a Lifeline," WBUR, October 16, 2014.

27. Interview with Yifat Susskind.

28. Ibid.

29. Ibid.

30. Ibid.

31. Somini Sengputa, "Finding a Path Back to Iraq, and Toward Securing Women's Freedom," *New York Times*, November 28, 2015.

32. Ibid.

33. Nick Cumming-Bruce, "5,500 Iraqis Killed Since Islamic State Began Its Military Drive, U.N. Says," *New York Times*, October 3, 2014.

34. Jasmina Tešanovic, "Mothering in War," in *Mothers of Adult Children*, edited by Marguerite Guzmán Bouvard (New York: Lexington Books, 2013).

35. Interview with Yifat Susskind.

36. Ibid.

37. Ibid.

38. Ibid.

39. Ibid.

40. Lisa Davis, *Seeking Accountability and Effective Response for Gender-Based Violence against Syrian Women: Women's Inclusion in the Peace Processes* (New York: CUNY and MADRE, 2014).

41. Ibid.
42. Ibid.
43. Lisa Davis, "Lifting the Ban on Women's Shelters in Iraq: Promoting Change in Conflict," *50.50 Inclusive Democracy*, October 14, 2015, https://www.opendemocracy.net/5050/lisa-davis/lifting-ban-on-women%E2%80%99s-shelters-in-iraq-promoting-change-in-conflict.
44. Ibid.
45. Interview with Yifat Susskind.
46. Ibid.
47. news@amazonwatch.org.
48. Interview with Yifat Susskind.
49. Somini Sengupta, "U.N. Report Says Progress for Women Is Unequal," *New York Times*, February 12, 2014.
50. Ibid.

CHAPTER 11

1. Loung Ung, *First They Killed My Father* (New York: Harper-Collins, 2000).
2. Richard Bernstein, "The Insoluble Question," *New York Review of Books*, April 3, 2014, 64–65.
3. Joel Brinkley, *Cambodia's Curse: The Modern History of a Troubled Land* (Philadelphia: Public Affairs, 2012), 160.
4. Ung, *First They Killed My Father*, 288.
5. Mia Cloonan, a social worker in Boston familiar with such cases has confirmed this, March 23, 2014.
6. Loung Ung, *Lulu in the Sky* (New York: HarperCollins, 2012), 280.
7. Brinkley, *Cambodia's Curse*, 269–72.
8. Ibid., 289.
9. Ibid., 207.
10. Ibid., 209.
11. Ibid., 219.
12. Interview with Alan Lightman, November 2014.

13. Ibid.
14. Ibid.
15. Ibid.
16. Ibid.
17. Ibid.
18. Ibid.
19. Ibid.
20. Ibid.
21. Ibid.
22. Ibid.
23. Ibid.
24. Ibid.
25. Interview with Chandy Eng, February 2014, courtesy of Dr. Lightman.
26. Brinkley, *Cambodia's Curse*, 355–57.
27. Ibid.
28. "Cambodian Democracy: Bruised, Bloodied and Probably Broken," *The Economist*, January 11, 2014.
29. Ibid.
30. Thomas Fuller, "Cambodia Cracks Down on Protest with Evictions and Ban on Assembly," *New York Times*, January 4, 2014.
31. "Time to Deal," *The Economist*, April 19, 2014.
32. Thomas Fuller, "In Cambodia, Voicing the Struggle," *New York Times*, March 13, 2014.
33. Ibid.
34. Email from Sivcheh Chheng, April 24, 2015.
35. Interview with Alan Lightman.

CHAPTER 12

1. Interview with Vidya Sri, January 2013.
2. Ibid.
3. Ibid.
4. Ibid.
5. Ibid.

6. Ibid.
7. Ibid.
8. Ibid.
9. Ibid.
10. Ibid.
11. Ibid.
12. Ibid.
13. Ibid.
14. Aisha K. Gill and Sundari Anitha, *Forced Marriage: Introducing a Social Justice and Human Rights Perspective* (London: Zed Books, 2011), 25.
15. Mosi Secret, "Court Documents Detail a Deadly Family Feud from Brooklyn to Pakistan," *New York Times*, May 23, 2013.
16. Gangashakti.org.
17. Gill and Anitha, *Forced Marriage*, 31.
18. Vidya Sri and Darakshan Raja, *Voices from the Frontline: Addressing Forced Marriage within the United States* (New York: Gangashakti, 2013), 3.
19. Ibid., 9.
20. United Nations Secretary-General, *Ending Violence against Women: Study of the Secretary-General* (New York: United Nations, 2006), 42.
21. Interview with Vidya Sri.
22. Ibid.
23. Mike Deak, "Manavi Offers Safe Harbor to South Asian Victims of Abuse in Central New Jersey," *Courier News*, April 13, 2014.
24. "Indian Mothers-In-Law, Curse of the Mummyji," *The Economist*, December 21, 2013.
25. Deak, "Manavi Offers Safe Harbor."
26. Ibid.
27. Tahirih Justice Center, "Forced Marriage Policy," http://www.tahirih.org/what-we-do/policy-advocacy/forced-marriage-policy/, accessed November 24, 2015.
28. Ibid.
29. Jasvinder Sanghera, *Shame* (London: Hodder and Stoughton, 2007).
30. Sri and Raja, *Voices from the Frontline*, 28.

31. Interview with Vidya Sri.

32. Sri and Raja, *Voices from the Frontline*, 12.

33. Interview with Vidya Sri.

34. Sri and Raja, *Voices from the Frontline*, 13–16.

35. Sanghera, *Shame*.

36. Sri and Raja, *Voices from the Frontline*, 13–16.

37. Ibid.

38. Ibid.

39. Ibid.

40. Ibid.

41. Sri and Raja, *Voices from the Frontline*, 8.

42. Ibid.

43. Ibid.

44. Jasvinder Sanghera, *Daughters of Shame* (London: Hodder & Stoughton, 2009).

45. Interview with Vidya Sri.

46. Amartya Sen, "India's Women: The Mixed Truth," *New York Review of Books*, October 10, 2013.

CHAPTER 13

1. Interview with Eric L. Adams, April 2014.

2. Ibid.

3. Eric L. Adams, "We Must Stop Police Abuse of Black Men," *New York Times*, February 5, 2014.

4. Ibid.

5. Charles R. Epp, Steven Maynard-Moody, and Donald Haider-Markel, *Pulled Over: How Police Stops Define Race and Citizenship* (Chicago: University of Chicago Press, 2014), 30–33.

6. Ibid., 34.

7. Ibid., 35.

8. Ibid., 154.

9. Alice Goffman, *On the Run: Fugitive Life in an American City* (Chicago: University of Chicago Press, 2014), 3–10.

10. Ibid., 20.

11. Ibid., 33.

12. NPR, August 2, 2015.

13. Steven Hsieh, "One Year After Ferguson Protests Just a Few Reforms Have Succeeded," *The Nation*, August 10, 2015.

14. Monica Davey, "Ferguson Commission, Citing Region's Racial Inequity, Urges Broad Changes," *New York Times*, September 14, 2015.

15. Gene Demby, "How Black Reporters Report on Black Death," NPR, August 19, 2015.

16. Ibid.

17. Interview with Eric L. Adams.

18. Ibid.

19. Joaquin Sapien, "Racist Posts on NY Cop Blog Raise Ire at Time of Tension," *Pro Publica*, April 16, 2015.

20. Francis Robles, "Racist Police Emails Put Florida Cases in Doubt," *New York Times*, May 16, 2015.

21. Timothy Williams, "Inquiry to Examine the Extent of Racial Bias in the San Francisco Police," *New York Times*, May 8, 2015.

22. Ibid.

23. David Goodman and Al Baker, "New Challenges to Secrecy That Protects Police Files," *New York Times*, February 5, 2015.

24. Ibid.

25. Benjamin Mueller, Al Baker, and Liz Robbins, "Swift Apologies in Harsh Arrest of a Tennis Star," *New York Times*, September 11, 2015.

26. Michael Greenberg, "The NY Police vs. the Mayor," *New York Review of Books*, February 5, 2015.

27. Ibid.

28. Ibid.

29. Ibid.

30. Rachel L. Swarns, "Police Hiring Process Stymies Black Applicant," *New York Times*, July 20, 2015.

31. Interview with Eric L. Adams.

32. Ibid.

33. "Briefing: American Prisons: The Right Choices," *The Economist*, June 20, 2015.

34. Ibid.

35. Ibid.

36. Interview with Eric L. Adams.

37. Adams, "We Must Stop Police Abuse of Black Men."

38. Jonathan Martin, "Denouncing Violence, but Avoiding Talk of Policy," *New York Times*, July 25, 2015.

39. "Policing. Don't Shoot," *The Economist*, December 13, 2014.

40. Richard A. Oppel Jr., "Wielding Search Data to Challenge and Change Police Policy," *New York Times*, November 21, 2014.

41. Ibid.

42. Ibid.

43. Nicholas Fandos, "A Study Documents the Paucity of Black Elected Prosecutors: Zero in Most States," *New York Times*, July 6, 2015.

44. "How Race Skews Prosecution," *New York Times*, July 14, 2014.

45. Albert Samaha, "Indefensible: The Story of New Orleans' Public Defenders," *Buzzfeed*, August 14, 2015.

46. Adam Liptak, "New Questions on Racial Gap in Filling Juries," *New York Times*, August 17, 2015.

47. Matt Apuzzo, "Justice Department Presses Agenda at Local Levels," *New York Times*, August 20, 2015.

48. Richard Fausset, "Settlement Reached in Shooting by Officer," *New York Times*, October 9, 2015.

49. Monica Davey and Mitch Smith, "Chicago Shopping District Becomes State for Protests," *New York Times*, November 28, 2015.

50. Ibid.

51. Gregory Aisch and Haeyoun Park, "In Chicago, Many Police Complaints, but Few Consequences," *New York Times*, December 18, 2015.

52. Carrie Johnson, "Justice Department Launches Civil Rights Investigation into Chicago Police Department," NPR, December 7, 2015.

53. Ibid.

54. Eric L. Adams, "More Scrutiny, Better Policing," *New York Times*, November 14, 2015.

55. Spencer Ackerman and Zach Stafford, "Chicago Police Detained Thousands of Black Americans at Interrogation Facility," *Guardian*, August 6, 2015.

56. Adams, "More Scrutiny, Better Policing."

57. Ibid.

58. Jon Wiener, "New ACLU Cellphone App Automatically Preserves Video of Police Encounters," *The Nation*, May 1, 2015.

59 "After Officer Shooting, Community Leaders Praise Transparency and Call for More," WBUR, March 31, 2015.

60. Marguerite Guzmán Bouvard, *Women Reshaping Human Rights: How Extraordinary Women Are Changing the World* (New York: Rowman & Littlefield, 1996).

61. Charles M. Blow, "Black Lives and Books of the Dead," *New York Times*, July 10, 2015.

62. John Nichols, "Black Lives Matter, Black Citizens Matter, Black Families Matter," *The Nation*, September 28, 2015.

Bibliography

Akpan, Uwem. *Say You're One of Them*. New York: Back Bay Books, 2008.

Alandor, Yamiche. "Texting Increases Human Trafficking Victims' Access to Help." *USA Today*, March 28, 2013.

Batmanghelidjh, Camila. *Shattered Lives: Children Who Live with Courage and Dignity*. London: Jessica Kingley Publishers, 2006.

Bebinger, Martha. "Why Some Bostonians Refuse Shelter in the Dead of Winter, and How They Survive." WBUR, February 19, 2014.

Becket, Lois. "The PTSD Crisis That's Being Ignored: Americans Wounded in Their Own Neighborhoods." *Pro Publica*, February 2, 2014.

Beresford-Kroeger, Diana. *The Global Forest: 40 Ways Trees Can Save Us*. New York: Penguin, 2010.

Bernstein, Richard. "The Insoluble Question." *New York Review of Books*, April 3, 2014.

Boeri, David. "Brutal Gang Violence Reigns in El Salvador." WBUR, December 16, 2014.

Bolkovac, Kathryn, with Cari Lynn. *The Whistle Blower: Sex Trafficking, Military Contractors, and One Woman's Fight for Justice*. New York: Palgrave Macmillan. 2010.

Bouvard, Marguerite Guzman. *Women Reshaping Human Rights: How Extraordinary Women Are Changing the World.* New York: Rowman & Littlefield, 1996.

"Briefing American Prisons: The Right Choices." *The Economist,* June 20, 2015.

Brinkley, Joel. *Cambodia's Curse: The Modern History of a Troubled Land.* Philadelphia, PA: Public Affairs, 2012.

Burgos Debray, Elizabeth. *I Regoberta Menchu: An Indian Woman in Guatemala.* New York: Versos, 1984.

Burnett, John. "US Border Patrol's Response to Violence in Question." NPR, May 15, 2014.

Burns, Helen Marie, and Sheila Carney. *Praying with Catherine McAuley.* Winona, MN: St. Mary's Press, 1996.

"Cambodian Democracy; Bruised, Bloody and Probably Broken." *The Economist,* January 11, 2014.

Canada, Geffrey. *Fist, Stick, Knife, Gun: A Personal History of Violence.* Boston: Beacon Press, 2010.

"Chad: No Protection from Rape and Violence for Displaced Women and Girls in Eastern Chad." *Amnesty International,* July 27, 2007.

Davie, Caroline. *Inquirer,* August 6, 2013.

Deak, Mike. "Monavi Offers Safe Harbor to South Asian Victims of Abuse in Central New Jersey." *Courier News,* April 13, 2014.

"Deliverance: No Way Out Human Trafficking in Kansas City." *Bostonia,* Winter–Spring 2015.

Demby, Gene. "How Black Reporters Report on Black Deaths." NPR, August 19, 2015.

Ehrenreich, Barbara. *Nickel and Dimed: On (Not) Getting by in America.* New York: Picador, Henry Holt, 2001.

Emanuel, Gabrielle. "McInnis House Provides End-of-Life Care for the Undocumented and Homeless." WBUR, June 28, 2014.

Enwemeka, Zeninjor. "After Officer Shooting, Community Leaders Praise Transparency and Call for More." WBUR, April 1, 2015.

Epp, Charles R., Steven Maynard-Moody, and Donald Haider-Markel. *Pulled Over: How Police Stops Define Citizenship.* Chicago: University of Chicago Press, 2014.

Fischer, Mary A. "Slave in the Garage." *Readers Digest*, May 2008.

Flores, Theresa L. *The Slave across the Street*. Idaho: Ampelon Publishing, 2010.

"France's National Front; On the March." *The Economist*, March 29, 2014.

Gill, Aisha K., and Sundari Anitha. *Forced Marriage*. London: Zed Books Ltd., 2011.

Glenny, Misha. *The Fall of Yugoslavia: The Third Balkan War*. New York: Penguin, 1992.

Goffman, Alice. *On the Run: Fugitive Life in an American City*. Chicago: University of Chicago Press, 2014.

Gordy, Cynthia. "Why The Ferguson Commission Co-Chair Believes New Report Will Bring Change to St. Louis." *Pro Publica*, November 26, 2015.

Green, Melissa Fay. "The Ancient Tree Archive." *Readers Digest*, April 2014.

Greenberg, Michael. "The NY Police vs. the Mayor." *New York Review of Books*, January 8, 2015.

Griswold, Eliza. *The Tenth Parallel: Dispatches from the Fault Line between Christianity and Islam*. New York: Ferrar Strauss & Giroux, 2010.

Havel, Vaclav. *Living in Truth*. UK: Faber and Faber Limited, 1989.

Heieh, Steven. "After Ferguson Protest Just a Few Reforms Have Succeeded." *The Nation*, August 12, 2015.

"Indian Mothers-In-Law, Curse of the Mummyji." *The Economist*, December 21, 2013.

Janbek, Dana. "For Syrian Refugees in Jordan the Cell Phone Is a Lifeline." WBUR, October 19, 2014.

Kellermann, Arthur L., and Frederick P. Rivera. "Silencing the Science on Gun Research." *Journal of American Medicine*, 309, no. 6 (2013): 549–50.

Kids Need of Defense, *Annual Report, 2014*.

KIND Pro Bono Attorney of the Month, June 2015. Courtesy of Wendy Young.

Laska, Vera. *Women in the Resistance and in the Holocaust*. Westport, CT: Greenwood Press, 1983.

Le Bon, Jon. "How the Feds Help McDonald Junk Food," *Mother Jones,* June 23, 2014.

LeBlanc, Steve. "The Quest to End Homelessness in Mass." WBUR, January 1, 2014.

Lloyd, Rachel. *Girls Like Us*. New York: HarperPerennial, 2012.

Lurie, Julia. "Black and Hispanic Kids Have a 50 Percent Chance of Developing Diabetes." *Mother Jones*, August 13, 2014.

Maathai, Wangari. *The Greenbelt Movement: Sharing the Approach and the Experience*. New York: Lantern Books, 2004.

Maine State Housing Authority. "Homeless Department Memorandum," July 15, 2013.

Marchione, Marilynn. "Doctors Target Gun Violence as a Social Disease." *USA Today*, August 12, 2012.

Martin, Philip. "Human Trafficking: The Crisis in Boston." WBUR, February 21, 2015.

———. "Sexual and Human Trafficking." WBUR, March 2, 2015.

McNamara, Eileen. "Gun Violence in Boston." WBUR, May 3, 2013.

Mitchell, Bill. "Risks of Living on Street in Bitter Cold: When Not to Walk on By." WBUR, January 31, 2014.

Moody Jr., Raymond A. *The Light Beyond: New Explorations by the Author of Life after Life*. New York: Bantam Books, 1989.

Moore, Jonathan. "In a Polarized Age What Does We the People Really Mean?" WBUR, March 17, 2014.

Nichols, John. "Black Lives Matter, Black Citizens Matter, Black Families Matter." *The Nation*, September 28, 2015.

Norton, Michael. "National Organization to Review Mass. Child Protection Agency." WBUR, January 9, 2014.

Ocasio, Linda. "Sex and Labor Trafficking in the U.S.: A Q&A on the 21st Century Slave Trade." *The Star Ledger*, March 4, 2013.

Pakenham, Thomas. *Remarkable Trees of the World*. New York: W.W. Norton, 2003.

"Policing. Don't Shoot." *The Economist*, December 13, 2014.

Ramirez, Alejandro. "Homelessness in Boston 1 Year after Losing the Long Island Shelter." WBUR, August 11, 2015.

Regan, Mary Joanna, and Isabelle Keiss. *Tender Courage: A Reflection on the Life and Spirit of Catherine McAuley, First Sister of Mercy.* Chicago: Franciscan Herald Press, 1988.

Regan, Keith. "Partners of the Year: Connection between More than Words and Constant Contact Easy to See." *Boston Business Journal*, September 12, 2014. http://www.bizjournals.com/boston/print-edition/2014/09/12/partners-of-the-year-connection-between-more-than.html.

Rios, Simon. "800 Young Immigrants Have Arrived in Massachusetts since January." WBUR, July 25, 2014.

Ritz, Erica. "FBI Rescues 105 Children from Horrific Sex Trafficking Operations in 76 U.S. Cities." WBUR, July 29, 2013.

Robbins, Jim. *The Man Who Planted Trees: Lost Groves, Champion Trees and an Urgent Plan to Save the Planet.* New York: Spiegel & Grau, 2012.

Rusesabagina, Paul. *An Ordinary Man.* New York: Penguin Books, 2006.

Ruskin, Gary. "The Calorie Control Council." Posted on January 17, 2015. *The Organic Consumers Association.*

Samaha, Albert. "The Story of the New Orleans' Public Defender." *Buzzfeed*, August 13, 2015.

Sanghera, Jasvinder. *Daughters of Shame.* London: Holder & Stoughton, 2009.

———. *Shame.* London: Index Books Ltd., 2007.

Sapien, Joaquin. "Racist Posts on NY Cop Blog Raise Ire at a Time of Tension." *Pro Publica*, April 16, 2015.

Seligman, Adam. *The Problem of Trust.* Princeton, NJ: Princeton University Press.

Sen, Amartya. "India's Women: The Missed Truth." *New York Review of Books*, October 10, 2013.

Sneed, Tierney. "How Big Data Battles Human Trafficking," *U.S. News and World Report*, January 14, 2015.

Spooner, Russell. *In Search of Sanity*. New York: iUniverse, 2005.

Straziuo, Jason. "U.N. Expresses Horror at South Sudan Massacre." *USA Today*, April 24, 2014.

Susskind, Yifat. Appearance on TED, a nonprofit television show sponsored by PBS, WBUR, and the Corporation for Public Broadcasting.

Swasy, Benjamin. "Boston Metro Area's Income; Poverty Rate Unchanged in 2012." WBUR, September 9, 2013.

"Tales from the Streets." *The Economist*, December 7, 2013, 23.

Tešanovic, Tasmina. "Mothering in War." In *Mothers of Adult Children*, ed. Marguerite Bouvard. New York: Lexington Books, 2013.

"Time to Deal." *The Economist*, April 19, 2014.

Tirado, Linda. *Hand to Mouth: Living in Bootstrap America*. New York: G.P. Putnam's Sons. 2014.

Torrey, Fuller, E. *Out of the Shadows: Confronting America's Mental Illness Crisis*. New York: Wiley, 1997.

Ung, Luong. *First They Killed My Father*. New York: HarperCollins, 2000.

———. *Lulu in the Sky*. New York: HarperCollins, 2012.

Watman, Melinda J. "Obesity: A Disease by Any Other Name." WBUR, April 5, 2014.

Weiner, Jon. "New ACLU Cellphone an App Automatically Preserves Videos of Police Encounters." *The Nation*, May 5, 2015.

Year End Report of MTW, 2014.

Young, Wendy, and Megan McKenna. "The Measure of a Society: The Treatment of Unaccompanied Refugee and Immigrant Children in the United States." *Harvard Law Review*, 2010.

Zarkovic, Radmilla Monojlovic, ed. *Sjecam Se: I Remember*. San Francisco: Aunt Lute Books, 1997.

Zehr, Howard. *Changing Lenses: A New Focus for Crime and Justice*, 3rd ed. Scottsdale, PA: Herald Press, 2005.

$\mathcal{I}_n d e x$